COOKING WITH HERBS

SUSAN BELSINGER
CAROLYN DILLE

CBI A CBI BOOK
Published by Van Nostrand Reinhold Company

D0188132

Production Editor / Rebecca Handler
Text Design / Sheryl Avruch
Compositor / Waldman Graphics
Cover Design and Illustrations / Christy Rosso
Insert Photography / Susan Belsinger and Carolyn Dille
Plants for illustrations furnished by Cricket Hill Herb Farm, Rowley, MA.

A CBI Book
(CBI is an imprint of Van Nostrand Reinhold Company Inc.)

Printed in the United States of America

Published by Van Nostrand Reinhold Company Inc.
135 West 50th Street
New York, New York 10020

Van Nostrand Reinhold Company Limited
Molly Millars Lane
Wokingham, Berkshire RG11 2PY, England

Van Nostrand Reinhold
480 LaTrobe Street
Melbourne, Victoria 3000, Australia

Macmillan of Canada
Division of Gage Publishing Limited
164 Commander Boulevard
Agincourt, Ontario M1S 3C7, Canada

16 15 14 13 12 11 10 9 8 7 6 5 4 3

Library of Congress Cataloging in Publication Data

Belsinger, Susan.
  Cooking with herbs.

  Bibliography: p.
  Includes index.
  1. Cookery (Herbs) 2. Herb gardening. I. Dille, Carolyn. II. Title.
TX819.H4B39 1983   641.6′57   83-17190
ISBN 0-8436-2225-3
ISBN 0-8436-2226-1 (pbk.)

To Dick and Tomaso

With unflagging appetite
and near unfailing cheer
you greeted the next rewrite
and still called us dear.
Then programmed the computers
and tilled the garden earth,
Meanwhile, behaved like swains and suitors,
and rallied the cooks with wine and mirth.

CONTENTS

FOREWORD

THE WORLD OF herbs, once the province of the initiated few, is expanding to become everyone's experience, delight, and recreation. For all these new garden enthusiasts, as well as those who remember the early days of the herb revival, this well-arranged cookbook will be rewarding reading. The arrangement of the book is interesting, clear, and practical. The herbs form the chapter heading, the recipes follow. I find this the simplest and most satisfying way to decide what original and interesting things to do with long rows of fragrant and prolific plants.

Herbs find their way into so many facets of our lives; they have inspired designers, historians, romantics, craftsmen, perfumers, doctors, religious groups, alchemists, witches, astrologers, and scientists, who have all found virtues in these humble plants. The interest of the cook, along with the physician, is probably the oldest and the most vital of all. The kitchen garden is a very ancient form of gardening, often a feature of castles and manor houses in Europe. Many of these that were neglected for years are being restored and now generate enthusiasm and curiosity in all who visit them. The grounds around our Early American homes are also being planted with these gardens once grown for "Meate and Medicine."

The interest is great but application of practical uses lags and many enthusiasts are presented with burgeoning crops that often go unharvested and unused for want of knowledge. For all the gardeners who find an overabundance of the twenty herbs here described, Belsinger and Dille have provided the answers. The multiple ways to season with basil is one example; it becomes no longer common but truly the "King of Herbs." Lemon balm, so prolific and so seldom used, has most intriguing and delicious recipes. Coriander, chervil, and the cresses are presented in a fashion that invites trying new taste experiences. *Cooking With Herbs* will expand your conception of herb cookery and certainly enrich your gardening life.

Adelma Grenier Simmons
Caprilands 1982

PREFACE

The pride of cooks, ancient treasures,
herbs delight, inform, inspire;
bring to fullness the table's pleasures
without the surfeit of desire;
regale us with their scent and savor,
and renew our palates with finest flavor.

HERBS APPEAL TO us for many reasons; the most important is that of the magical transformations they work in the kitchen. The simplest ingredients—sun-ripened tomatoes, virgin olive oil, and a little salt—become an extraordinary salad when strewn with fresh basil leaves. A sprinkling of minced sage worked into bread dough graces the kitchen with rich fragrance while the loaves are baking.

The twenty best-known culinary herbs form the foundation of the oldest and finest cooking traditions. This book is a culinary celebration of these herbs as well as a guide to growing, harvesting, and preserving your own supply.

The rewards of using aromatic plants are many. The variety and combinations of flavor they offer are infinite. The finesse of fine food in restaurants depends partly on fresh herbs; cooks at home can create equally memorable meals using them. Herbs add so much zest and flavor to food that most dishes need less salt. Garnishing with herbs decorates food naturally and palatably. In pots, tubs, planter boxes, or the garden, the liveliness of herbs stimulates the cook's creativity. Growing your own is not only fun, but it also makes possible the use of herbs that cannot be bought.

Cooking with fresh herbs influences us to think of food in new ways. The amounts to use, and the diversity of foods they flavor, encourage improvisation and help each cook develop a personal taste aesthetic. Although we have worked to make our recipes clear and delicious, they still offer possibilities for individual imagination and experimentation.

We believe that herbs are invaluable ingredients in the current renaissance of American cooking. From the everyday cook to the restaurant chef, Americans are evolving their own cuisine, characterized by a new emphasis on fresh foods and herbs, simple but flavorful dishes, and the merging of regional American with ethnic and foreign foods.

Of course, using herbs to enhance the flavor of food is hardly a new idea. One of the most fascinating aspects of culinary herbs is the way various cultures use them. We have had an opportunity to experience this firsthand while living and cooking in Greece, Italy, Morocco, Mexico, and various areas of the United States. Much of this personal involvement is reflected in our recipes.

In addition to recipes, our book provides some special features to make the cultivation of herbs easier, to illustrate specific uses for them, and to bring alive their enchanting legends. The chapter for each herb begins with an introduction discussing herblore, culinary suggestions, and cultivation information. In the final chapter, "Working With Herbs," the generally simple requirements for growing herbs are summarized in a chart prepared by a professional herb grower. This chapter also lists complementary herb combinations to help the cook understand which herbs harmonize and work together to create variety and subtlety in new dishes or old favorites. The use of dried herbs in place of fresh is reviewed in this chapter.

Nothing else captures the essence of fresh herbs, but there are times when they are just not available. The last chapter explains how to harvest, dry, and freeze them. The vinegar and oil section elaborates on these wonderful condiments, which greatly expand the cook's repertoire. The shelf in our kitchen, which is lined with jewel-like bottles in tones of topaz, rose quartz, and emerald, offers us more than simple infusions. In a very real way, these represent kitchen wealth, gladdening as they do the senses of sight, taste, and smell.

Our list of sources for plants, seeds, and dried herbs (see the Appendix) is the most complete we have seen and will make obtaining herbs easy for you. We hope the selected bibliography will have you reading herb books as eagerly as we do.

We find herbs even more important kitchen tools than good knives or pots (as much as we value these), since they add flavor and soul to our food. A snip of last summer's chives, brought in to winter over on the sill, does wonders for any vegetable. A pot-bound rosemary, blooming indoors as the snow falls, cheers the cook and livens the stew.

We hope that you find, as we do, that herbal alchemy is a magic every cook should know, and one that brings pleasure to all who come under its spell.

Acknowledgments

One of the reasons that writing this book was such a gratifying project was the sharing of skills and ideas with cooks, herbalists, writers, editors, families, and friends.

Our warmest thanks to the following people for their generosity, support, and expert advice: Lynn Armstrong, Don Barr, Audrey and Robert Belsinger, Thomas De Baggio, Joel Butler, Stuart Cooper, Ruth Glick, *Gourmet Magazine,* Dr. Sharon Harsher, Linda Hayes, Jean Hedges, Doneth Hinkleman, Harriet Rothenberg, Marguerite and Warren Sargent, Adelma Grenier Simmons, Alice Waters, and Nanette Wizer.

And to all those friends whose good nature, wit, and willingness to help made the pleasures of the table and the work of the cooks light and satisfying, a special fond thanks.

COOKING
WITH
HERBS

BASIL

BASIL

Basil is summer's prince,
with jeweled leaves and sweetest scent.

RICHLY FRAGRANT and handsome, basil inherits its name from the Greek word for king. Its aroma is as complex as a perfume, with a base of sweet grasses that grow by meadow streams, clove, orange, mint, and hyacinth. Of the sixty-odd varieties, most are cultivated for use in perfumes. Basil's scent probably inspired the stories of romantic and sensual love in European herblore. The villagers of Crete, southern Italy, and Spain used to give pots of it to newlyweds and placed its sprigs around the doors and windows of their houses. On a more homely note, basil was given as a house gift in Renaissance England to keep flies away.

Cooking with fresh basil has been recognized as a special treat for hundreds of years. Its cultivation as a potherb was noted in tenth-century France, where it is still called *l'herbe royale*. Old and current recipes use the flavorful leaves with all varieties of meats, including game, in soups, with cooked vegetables and salads, in egg dishes, with fresh cheeses or seafood, and for flavoring vinegars and oils.

Italians seldom eat tomatoes, cooked or raw, without basil; it is so essential to Italian cooks that field or greenhouse basil is available throughout the year. Our first dish of summer pesto in Italy so captivated us that basil remains our favorite herb. Each summer we have to restrain ourselves from adding it to everything. But this abandon can have intriguing results. Try substituting basil for dill with cucumbers or fish, or using it in place of lettuce on cheese sandwiches. Lavish basil over vegetables and green salads and add it to marinades and sauces.

To retain the aroma and flavor of the fresh herb, cook it briefly, or add a chiffonade as a garnish if the dish requires long cooking. A simple butter with lots of finely minced basil is excellent with all fresh vegetables and seafood, especially with lobster and salmon.

Growing basil is relatively simple. The main culinary varieties have a range of aromas and uses. Bush basil, *Ocimum minimum,* is a fine small variety, which can be grown in pots; sweet basil, *Ocimum basilicum,* is the most flavorful and the best outdoor plant. Lettuce leaf basil is the kind most commonly sold at greengrocers; its flavor is less intense than sweet basil, but still very aromatic. Purple basil has a more pungent perfume and is slightly more bitter than the others; it is the best for vinegar.

There are two ways to insure a plentiful supply of basil for both summer and winter. Cutting the plants when they are 10 to 12 inches tall just above the bottom set of leaves results in continuous new growth. Or, sowing seeds three times during the growing season (every four to six weeks) also provides abundant fresh leaves. Sow the tiny seeds in a rich, well-drained soil that is warm.

Basil transplants easily and can be started indoors in cold climates. Allow a 12-inch radius around each plant when transplanting. In general, basil flourishes outdoors but does not do well inside. Sunshine and light fertilization once a month are necessary for it to thrive. Care must be taken to pinch back the leaves so that flowers do not develop; this practice prevents the plants from going to seed and the leaves from becoming bitter.

If your growing space is limited, buy as much as you like during the season and preserve it for use during the winter. In the market, look for deep green leaves with no dark spots, a full bushy growth, and pronounced aroma. To keep fresh bunches of basil for more than a day, do not rinse the leaves, as water tends to turn them dark. Put the stems in water and keep the basil out of sunlight. The magic of sniffing a freshly cut bouquet of basil from your own garden or balcony is one of the small enchantments that seduces herb growers.

Although summer ends, basil devotees need not despair. There are several good ways to preserve the herb. Mincing two parts basil with one part parsley leaves and freezing the mixture in convenient amounts (1 tablespoon to 1/2 cup) gives moderate flavor and color for a variety of uses. A little olive oil can be stirred in; this mixture is especially good for pesto. Whole leaves can be laid on a baking sheet, frozen, and then packed in convenient-sized containers. Layering whole leaves between salt or olive oil will turn the leaves dark, but they can be used in recipes that insist on fresh basil. To preserve basil using these methods, make sure the leaves are brushed free of dirt.

Basil preserved in oil can be stored in the refrigerator for up to a year. Salt-packed basil will keep from four to six months in a cool dark place; it should be rinsed lightly before use. Although dried basil loses much of its characteristic aroma, it is a pleasant and useful herb. To dry, hang bunches upside down in a warm place away from direct sunlight until the leaves are dry and crackly. Fresh or dried, basil reigns in the following recipes.

Antipasto di Pomodoro e Basilico

This appetizer is traditionally made with *Mozzarella di Bufala*. Since it is very difficult to get this cheese in the United States, we use a good Italian Fontina. It makes a fine beginning to a meal when the days are very hot.

4 large, firm, summer-ripe tomatoes	salt and freshly ground pepper to taste
1 medium red onion	1/2 cup packed fresh basil leaves
1/2 cup virgin olive oil	1/2 pound Italian Fontina cheese, well chilled

Cut the tomatoes into slices, 3/8 inch to 1/2 inch thick. Cut the onion in half lengthwise, then into very thin slices crosswise. Sprinkle the vegetables with the olive oil, salt, and pepper. Cut the basil in a chiffonade and toss it gently with the tomatoes and onions.

Cut the well-chilled Fontina into 1/4-inch thick slices. Add the cheese to the antipasto, coating it well with the oil. Arrange the vegetables and cheese on a platter and marinate them in the refrigerator for 2 hours. Bring to a cool room temperature before serving.

Serves 6.

Cucumber Basil Tea Sandwiches

1/2 pound cream cheese, softened	1 small cucumber
1 to 2 tablespoons half-and-half cream	24 basil leaves
1 small loaf rye or whole wheat bread, trimmed to round slices	

Thin the cream cheese with the cream until it is the consistency of soft butter. Spread the cheese on the bread slices.

Peel the cumcumber, if the skin is bitter, and slice it thinly. Arrange the cucumber slices on the bread slices. Put a whole, large leaf of basil on each sandwich.

Yields 24 tea sandwiches or canapes.

Basil Almond Deviled Eggs

6 large eggs, at room temperature	1/2 teaspoon paprika
1/4 cup toasted almonds	1/2 teaspoon salt, or to taste
1/3 cup sour cream	1/4 cup packed fresh basil leaves
1 1/2 teaspoons Dijon mustard	Garnish: 12 small basil leaves

Cover the eggs with warm water in a saucepan. Bring to a simmer and cook for 8 to 10 minutes. Cool the eggs under cold water. Shell the eggs and cut in half lengthwise. Remove the yolks and press through a sieve into a small bowl.

Chop the almonds to the size of tiny peas. Mix the sour cream, mustard, paprika, and salt very well. Add this mixture and the nuts to the yolks and combine thoroughly. Adjust seasoning if necessary.

Mince the 1/4 cup basil leaves finely, add to the yolks, cover, and chill for 1 hour. Fill the egg whites with the yolk mixture using a teaspoon or pastry bag with a wide tip. Garnish each egg with a basil leaf.

Yields 12 egg halves.

Potato Pesto Pizza

This pizza is so special that it is worth heating up the oven in summer when the basil and potatoes are at their peak. It tastes wonderful in the winter, too, with frozen or preserved basil substituted for the fresh.

Pizza Dough

1 tablespoon active dry yeast	1/4 cup whole wheat flour
pinch of sugar	2/3 cup warm water
1/4 cup warm water	1 tablespoon olive oil
2 cups unbleached white flour	1/2 teaspoon salt

Dissolve the yeast and sugar in 1/4 cup warm water. Mix the flours and make a well. When the yeast is active, add it to the well. Let the sponge rise about 10 minutes.

Gradually add 2/3 cup warm water. About half way through this step, stir in the olive oil and salt. Incorporate as much flour as the sponge will take and still remain a bit sticky, though very lively.

Knead the dough lightly for 10 minutes. Let the dough rise for 45 minutes to 1 1/2 hours, until doubled in bulk. Punch the dough down and let it rest for 15 minutes before forming into pizza shapes.

Pizza Topping

6 to 8 new potatoes, about 2 inches in diameter	about 1/2 cup virgin olive oil
about 1 tablespoon olive oil	about 3/4 cup freshly grated Parmesan cheese
2 garlic cloves, unpeeled and mashed	1 small red onion
3 to 4 large garlic cloves, peeled	salt and pepper to taste
1 cup packed basil leaves	

Preheat oven to 350° F.

Scrub the potatoes, dry, and rub with a little olive oil. Place them in a baking dish with the mashed garlic and roast for about 20 minutes, or until they are just tender. Remove from the oven and cool to room temperature.

Slice the peeled garlic thinly. Put the garlic, basil, and about 1/4 cup olive oil in a large mortar, or in a blender or food processor. Pound or blend to a smooth paste. Add the cheese and more olive oil little by little.

Taste the pesto for balance and consistency, adding more cheese or olive oil if necessary.

Slice the potatoes into 1/4-inch rounds and the onion into 1/8-inch slices.

Preheat a baker's tile in a 500° F. oven for 15 minutes.

Divide the pizza dough into two equal parts. Form one piece of dough into a 9- or 10-inch round on a lightly floured pizza paddle. Brush the top lighly with olive oil and arrange half the potato and onion slices on it. Salt and pepper lightly.

Slide the pizza onto the baker's tile and bake for 5 to 6 minutes, until the crust is puffed around the edge and a light golden brown. Remove the pizza using the paddle and spread half the pesto over it. Return the pizza to the oven for 1 to 2 minutes, until the bottom crust is done and the pesto just begins to bubble.

Remove the pizza to a cutting board and cut into 8 pieces. Serve immediately. Repeat the procedure for the other pizza.

Serves 3 or 4 as an appetizer.

Basil Mayonnaise

Good mayonnaise can be prepared in many ways, even in a soup bowl using a fork to blend the egg and oil. We like the texture that results from making mayonnaise in a mortar and pestle. This recipe is good with anything from the grill, especially chicken, fish, eggplant, onions, and peppers.

1 garlic clove	*juice of 1 lemon*
about 1/2 cup basil leaves	*salt*
1 large egg yolk, at room temperature	*3/4 cup light olive oil or salad oil*

Peel the garlic and chop it roughly. Put it in the mortar and pound it to a paste. Chop the basil leaves roughly, add to the mortar, and pound them until they make a paste.

Stir in the egg yolk, about 1 teaspoon lemon juice, and a pinch of salt. Begin to add the oil a few drops at a time, stirring constantly. When about 1/4 cup has been added, pour in the remainder in a fine stream until the oil has been used and the emulsion has formed. Season with salt and lemon juice.

Yields about 1 cup.

Basic Basil Tomato Sauce

1 large carrot	1/2 cup packed basil leaves, or 1 tablespoon dried basil
1 small red onion	2 whole garlic cloves, peeled
2 pounds fresh, red plum tomatoes, or 1 28-ounce can plum tomatoes	1/2 teaspoon salt, or to taste

Grate the carrot and chop the onion coarsely. Combine them in a heavy 2-quart saucepan with the tomatoes, basil, and garlic. Add 1/2 teaspoon salt, cover, and simmer over moderate heat for 30 minutes. Remove from the heat and taste for salt.

Pass the sauce through a food mill or use a food processor to make a medium-fine puree. The sauce will probably have to be divided into 2 batches for the food processor.

Serve the sauce over Cannelloni al Basilico (see Index) or other pasta dishes, or use as a base tomato sauce.

Yields 1 quart.

Pesto Alberto

We named this sauce after our friend who made the first pesto we ate in Toscana. Pesto is a wonderfully simple sauce that depends on the best ingredients, combined in a well-balanced manner, to embody the flavor that makes it a classic. The finest Italian Parmesan cheese should be used. Italian, Spanish, or western United States pine nuts are the best. Buy the nuts from a good supplier, as they go rancid quickly. Basil and garlic vary in strength, so adjust the amounts accordingly. There's nothing more to say than *Buon appetito!*

about 6 garlic cloves, peeled	1 cup packed Italian parsley leaves
1/2 cup pine nuts	about 1/2 cup freshly grated Parmesan cheese
1 cup packed fresh basil leaves, plus perhaps another 8 to 10 leaves	about 1 cup virgin olive oil

Prepare the pesto using a large mortar, or a blender or food processor. If you use the mortar and pestle, pound the garlic first, then add the pine nuts. Finally, pound the basil and parsley. Then stir in the cheese and oil and blend until you have a smooth paste. If using a blender or processor, add all the ingredients together and blend to a smooth paste. Serve over hot or cold pasta or with minestrone.

Yields about 2 1/2 cups, enough for 6 portions of pasta.

Salsa Italiana

We like this sauce so much we eat it on homemade bread and even by the spoonful. Using homemade bread for the crumbs makes a far superior sauce.

1 cup soft Italian or French bread crumbs, crusts removed	1 cup packed Italian parsley leaves
1/4 cup white wine vinegar	2 medium garlic cloves
1/2 cup water	1 teaspoon red pepper flakes
1 cup virgin olive oil	salt to taste
1 cup packed basil leaves	

Soak the bread crumbs in the vinegar and water for 15 minutes. Squeeze the crumbs dry and put them in a blender or food processor. Add the olive oil, basil and parsley, garlic, and red pepper. Blend or process for 1 minute, scrape down, and blend for 30 seconds. Season with salt and red pepper flakes if desired. Serve at room temperature with roasted or broiled meats, or with cauliflower, chard, or broccoli.

Yields about 2 1/2 cups.

Spinach Basil Soup

1 pound fresh spinach leaves	1 cup heavy whipping cream
3 tablespoons unsalted butter	1 1/2 cups milk
1 medium onion, finely diced	salt and white pepper to taste
1/2 cup packed fresh basil leaves	Garnish: 2 tablespoons freshly grated Parmesan cheese
3 medium garlic cloves, finely minced	6 basil leaves, shredded
2 1/2 cups chicken or vegetable stock	

Wash and stem the spinach. Place in a stainless steel pot, cover, and heat over low heat until the spinach is just wilted.

Melt the butter in a skillet over low heat and saute the onion until it is translucent.

Add the spinach and its cooking liquor to a 3-quart soup pan along with the basil leaves, garlic, onions, and stock. Simmer over moderate heat for 5 minutes, then add the cream and milk and lower the heat. Simmer for 10 minutes and season with salt and pepper.

Puree 2 cups of soup, one cup at a time, in a blender or food processor. Return the pureed soup to the pan and let stand, covered, for 5 minutes. Pour into warm soup bowls and garnish with the Parmesan cheese and shredded basil.

Serves 6.

Cannelloni al Basilico

Filling

2 large eggs	2 cups freshly grated Parmesan cheese
1 pound ricotta cheese	1 teaspoon salt, or to taste
1 cup packed fresh basil leaves, finely chopped	about 1 teaspoon freshly grated nutmeg

Beat the eggs well and mix with the ricotta cheese. Stir in the basil and Parmesan cheese. Season with salt and nutmeg.

Pasta

3 cups unbleached white flour	3 teaspoons olive oil
3 large eggs	1 1/2 teaspoons salt

Sift the flour and mound it on a smooth surface; make a well in the center. Beat the eggs, olive oil, and salt in a small bowl until the mixture is homogenous. Add the egg mixture to the well and stir into the flour from the bottom of the well, with a fork, until the dough in the center is smooth and shiny. With the hands, incorporate the flour from the outside under the center, kneading gently until the mass of dough is consistent but still soft. All the flour may not be incorporated at this point.

Sift the remaining flour and reserve for flouring the dough later. Divide the dough into three equal pieces. Cover the pieces with plastic wrap and rest the dough for about 20 minutes.

To roll the dough, put one piece through the pasta machine on the widest setting. If it is still sticky, flour it lightly on both sides and fold it into thirds. Always put an open side into the machine when adding folded dough. Put the dough through the widest setting twice more, folding it into thirds and flouring if necessary.

Advance the rollers and put the dough through the machine without folding. Continue rolling the dough once through each setting without folding, flouring if necessary. The final setting of pasta machines varies; the ideal thickness for cannelloni is a little less than a millimeter. The pasta will be difficult to handle if it is rolled too thin.

When the pasta has been rolled to the correct thickness, trim the odd-shaped pieces from the ends, reserving them for another use, and cut the pasta into 4-inch lengths. Set the pieces of cut pasta on a smooth, lightly floured surface so that they do not touch. Roll and cut the remaining two pieces of dough.

Assembling the Cannelloni

5 quarts well-salted water	3 to 4 tablespoons unsalted butter
3 quarts cold water	1 recipe Basic Basil Tomato Sauce (see Index)
3 tablespoons light salad oil	

Bring the 5 quarts of water to a boil. Put the cold water and oil in another pot or a large bowl. Drop the pasta, 4 sheets at a time, into the boiling water and cook for 10 seconds. Do not overcook. Remove the pasta with a large strainer or slotted spoon to the cold water. Repeat until all the pasta is parcooked. Drain the water from the cold water and oil pot and add fresh cold water.

Working carefully, transfer the pasta to 2 or 3 dry cotton tea towels. Butter 2 9-by-12-inch shallow casseroles. Place a sheet of pasta in a casserole and spread about 3 tablespoons of filling across the upper third of it. Roll the cannelloni so that the seam side is on the bottom of the casserole. Continue filling and rolling. Eight cannelloni will fit in each casserole.

Cover the cannelloni with the sauce.

Preheat the oven to 375° F. and bake the cannelloni for 25 minutes. The edges should be slightly brown and crunchy.

Yields 16 cannelloni.

Basil Broiled Lamb Chops

When grilling these chops, using charcoal made from pieces of real wood, usually mesquite or hickory, gives a much better flavor than the briquette-type, which is chemically treated.

8 loin lamb chops	1 tablespoon soy sauce
1 small onion	1 teaspoon freshly cracked black pepper
1 large garlic clove	1/3 cup packed fresh basil leaves
3 tablespoons olive oil	salt to taste
2 tablespoons honey	

Trim the chops of excess fat, leaving about 1/4 inch. Slice the onion thinly. Peel and mash the garlic lightly. Combine the onion and garlic with the olive oil, honey, soy sauce, and pepper in a dish just large enough to hold all the chops. Bruise the basil leaves in the marinade. Add the chops to the dish and marinate at a cool room temperature for 3 to 4 hours, turning them occasionally.

Prepare a medium-hot wood charcoal fire or preheat the broiler. Pat the excess marinade from the chops and salt them lightly. Grill the chops 5 inches from the flame for 4 to 6 minutes on each side, depending on desired doneness. Meanwhile, strain the marinade.

When the chops are done, transfer them to a platter and rest them for 2 to 3 minutes in a warm place. Pour the accumulated juices into the strained marinade, transfer the sauce to a skillet, and reduce by half. Pour the sauce over the chops and serve immediately.

Serves 4.

Fragrant Pilaf

All flavors come together well in this pilaf. It is rather rich and goes best with simple grilled meats, especially duck and squab. Wild rice quality varies greatly. If you can, buy it in bulk and choose evenly shaped grains, rather than broken bits. It is best to find one brand or supply that you like so that you can establish the cooking time, which also varies greatly.

1 cup wild rice	*1 medium onion, finely diced*
6 cups chicken or vegetable stock	*1 teaspoon salt, or to taste*
2 cups coarse bulgur wheat	*1/2 cup packed fresh basil leaves, or 1 tablespoon plus 1 teaspoon dried basil*
1/2 cup unsalted clarified butter	*1 tablespoon fresh oregano leaves, or 1 teaspoon dried oregano*
1 large carrot, finely diced	*1/2 cup raw cashew nuts*
1 large celery rib, finely diced	

Cook the rice in 3 to 4 cups boiling, lightly salted water for 15 to 30 minutes, or until the rice just begins to open. Drain it and cover. In another pan bring the stock to a simmer and keep it hot.

Saute the bulgur in 1/4 cup butter over medium heat for 2 to 3 minutes. Add the drained rice and saute for another 2 to 3 minutes. Remove the grains to a large casserole.

Saute the carrot, celery, and onion in the remaining 1/4 cup butter over medium heat for 5 minutes. Mix the vegetables and grains together and add 3 cups stock. Salt to taste. Cover and simmer for 15 minutes, adding 1/2 cup stock at a time as necessary.

Mince the fresh basil and oregano finely, or crumble the dried herbs. Add the herbs and cashews to the pilaf. Uncover the pan and cook over low heat for about 10 minutes, or until the grains are just cooked through.

Serves 8.

Basil Stewed Tomatoes

Stewed tomatoes were family favorites for both of us. This version is the best we have eaten. It is especially good with roasted chicken and mashed potatoes.

1 medium onion, coarsely chopped	3 garlic cloves, finely minced
1 medium celery rib, coarsely chopped	2 teaspoons honey
1/4 cup olive oil	1/4 teaspoon cayenne pepper
6 large ripe tomatoes, or 1 28-ounce can tomatoes	salt
8 large basil leaves, or 1/2 teaspoon dried, crumbled basil	1 cup coarse whole grain bread crumbs
1/4 cup packed parsley leaves	

Saute the onion and celery in the olive oil for about 8 minutes over medium heat. Cut the tomatoes into eighths, or coarsely chop the canned tomatoes, and add them to the vegetables. Coarsely chop the basil and parsley leaves and add them to the tomatoes with the garlic, honey, cayenne, and salt to taste. Simmer uncovered for 20 minutes. Stir in the bread crumbs and simmer 5 minutes longer. Cover and let stand for 5 minutes. Serve in a heated serving dish.

Serves 4 to 6.

Carrots with Basil

1 1/2 pounds small sweet carrots	1/4 cup virgin olive oil
1/3 cup fresh basil leaves, or 1 tablespoon dried basil	1/2 teaspoon salt, or to taste

Scrub the carrots well, trim the tops and tips, and drop them whole into abundant boiling, lightly salted water. Cook for 7 to 10 minutes, depending on the size of the carrots. Drain the carrots and rinse under cold water.

Coarsely chop the fresh basil, or lighly crumble the dried basil, into a small bowl with the olive oil and salt.

Rub the skins from the carrots and cut each carrot into quarters lengthwise. Cut the quarters in half crosswise. Saute the carrots in the basil oil over medium-low heat for 3 to 4 minutes, stirring to coat the carrots well. Serve hot on a warmed platter.

Serves 6.

Basil Potato Salad

Because we love potato salads, we are always trying new combinations. We find this one particularly good for picnics as it has no mayonnaise.

3 pounds new potatoes	8 salt-packed anchovy fillets
1 1/2 pounds fresh small peas, in the shell	5 small, firm, summer tomatoes
2 tablespoons olive oil	1 small red onion
1 teaspoon honey	1 teaspoon salt
1/4 cup water	cold water
1/2 cup packed fresh basil leaves	

Scrub the potatoes well and boil them whole, with their skins, until they are firm but tender. Drain, rinse with cold water for 2 minutes, and set aside to cool.

Shell the peas and combine them in a small pan with the olive oil, honey, and water. Cover and simmer for 4 minutes. Remove from the heat, drain, and set aside to cool.

Chop the basil and 4 anchovy fillets coarsely, reserving 4 fillets for garnish. Cut each tomato into sixths. Thinly slice the onion. Put the slices in a small bowl with the salt and cold water to cover, and reserve. Cut the potatoes into 1-inch cubes. In a large bowl, mix the potatoes, tomatoes, peas, anchovies, and basil.

Dressing

3/4 cup virgin olive oil	salt and pepper to taste
1/4 cup lemon juice	

Combine the dressing ingredients and toss lightly with the salad vegetables. Season with salt and pepper.

Garnish

1 large head romaine or red leaf lettuce	12 basil leaves
reserved onion slices	reserved anchovy fillets, split lengthwise
1 small, firm, ripe tomato	

Line a large salad platter with the lettuce leaves. Drain the onions well and pat them dry. Arrange the salad on the lettuce and scatter the onion rings over it. Cut the tomato into eighths and arrange the wedges on the salad. Complete the garnish with basil leaves and anchovy fillets.

Serves 8 to 10.

Basil Lime Marmalade

6 limes	5 cups sugar
3 lemons	10 5-to-6-inch basil sprigs
3 times as much water as the volume of limes and lemons	12 basil leaves

Scrub the limes and lemons well. Cut them into very thin slices, reserving the juice. Cut the slices in half. Measure the fruit and juice and transfer it to a large bowl, covering it with 3 times as much water. Let stand at room temperature for 24 hours.

Transfer the fruit and water to a stainless or enameled pan and add sugar and basil sprigs. Simmer for 45 minutes, uncovered, until the liquid sheets from a metal spoon, or a jelly thermometer reaches 222° F.

Remove the sprigs of basil from the marmalade. Place 1 basil leaf in each of 6 hot, half-pint jelly jars. Fill each jar half full of marmalade and add another basil leaf to each jar. Fill the jars to 1/2 inch from the top, wipe the rims, and seal. Let cool to room temperature and store in a cool, dry place.

Yields 6 half-pints.

YOUNG BAY TREE

BAY

*A crown of bay good fortune brings
to poets, cooks, scholars, kings.*

B AY IS THE SUPERLATIVE herb for many herbalists: the most beautiful, the most fragrant, the most versatile, the most useful medicinally. Nothing bad is said about bay; rather, cooks and herbalists from early civilizations on have been unanimous in recording its virtues. The classical legend of bay's origin was Daphne's transformation into the laurel tree during Apollo's pursuit. Apollo was so astounded by the tree's beauty that he claimed the laurel as his own and dedicated it to reward the highest achievements of Greek civilization. Bay was first an herb of poets, and also of oracles, warriors, statesmen, and doctors.

Because bay was so associated with the gods and people of high esteem, it gained the reputation of protecting against all manner of natural and human disasters. Sorcerers and poisoners could not harm the person who carried bay. It was a widely held belief that lightning would not strike where bay was planted. The Caesars appropriated bay as their special protector against accidents and conspiracies. Though not notably successful, its efficacy in this field was maintained even in sixteenth- and seventeenth-century England. Witches and devils were supposed to be rendered helpless by it.

Bay, along with rosemary, was taken to weddings and funerals, being "good for the unborn, living and dead." It was the symbol of wisdom, both acquired and intuitive. Baccalaureate is from the Latin for laurel berries, which were given to Greek students of the classical period. As bay is a narcotic and stimulant in large amounts, it was an important part of the

Delphic rites. Apollo's priestesses chewed bay before prophesying. Later, even placing bay beneath pillows was thought to bring prescient dreams.

The medicinal uses of the herb were always important; bay was used as often as garlic to protect against epidemics. Considered an antirheumatic, it was drunk as a tea and used in baths. The Romans used bay leaves and berries for the treatment of liver disorders. Culpeper said that bay berries were "effectual against the poisons of all venomous creatures and the sting of wasps and bees." Oil from the berries was rubbed on sprains and used as eardrops.

The culinary history of bay has been even more constant; it is still an essential herb in European cuisines. Strangely, though bay is likely of Middle Eastern origin, we can find no mention of it in records of Chinese cuisine. In the past, when people appreciated more and stronger herbal flavors, bay was commonly ground and sprinkled over fresh vegetables, and cooked or marinated in fruit compotes. Now it is cooked with every variety of meat and most fish and shellfish. Bay leaves are used in the stuffings of or simply alongside many roasted fowl dishes. Its sweet balsamic aroma wafts from freshly baked breads and puddings. It is essential to bouquets garnis for soups and stews. We believe that bay, *Laurus nobilis,* adds depth and warmth to most kinds of sweets and savouries.

The main contribution of bay to foods is its fragrance, sweet but not cloying, pervasive but not overpowering. If you are fortunate enough to have walked through a forest with many bay trees, you can appreciate the incredibly refreshing power of bay's scent. Its blend of balsam and honey, with faint tones of rose, clove, orange, mint, and other more ethereal echoes, must be an ideal of master perfumers. The peak of bay's aroma is reached three days to a week after it has been picked. This brief drying time concentrates the oils just enough.

The taste of bay is sharp, slightly peppery, and of medium bitterness. Most cooks now use the whole leaves and remove them before serving, although traditionally the guest whose portion contained the leaf was due to receive some minor or major fortune. Commercially dried bay should be bought carefully from a spice merchant. We do not recommend picking bay in the wild, as some commonly called bays or laurels are highly poisonous. The California bay, *Umbellularia californica,* which we have picked in the woods there, has an aroma much like *Laurus nobilis* but the taste is more bitter and the scent dissipates more easily during cooking.

The effort to grow this noble herb is rewarded with a beautiful evergreen bush or tree that enhances any garden or home having the necessary growing conditions. The plants are expensive because seed germination is very chancy and other methods of propagation are quite slow. We prefer to buy plants from growers we trust, since bay should be well rooted and this can take up to a year. Bay prefers humid, warm summers, sunlight from above all year long, and winters of 55° to 40° Fahrenheit. These requirements make bay problematic in a closed environment. But if you possess a cool cellar or hallway with artificial lighting or a skylight, and take care of its seasonal placement, bay can be exceptional as an interior plant. In climates with freezing temperatures, it must be planted in large tubs and wintered in a protected area. Pay attention to light, moisture, and fertilization whether you plant in the garden or in a container.

Here we laurel some of bay's perennial goodness.

Four Meat Terrine

Prosciutto varies greatly in quality; the finest is from Italy, but its importation is restricted. In this country, it is best to buy domestic prosciutto from an Italian delicatessen. Areas with Italian populations often have locally cured, bone-in prosciutto. This is much better than commercial prosciutto, which is dry and salty. If you cannot get prosciutto, substitute half boiled ham and half fresh salt pork.

1 pound fresh pork fat, very thinly sliced	*2 eggs*
2 bay leaves, preferably fresh	*3 tablespoons Armagnac or Cognac*
1/2 cup whipping cream	*2 teaspoons salt*
1/4 pound prosciutto, thinly sliced	*about 1 teaspoon freshly grated nutmeg*
1/2 pound ground veal	*about 1 teaspoon freshly ground black pepper*
1/2 pound ground pork	*Garnish: 3 fresh bay leaves*
1/2 pound chicken livers	

Line a 1 1/2-quart rectangular terrine with the pork fat. Scald the bay leaves in the cream and set the cream aside to cool.

In a food processor, make a paste of the prosciutto, veal, pork, and chicken livers. The paste should not be completely smooth. Remove the bay leaves from the cream and reserve them. Add the cream, eggs, Armagnac, salt, nutmeg, and pepper to the meats. Blend the forcemeat together. The forcemeat should be well seasoned.

Preheat the oven to 350° F.

Place one of the reserved bay leaves on the bottom center of the fat-lined terrine. Spread the forcemeat in the terrine. Put the other bay leaf on top and cover the forcemeat with foil. Cover the terrine and bake for 1 hour and 15 minutes.

Take the terrine from the oven and remove the cover. Place a weight on the terrine and cool to room temperature. Chill the terrine for 24 hours with the weight on. Remove the weight and carefully unmold the terrine. Garnish the top of the terrine with fresh bay leaves. Slice in 3/8-inch slices.

Serves 12 to 16.

Spiced Mushrooms

1 1/2 pounds medium-sized button mushrooms	1 cup dry white wine
1/3 cup light olive oil	2 large bay leaves, preferably fresh
1 teaspoon fenugreek seeds	1 teaspoon salt, or to taste
6 black peppercorns	1/4 cup red wine vinegar
1 teaspoon pickling spice	

Brush and stem the mushrooms. Reserve the stems for another use. Heat the olive oil in a large skillet over moderate heat and saute the mushrooms for 3 minutes, shaking the pan to coat them with oil.

Tie the fenugreek seeds, peppercorns, and pickling spice in cheesecloth, or put them in a bouquet garni bag. Add the spice bag, white wine, bay leaves, salt, and vinegar to the pan with the mushrooms. Simmer the mushrooms for 10 minutes, turning them once.

Remove the mushrooms and marinade to a glass or ceramic dish and cool them to room temperature, turning them occasionally. Cover and chill them for at least 4 hours. Let the mushrooms come to a cool room temperature. Remove the spice bag and bay leaves before serving.

Serves 6 to 8.

Bay Hot Cross Buns

This recipe works very well if 2 cups of whole wheat flour replace 2 cups of white flour.

1 cup milk	*about 8 cups unbleached white flour*
3 bay leaves, preferably fresh	*2 large eggs, lighly beaten*
1/4 cup light honey	*1 teaspoon salt*
2/3 cup currants	*1/2 cup water*
2 1/2 cups warm water	*1/2 cup unsalted butter, melted*
2 tablespoons plus 1 teaspoon active dry yeast	*1 egg white*

Scald the milk with the bay leaves. Remove from the heat and dissolve the honey in the mixture. Soak the currants in 2 cups of warm water for 15 minutes. Drain and squeeze the excess water from them. Discard the soaking water.

Dissolve the yeast in 1/2 cup warm water. Sift 8 cups of flour into a large bowl. Add the eggs, salt, and 1/2 cup water to the milk and honey.

When the yeast is active, add it to the flour along with the milk mixture, melted butter, and currants. Stir the liquid with a wooden spoon to incorporate about half of the flour. Remove the dough to a smooth surface and knead in the rest of the flour. After the flour has been incorporated, knead for 10 minutes. The dough should be smooth and soft but not sticky.

Place the dough in a lightly buttered bowl, cover it with a tea towel, and let the dough double in bulk, about 1 hour. Punch the dough down and divide it in half. Roll each portion into a long cylinder about 3 inches in diameter. Cut the cylinders into 1-inch slices and roll each slice into a ball.

Preheat the oven to 375° F.

Place the balls on lightly buttered baking sheets and let them rise for 10 minutes in a warm place. Slash the top of each ball in a cross shape with a sharp knife. Beat the egg white until frothy and brush each ball lightly with it. Bake the buns for 15 to 20 minutes, until they are a rich golden brown. Remove the buns from the oven and let them cool to room temperature. Drizzle them with Simple Icing (recipe follows) along the slash marks, if desired.

Yields about 36 buns.

Simple Icing

1 tablespoon lemon juice	1 cup confectioner's sugar
1 tablespoon water	

In a small bowl, combine all ingredients and whisk until smooth. Drizzle the icing over Bay Hot Cross Buns or other sweet rolls.
   Yields about 1/2 cup.

Pecan Tomato Sauce with Bay

2 pounds plum tomatoes	pinch of cayenne pepper
1 small red onion, diced	salt to taste
1/2 cup light olive oil	2/3 cup shelled pecans
2 garlic cloves, minced	Garnish: 2 to 3 tablespoons unsalted butter
3 bay leaves	freshly grated Parmesan cheese

Blanch the tomatoes for 10 seconds, then peel, seed, and dice them. Cook the onion in the olive oil over moderate heat for about 10 minutes. Add the tomatoes to the onions along with the garlic, bay leaves, cayenne, and a little salt. Simmer the sauce for 20 minutes.
   Make a medium-fine meal of the pecans and stir them into the sauce. Adjust the seasoning and simmer for 3 to 4 minutes. Serve over Paglia e Fieno (recipe follows) or other hot pasta. Garnish with butter and Parmesan cheese.
   Serves 4 to 6.

Paglia e Fieno

We include the recipes for egg and spinach pasta here because this combination goes well with the Pecan Tomato Sauce with Bay. The "straw and hay" can be used for other pasta shapes, such as lasagna, *pappardelle*, or *taglierini*.

Egg Pasta

2 cups unbleached white flour	2 teaspoons olive oil
2 large eggs	1 teaspoon salt

Sift the flour into a mound on a smooth surface and make a well in the center. Beat the eggs, olive oil, and salt lightly in a small bowl.

Add the egg mixture to the well, stirring the mixture into the flour from the bottom of the well with a fork until the dough in the center is smooth and shiny.

Begin to incorporate the rest of the flour from the outside under the center, kneading gently with the hands, until the mass of dough is consistent but still a little soft. All the flour may not be incorporated at this time.

Sift the remaining flour and divide the dough into 2 pieces. If the dough is very stiff, cover it with plastic wrap and let it rest for 15 to 30 minutes. If it is still soft, knead in the rest of the flour and let it rest, covered, for about 10 minutes.

Unwrap one piece of dough and flour it lightly. Put it through a pasta machine using the widest setting. Fold the dough into thirds and put it through the machine using the widest setting twice more, folding each time.

Advance the rollers one step and put the dough through once without folding. Follow this procedure until the dough is as thin as desired. A thickness of about 1 millimeter is right for *fettuccine* or *tagliatelle*. Flour the dough lightly and roll it through the fettuccine cutting blades. Cut the pasta 6 to 8 inches long. Roll and cut the other piece of dough. Curl the pasta into nests or toss it to prevent sticking.

Serves 4 as a pasta course.

Spinach Pasta

1 pound tender spinach	1/2 teaspoon salt
2 large eggs	3 cups unbleached white flour
2 teaspoons olive oil	

Wash and stem the spinach. Wilt it in a covered pan, without adding extra water, over very low heat for 2 to 3 minutes. Remove the spinach from the pan and spread it to cool. When the spinach is cool enough to handle, squeeze it very dry in 3 or 4 batches. Mince it finely and place it in a bowl. Add the eggs, olive oil, and salt to the bowl and stir the mixture well.

Sift the flour into a mound on a smooth surface and make a well in the center. Add the spinach mixture to the well and proceed as for the egg dough, following the kneading, rolling, and cutting directions. Spinach pasta is stickier than egg pasta, so it may need to be floured between rollings.

Serves 6 as a pasta course.

Cooking the Pasta

1 recipe Egg Pasta	6 to 8 quarts boiling water
1 recipe Spinach Pasta	salt

To serve 6 as a pasta course, or 4 as a main course, use half of each recipe. Save the rest of the pasta for another dish. After cutting, allow the pasta to stand for 10 to 15 minutes before cooking. If you make the pasta hours in advance, keep it on a lightly floured baking sheet, covered, in the refrigerator.

Salt the water heavily and bring it to a boil. Add the pasta and cook it al dente, about 30 seconds. Drain the pasta well and put it in a large, warmed serving bowl. Toss it with half of the Pecan Tomato Sauce with Bay (see previous recipe). Pour the rest of the sauce on top and serve immediately.

Corn and Potato Chowder

2 large celery ribs	2 cups half-and-half cream
3 large leeks	1/3 cup chopped parsley
4 large, waxy potatoes	salt
4 tablespoons unsalted butter	freshly ground pepper to taste
1 1/2 quarts chicken or vegetable stock	Optional: curry powder to taste
3 bay leaves	1/2 cup freshly grated Parmesan cheese
4 ears of corn, husked	

Wash and trim the celery, leeks, and potatoes. Peel the potatoes and cut the green parts from the leeks. Rough chop the vegetables and sweat them in butter in a soup pot for 10 minutes. Add the stock and bay leaves. Bring the soup to a boil, reduce the heat to a simmer, and cover.

Remove the kernels from the corn and add them to the soup. Simmer covered for 10 minutes. Then stir in the cream and parsley. Season the soup with salt and pepper. Add the curry powder if desired.

Heat the soup over low heat until just hot. Just before serving stir in the cheese. Serve in warm soup bowls.

Serves 8.

Brisket of Beef with Bay Mustard Sauce

2 1/2- to 3-pound brisket of beef	1 pound green cabbage
2 bay leaves, preferably fresh	6 medium-sized brown potatoes
2 quarts beef stock	24 pearl onions
6 juniper berries	salt
10 black peppercorns	

Place 1 bay leaf in the center of the brisket. Roll and tie the brisket. Put the brisket and the stock in a large pot and bring the stock to a boil. Reduce the heat to a simmer. Make a small bouquet garni by tying 1 bay leaf, the juniper berries, and the peppercorns in cheesecloth. Add the bouquet garni to the pot and simmer for 2 1/2 hours.

Wash the cabbage and discard the outer leaves. Core the cabbage and cut it lengthwise into eighths. Peel the potatoes and cut them lengthwise into eighths. Peel the onions and slash the stem ends.

Remove the brisket from the stock, cover it, and keep it warm. Season the stock with salt, then reserve 1 cup of it for the sauce. Add the potatoes to the stock. Cover and simmer for about 5 minutes. Add the onions and simmer for another 5 minutes. Add the cabbage and cook the vegetables until the potatoes are just done.

Remove the vegetables with a slotted spoon and arrange them on a warm serving platter. Remove the string from the brisket and slice it into 1/2-inch slices on a slight diagonal. Take the bay leaf from the meat. Arrange the meat in the center of the platter. Spoon some Bay Mustard Sauce (see following recipe) over the meat and vegetables and serve the rest of the sauce separately. Serve hot.

Serves 6 to 8.

Bay Mustard Sauce

2 tablespoons unsalted butter	1 cup reserved beef stock
2 tablespoons flour	3 tablespoons Dijon mustard
1 cup half-and-half cream	salt
1 bay leaf, preferably fresh	

Make a roux of the butter and flour in a heavy saucepan. Scald the cream with the bay leaf in another pan. Add the scalded cream and beef stock to the roux, stirring constantly. When the sauce is smooth, add the mustard and season with salt. Cook over very low heat for 10 minutes. Remove the bay leaf before serving.

Yields about 2 cups.

Hungarian Baked Vegetable Stew

4 large shallots	1 tart green apple
1 medium-sized red or green sweet pepper	4 medium-sized firm, ripe tomatoes
1 medium-sized red onion	about 1 1/2 teaspoons salt
4 tablespoons light olive oil	1 tablespoon light honey
3 garlic cloves, minced	1 teaspoon Hungarian paprika
3 bay leaves	1 teaspoon ground chili pepper
1 pound waxy potatoes	1/2 cup chopped parsley
2 large carrots	3 cups Hungarian red wine, or other rich red wine
2 rutabagas, about 4 inches in diameter	Garnish: about 1/2 cup sour cream

Dice the shallots finely. Seed the pepper, peel the onion, and cut them in a medium dice. Heat the olive oil in a large skillet over moderate heat and add the shallot, pepper, and onion. Stir in the garlic and bay leaves and cook for about 5 minutes.

Wash, peel if necessary, and rough chop the potatoes, carrots, rutabagas, apple, and tomatoes. Add these to the skillet and cook for about 5 minutes.

Preheat the oven to 350° F.

Stir in the salt, honey, paprika, chili pepper, parsley, and red wine. Mix the ingredients thoroughly and transfer them to a lightly oiled, earthenware or ceramic casserole. Cover the casserole and bake for 1 hour. Reduce the heat to 300° F. and bake 1 hour longer. Remove the casserole from the oven and let it stand, covered, for about 15 minutes. Serve from the casserole into individual bowls, and garnish with sour cream.

Serves 8.

Salt Cod in Tomato Sauce

Salt cod is a neglected food in this country. If well prepared, it is succulent and delicious. It is important to buy the fleshy white cod, available at Italian delicatessens, rather than the extremely dry yellow cod.

1 pound salt cod	1 pound plum tomatoes, diced, or 1 14-ounce can plum tomatoes, diced
1 medium onion	2 garlic cloves
4 whole cloves	freshly ground black pepper to taste
3 tablespoons light olive oil	1/4 cup minced parsley
1 large bay leaf	

Soak the cod in 6 to 8 quarts cold water for 48 hours in the refrigerator. Change the water 3 times. Before cooking the cod, remove any skin, bones, and dark spots.

Cut the cod into 1-inch strips. Peel and cut the onion into quarters. Stud each quarter with a whole clove. Heat the olive oil over moderate heat in a large skillet and saute the onion and bay leaf for 5 minutes.

Add the tomatoes, cod, garlic, and pepper. Simmer, covered, about 15 minutes. Add the parsley and simmer 5 minutes longer. Serve hot with plain rice or boiled potatoes.

Serves 4.

Brussel Sprouts with Walnut Cream Sauce

1 1/2 pounds fresh, small brussel sprouts	2 bay leaves
1 cup whipping cream	1 cup shelled walnuts
1 cup half-and-half cream	3 tablespoons freshly grated Parmesan cheese
1 garlic clove, slightly crushed	salt and freshly ground white pepper

Wash and trim the brussel sprouts. Steam them until just tender, about 5 minutes if they are very small. Keep them warm while you make the sauce.

Mix the creams in a saucepan and scald them with the garlic and bay leaves. Grind the walnuts to a fine meal. After the cream has cooked about 5 minutes, remove the garlic and bay leaves. Stir in the walnuts and the cheese. Adjust the seasoning and let the sauce stand, covered, for 5 minutes.

Pour some sauce in a warm serving dish and place the brussel sprouts on top. Pass the rest of the sauce separately. Serve very hot.

Serves 6 to 8.

Bay Rum Custard

This is always a favorite dessert in our herb classes. It is easy to make, and the bay and rum enhance the custard.

1 1/2 cups milk	1/4 cup light honey
1 cup half-and-half cream	large pinch of salt
2 large bay leaves, preferably fresh	2 tablespoons dark rum
4 egg yolks	

Scald the milk and cream in a saucepan with the bay leaves. When the mixture has cooled about 10 minutes, remove the bay leaves and slowly whisk in the egg yolks, honey, and salt. Stir in the rum.

Preheat the oven to 350° F.

Pour the custard into 6 lightly buttered custard cups, pot de creme pots, or a 1-quart souffle dish. Place the dishes in a pan of very hot water and bake. The individual custards will take about 25 to 30 minutes, the souffle dish about 45 to 50 minutes. Test the custard by shaking the dish slightly to see if it is set.

Remove the dishes from the hot water and cool to room temperature. Chill the custard 3 to 4 hours or overnight. Remove from the refrigerator about 1 hour before serving.

Serves 6.

CHERVIL

CHERVIL

*Like lace it looks
and tastes divine;
God send to cooks
fair chervil fine.*

CHERVIL IS ONE of the herbs whose lack causes us great distress. Since it cannot be bought fresh, we are careful to grow plenty of it for salads, which always seem a little dull without its sprightly sprigs. We're vigilant to keep it well cut back to prolong our seasonal enjoyment. And we put up with its fickle temperament just as we would indulge a favorite finicky aunt who comes for a short visit. The pleasure of chervil's company at dinner is well worth the effort of accommodating its special needs for water and shade. The fragile foliage lightens a shady corner in the garden and rewards the gardening cook with a graceful, amiable beauty, which pleases the palate and eye equally.

In the cook's realm, chervil has been treasured beginning with the Romans, who probably transplanted it throughout England and France. It was prized as the "finest salade herbe" in medieval times. Its lively, delicate flavor, compounded of parsley and mild anise with undertones of pear, continues to find favor, especially in France, where chervil reigns with parsley and tarragon. There, it is used with fish, oysters, poultry, and eggs, and in salads and sauces, especially *remoulades* and *ravigotes*. It is also excellent with carrots, cucumbers, asparagus, avocados, mushrooms, and potatoes.

In spite of its lacy, romantic appearance, chervil's history contains little fanciful lore. Because of its alleged powers of rejuvenation, many Europeans sipped chervil broth on Holy Thursday to symbolize the resurrection of Christ. Although not considered a powerful medicinal herb, chervil still had its advocates. Evelyn recommended it as a spring tonic and "chearing of the spirits," and Pliny thought it good for stomach disorders. During the time of the plague, chervil roots were boiled and eaten as a preventative. Another popular folk use of the herb was as a cure for hiccoughs.

Chervil is a bit fussy about its place in the garden, but, once established, it will do quite well and will self-sow with good results. Choose a partially shaded spot with very finely worked soil. The slender black seeds should be sown freely and covered lightly with fine soil. They must receive some light and be kept moist for germination, which will take from ten to four-teen days. In cool climates, it is best to sow directly in the ground as soon as it is warm. If you are an avid and experienced transplanter, sow the seeds in flats and transplant in the same manner as parsley. We find many of the Umbelliferae (chervil, parsley, dill, and coriander) tricky to transplant and get the best plants by garden sowing.

During the summer, it is important to water and harvest continuously to keep the plants from seeding; they have a way of seeding all too soon regardless of all the attention they receive. Chervil, like chives, benefits from cutting. Begin when the chervil is three to four inches tall and keep some of it at that height during the hottest summer months. The leaves will turn orange or red from too much heat and light. In very hot climates, sow the seed in the fall and early spring.

Because of the delicate handling it requires and its relative obscurity in the United States, chervil is practically unobtainable commercially, though some is grown for the restaurant trade. Many of chervil's essential oils evaporate in drying, so a reliable dried herb supplier should be selected. Dried chervil should be stored away from light in tightly closed glass jars. If you are successful in growing a large patch, you can freeze your surplus chervil in small batches, using either the whole tiny sprigs or chopping it coarsely with a bit of parsley.

But to really cherish chervil, use it during the season in any of the following dishes.

Cherry Tomatoes with Chervil Salmon Mousse

1/3 pound very fresh salmon	1/2 teaspoon Dijon mustard
2 tablespoons creme fraiche	salt and white pepper to taste
1/4 cup chopped chervil	1 pint basket of firm, ripe cherry tomatoes (about 40 tomatoes)

Skin and remove bones from the salmon, and cut into 1-inch chunks. In a food processor or blender, puree the salmon in batches with the creme fraiche, chervil, mustard, salt, and pepper. Carefully cut 1/8 inch from the tops of the cherry tomatoes and gently scoop out the centers with a finger or small knife. Transfer the salmon puree to a pastry bag fitted with a medium star tip, and pipe it into the tomatoes.

Yields about 40 stuffed tomatoes

Eggplant Caviar

This particular dish has been well received by many people; it is a simple yet different and delicious spread. If you do not have both kinds of nuts on hand, use all of one kind. However, the pecans lend a sweeter taste. If chervil is out of season, use 3 tablespoons fresh parsley and 2 tablespoons fresh tarragon.

1 large eggplant, about 1 1/2 pounds	5 tablespoons minced chervil
1/4 cup olive oil	2 dashes cayenne pepper
2 garlic cloves, chopped	salt to taste
1/2 cup walnuts	1 tablespoon lemon juice, or to taste
1/2 cup pecans	2 tablespoons poppy seeds
1 cup sour cream	

Cut a lengthwise slice, about 1 inch thick, from one side of the eggplant. Scoop the pulp out carefully, leaving a 1/4-inch shell. Rub the shell with lemon juice to prevent darkening. Cut the eggplant meat into chunks. Saute over low heat in the olive oil with the garlic for about 15 minutes, until the eggplant is tender and lightly browned.

In a food processor or blender, finely grind the nuts in batches; add the eggplant and puree. Add the sour cream, chervil, cayenne, and salt.

Process or blend to a smooth paste. Blend in the lemon juice and the poppy seeds. Taste for seasoning.

Fill the eggplant shell and chill for at least 3 hours. (The caviar will keep for 3 to 4 days in the refrigerator.) Remove from the refrigerator 1 hour before serving. Serve with thinly sliced baguettes or crudites.

Yields about 2 1/2 cups.

Snowpeas with Chervil Cream Cheese

These snowpeas make a delicate and pretty appetizer served with the Cherry Tomatoes with Chervil Salmon Mousse (see Index).

1/4 pound snowpeas	1 tablespoon finely minced chives
5 ounces natural cream cheese, softened	1/8 teaspoon paprika
2 tablespoons buttermilk	salt to taste
2 tablespoons minced chervil	

Wash and dry the snowpeas. Carefully slit each pod open along a rib and set the peas open side down. Combine the cream cheese, buttermilk, chervil, chives, paprika, and salt. Stir the mixture well.

To stuff each pea, hold it open at one end, take about 1 1/2 teaspoons of the cheese mixture on the tip of a small blunt knife, and spread it inside the pea. Or put the cheese mixture in a pastry bag fitted with a medium star tip and pipe it into the peas.

Yields about 30 stuffed snowpeas.

Chervil and Asparagus Soup

2 medium-small potatoes	3 tablespoons unsalted butter
1 1/2 pounds asparagus	1/2 cup minced chervil
4 cups chicken or vegetable stock, simmering	salt and pepper to taste
1 medium shallot	Garnish: 1/2 teaspoon minced chervil for each serving

Wash the potatoes, cut them in half, and bring them to a boil in 3 cups lightly salted water. Reduce the heat and simmer, uncovered, until the potatoes are fork tender. Remove the skins and set the potatoes aside.

Wash the asparagus and break off the tough stems. Break the tender stalks into 3 pieces and put the asparagus into a large pot with the simmering stock. Reduce the heat, cover, and cook the asparagus until just tender. Puree the asparagus, with the stock and potatoes, in batches in a food processor or blender, leaving some asparagus in pieces.

Mince the shallot and soften it in butter over low heat until it turns golden. Return the pureed soup to the pan, and add the shallot and butter, chervil, salt, and pepper. Bring the soup just to a simmer over low heat. Ladle into warm bowls and sprinkle each bowl with chervil.

Serves 6.

Scallops in Pastry Shells

1/2 pound puff paste	2 tablespoons minced chervil
1 cup whipping cream	1 tablespoon capers
1/2 pound scallops	salt and white pepper to taste
1 tablespoon clarified butter	

Preheat oven to 450° F.

Roll the puff into a 10-by-8-inch rectangle. Cut out 12 pastry shells using a 2 1/4-inch round cutter. Bake on a lightly buttered baking sheet for 8 to 10 minutes, until the shells are golden brown. Cool the shells to room temperature. Cut a 1/8-inch slice from the top of each shell and remove the uncooked center dough.

Reduce the cream to 3/4 cup over very low heat, about 35 to 40 minutes. Cut the scallops into bite-sized pieces and saute them in butter for 2 minutes. Remove the scallops and pan juices to a small bowl. Add the reduced cream to the bowl, with the chervil, capers, salt, and pepper.

Preheat the broiler.

Divide the scallop filling equally among the pastry shells and glaze for 2 minutes, 5 inches from the heat. Serve immediately.

Yields 12 small shells.

Chicken Breasts with Chervil

Stuffed and sauteed chicken breasts are a popular dish. We think that this is an excellent variation.

2 medium shallots	1 large egg
3 ounces mushrooms	about 1 cup flour
2 tablespoons unsalted butter	large pinch of salt
9 to 12 large chervil sprigs	about 1 cup fine bread crumbs
salt and pepper to taste	3 tablespoons clarified butter
2 whole chicken breasts	Garnish: 4 or 5 chervil sprigs

Finely dice the shallots and mushrooms and soften them in butter over low heat for 5 minutes. Remove from the heat. Mince 9 to 12 chervil sprigs; the yield should be about 1/2 cup loosely packed. In a small bowl, combine the minced chervil, shallots, mushrooms, salt, and pepper.

Bone and skin the chicken breasts. Flatten the 4 half breasts between waxed paper until about 3/8 inch thick.

Spread half the chervil mixture evenly on each of 2 breasts. Cover these with the other breasts and flour them well, patting the excess flour loose. Lightly beat the egg with about 1/4 teaspoon salt, and dip the floured breasts into the egg, coating them evenly. Coat the breasts with bread crumbs, patting the crumbs into the breasts and sealing the edges well.

Cover the breasts with plastic wrap or waxed paper, and freeze for 10 to 15 minutes, or refrigerate for up to 8 hours.

Saute the breasts in the clarified butter, over medium heat, for 4 to 5 minutes on each side. If the breasts have been refrigerated longer than 1 hour, lower the heat and increase the cooking time by about 2 minutes on each side. When they are a rich golden brown, serve them immediately on warm serving plates garnished with chervil sprigs.

Serves 2.

Baked Yams with Parmesan and Chervil

Use the dark orange-colored sweet potatoes, often sold as yams, for the best flavor.

2 pounds yams, or sweet potatoes	4 tablespoons minced chervil
3 tablespoons unsalted butter	salt and pepper to taste
1/2 cup freshly grated Parmesan cheese	

Preheat the oven to 350° F.

Wash the yams and split them lengthwise. Bake them, cut side down, in a lightly oiled baking dish for 40 minutes, or until fork tender. Leave the yams at room temperature until they are just cool enough to handle. Scoop the pulp into a large bowl, leaving 1/4-inch shells.

Mix the pulp with the butter, cheese, chervil, salt, and pepper. Mound the mixture into the yam shells and return to the oven for 10 minutes. Serve hot.

Serves 6 to 8.

Carrots in Chervil Vinaigrette

1 pound fingerling carrots	3 tablespoons white wine vinegar
1/2 cup packed chervil	1 tablespoon lemon juice, or to taste
1/3 cup safflower oil	salt and pepper to taste
1/3 cup light olive oil	

Peel and trim the carrots. Blanch them in lightly salted water for 3 to 4 minutes, until they are tender crisp. Refresh them under cold water and pat dry.

Finely mince the chervil and combine it with the oils, vinegar, and lemon juice. Season with salt and pepper. Toss the carrots in the vinaigrette, cover, and chill for at least 2 hours.

Serves 4 to 6.

Chervil Avocado Papaya Salad

Mache is a delicate French lettuce which we discuss in the last chapter under "Enjoying Herbs in Salads." Limestone lettuce is grown in areas fed by limestone springs; this gives the lettuce a subtle earthy flavor. Chervil complements these mild lettuces and has a special affinity for avocados too; the flavors here meld extremely well.

1 ripe avocado	12 or 16 mache or limestone lettuce leaves
1 ripe papaya	handful of chervil sprigs

Peel the avocado and papaya carefully. Halve them lengthwise, removing the avocado pit and papaya seeds. Carefully slice each half lengthwise in 1/4-inch slices. Gently alternate papaya slices with avocado slices to form 4 multistriped halves. Arrange a few lettuce or mache leaves and a small handful of chervil sprigs on each of 4 plates. Place a striped fruit half on each plate.

Dressing

1 to 1 1/2 tablespoons raspberry vinegar	4 tablespoons virgin olive oil
2 tablespoons hazelnut oil	

Combine all the ingredients and drizzle over the salads. Garnish each salad with a chervil blossom or two.
  Serves 4.

Jicama Chervil Cucumber Salad

1 small jicama, about 3/4 pound	1 large bunch escarole
1 large or 2 small cucumbers	1/2 cup chervil
1/3 pound prosciutto, thinly sliced	

Trim and peel the jicama. Cut enough jicama into 1/4-by-2-inch strips to measure 2 cups. Blanch the jicama for 2 to 3 minutes. Refresh under cold water, drain, pat dry, and chill. Cut the cucumber into 1/8-inch slices to measure about 1 1/2 cups. Julienne the prosciutto.

  Trim, wash, and dry the escarole. Tear the escarole into large pieces and arrange it on a platter. Mince the chervil and toss half of it with the jicama, cucumber, and prosciutto. Arrange the mixture in a shallow mound on the escarole.

Dressing

1/4 cup lemon juice	1/2 cup light olive oil
3 tablespoons walnut oil	salt and white pepper to taste

Blend all the ingredients with the reserved minced chervil. Drizzle the salad with the dressing and serve immediately.

Serves 6.

Pasta and Chervil Salad with Spring Vegetables

2 artichokes	1/2 pound capelli d'angelo pasta
about 1/2 cup olive oil	2 medium shallots
salt and pepper to taste	juice of 1/2 lemon, or to taste
about 2 pounds fresh fava beans	1/2 cup loosely packed chervil leaves

Pare the artichokes to the hearts and slice the hearts crosswise 1/8 inch thick. Saute the slices over medium heat in 1 tablespoon olive oil for 3 to 4 minutes. Salt and pepper them lightly. Remove to a plate and cool to room temperature.

Shell the fava beans and blanch them for 30 seconds. Refresh them with cold water and drain. Remove the tough outer covering.

Cook the pasta al dente and refresh with cold water. Drain thoroughly and toss with a little olive oil.

Mince the shallots finely, mix them with the remaining olive oil and the lemon juice, and season with salt and pepper.

Chop the chervil coarsely. Toss the chervil, pasta, favas, and artichokes with the shallot vinaigrette. Let stand at room temperature for about 30 minutes before serving.

Serves 6.

Honeydew Chervil Sorbet

This is one of those special and perfect flavor marriages. It is wonderfully refreshing at any point during a meal.

1/3 cup sugar	*4 tablespoons packed chervil*
1 cup boiling water	*1 cup Asti Spumante*
1 large honeydew melon	*Garnish: 10 small, edible summer flowers, preferably violets or borage blossoms*

Dissolve the sugar in the water and let the syrup cool. Remove the seeds from a large honeydew melon and scoop enough pulp to measure 3 1/2 cups. In a food processor or blender, puree the honeydew in batches with the syrup and chervil. Pour the puree into a thin metal bowl or pan and freeze for 1 hour.

About 10 minutes before serving, break up the sorbet and process or blend to a smooth puree. Transfer to chilled serving glasses or dishes and return to the freezer for 5 minutes. Garnish with blossoms or chervil sprigs.

Remove the sorbet from the freezer and break it up with a spoon, whisk, or mixer. Repeat the freezing once or twice, stirring in the Asti Spumante after the sorbet has been broken up for the last time.

About 10 minutes before serving, break up the sorbet and process or blend to a smooth puree. Transfer to chilled serving glasses or dishes and return to the freezer for 5 minutes. Garnish with blossoms or chervil sprigs.

Serves 8 to 10.

CHIVES IN BLOOM

CHIVES

No one grows a single chive
who wants his table's grace to thrive.

CHIVES BRIGHTEN all but the busiest or darkest kitchens, in cold climates or warm, in city, suburbs, or country. The slender, dark green leaves require minimal care and thrive on constant snipping to sprinkle over the plainest salad or the simplest soup. The history of chives is not one of great medicinal purpose, grand myth, or charming folklore; yet chives have been respected for at least 3,000 years for their compatibility with virtually every kind of food other than desserts. Their flavor, with the sweetness of a platonic onion and the echo of very young garlic, is ideal for refined palates and delicate foods.

Chives have found a niche in all cuisines of the Northern Hemisphere, though they are used differently according to the taste and genius of each. In Japanese food, they are the contrasting garnish for clear delicate soups. Russians favor them with fermented creams and milks and with beets and lamb. The Italians use them exclusively in summer green salads. For the French, chives have an affinity with egg dishes, light sauces, and lightly cooked vegetables. The English use of chives concentrates on fresh cheeses and salads. German cooks use them in mayonnaises and remoulades. Egyptians and Lebanese garnish spicy meat stews and sauces with chives.

Once the flavor of fresh chives is established in the cook's palate, it will suggest itself as a pleasing touch to many classic and impromptu dishes. An especially tasty green rice can be made by adding equal amounts of finely snipped chives and minced parsley to taste. A chive butter made of one-half cup snipped chives and one-half pound softened, unsalted butter should not be restricted to potatoes; it is excellent with grilled garden tomatoes, fresh corn, sweet peas, and summer squash. With the addition of a tablespoon or so of lemon juice, it adorns the finest fresh lobster or grilled meat.

Fresh chives have nothing to do with dried, and even frozen chives taste of the freezer after a few months. Chives require little effort to grow indoors and out and are insect and cold resistant, yet they add much to the essential herbal variety that stimulates the imagination and taste buds. We grow two varieties of chives. The most common, *Allium schoenoprasum,* has very small tubular leaves and one-inch lavender blossoms; garlic chives, *Allium tuberosum,* have flat broad leaves and larger white blossoms. We like the finer taste of common chives with light fare and the garlic flavor with robust dishes.

It is best to buy potted chives from a garden or herb supplier and repot them. Chives need a very light soil, very good drainage, and much light and moisture. Although they cluster, they prefer plenty of room to produce upright lush leaves. They can become laterally potbound and should be divided into clumps about one inch in diameter in the spring or fall, if they begin to droop or yellow. Pots may be moved to a colder, darker area in the winter, as chives require some winter rest.

The leaves should be snipped from the bottom, about one-half inch above soil level. The blossoms should be snipped off as they form in order to maintain the best flavor and tenderness. If your summer garden has abundant chives, cut the lavender blossoms and steep them in white wine vinegar for a beautifully colored and flavored salad vinegar. For a rare garden treat, we dip garlic chive blossoms in a light batter and fry them gently until golden brown.

Fresh chives are usually available in markets through spring and summer. These are often a large variety with a slightly coarser flavor. Home freezing of the whole leaves yields a fairly good flavor for up to three months. It is best to snip the chives as called for, straight from the freezer.

You will find that chives' gentle piquancy favors the cook with versatility.

Chive Avocado Soup

2 ripe Haas avocados	2 tablespoons plus 1 teaspoon fresh, snipped chives
1/4 cup sour cream	1/2 teaspoon salt
2 cups vegetable or chicken stock, at room temperature	freshly ground white pepper to taste

Peel and remove the seeds from the avocados. Puree the avocados with the sour cream. Blend the avocado puree with the stock, chives, salt, and pepper. Chill. Thirty minutes before serving, bring to a cool room temperature. Garnish with fresh chives or a leaf of your favorite herb.

Serves 4.

Caviar and Chive Omelette

2 large eggs	1 tablespoon fresh caviar
1 tablespoon cold water	1/2 teaspoon lime juice
1/4 teaspoon salt	Garnish: 1 1/2 tablespoons sour cream
1 teaspoon fresh, chopped basil, or 1/4 teaspoon crushed, dried basil	1 1/2 tablespoons fresh caviar
1 1/2 teaspoons unsalted butter	1 teaspoon snipped chives
1 tablespoon snipped chives	

In a small bowl, beat the eggs, water, salt, and basil well. Melt the butter in an omelette pan over moderate heat. Have all of your ingredients ready. When the butter sizzles, pour the eggs into the pan. Keeping the pan on the burner, shake the omelette for 1 minute.

Spoon 1 tablespoon chives and 1 tablespoon caviar in the center of the omelette. Sprinkle the lime juice over the filling. Continue to shake the pan until the eggs are barely set. Fold the omelette in half and remove to a warm plate. Garnish with sour cream, caviar, and chives.

Serves 1.

Chickpea and Chive Falafels

1/2 cup dried chickpeas	*1/2 teaspoon ground turmeric*
1 teaspoon salt	*1/2 teaspoon freshly ground cumin seed*
1 cup finely grated carrot	*1/4 teaspoon cayenne pepper*
4 tablespoons finely minced chives	*salt and pepper to taste*
3 tablespoons tahini	*2 tablespoons light sesame oil*

Soak the chickpeas overnight. Rinse and cover with 1 inch cold water in a 2-quart, heavy-bottomed pan. Add the salt and cook the chickpeas until tender, about 1 hour. Drain the chickpeas and mash them with a potato masher, or puree them lightly. Add the carrots, chives, tahini, turmeric, cumin, cayenne, salt, and pepper. Blend the mixture well and shape into 1 1/2-inch patties, about 1/2 inch thick.

In a large skillet, heat the sesame oil over moderately high heat and saute the patties for about 2 to 3 minutes on each side, or until golden brown. Remove pan from heat and cover for 3 minutes.

Yields about 18 patties or enough for 6 falafels.

Falafel Sauce

1/2 cup yogurt	*1 tablespoon tahini*
1/2 cup sour cream	*1/4 cup snipped chives*
1/2 cup prepared hot sauce	

Blend all the ingredients well. Cover and let flavors develop before using.
Yields about 1 1/2 cups.

Serving the Falafels

6 pita breads	*3 medium, firm-ripe tomatoes*
1 medium head red leaf lettuce	

Preheat oven to 350° F.

Cut a 1-inch strip off the top of each pita bread. Wrap the bread in foil and heat for 15 minutes. Wash, dry, and shred the lettuce. Cut the tomatoes into thin wedges.

Into each pita bread, put 3 patties, about 1/2 cup lettuce, and about 1/2 of a tomato. Serve the falafels with Falafel Sauce.

Serves 6.

Chicken in Chive Coconut Cream Sauce

3 1/2 pound frying chicken	1/3 cup minced parsley
1 tablespoon light sesame oil	2 teaspoons light sesame oil
1 cup dry white wine	10-ounce can unsweetened coconut cream
1 teaspoon salt	1/2 cup shelled pistachio nuts
1/2 cup snipped chives	

Remove the innards from the chicken and reserve for another use. Rinse the chicken, pat dry, and cut into serving pieces. In a large skillet, heat 1 tablespoon sesame oil and saute the chicken for 15 minutes, turning frequently. Drain the excess fat from the pan. Add the wine and salt, reduce the heat, cover, and simmer for 10 minutes.

In a small skillet, saute the chives and parsley in 2 teaspoons sesame oil, over low heat, for 5 minutes. Add the herbs and coconut cream to the chicken. Simmer, uncovered, for 10 minutes, stirring occasionally. Remove chicken to a warm serving platter and keep warm. Add the nuts to the sauce and simmer for 5 minutes. Nap the chicken with some of the sauce and serve the rest separately. Serve hot.

Serves 4.

Crab with Chive Mousseline

On the East Coast, we use backfin or lumb crabmeat. This crab has been cooked, but not frozen, and is very perishable. Cooked Dungeness crab can be used in place of the backfin crab, but the flavor will not be as delicate.

Mousseline

1/2 cup unsalted butter	1 tablespoon warm water
2 tablespoons lemon juice	2 egg yolks, well beaten
2 tablespoons dry vermouth	salt to taste
1 tablespoon water	3 tablespoons snipped chives
1/4 teaspoon white pepper	1/3 cup heavy whipping cream, whipped

Melt the butter and set aside. In a small, heavy-bottomed saucepan, simmer the lemon juice, vermouth, 1 tablespoon water, and white pepper until the mixture is reduced by one-third. Remove from the heat and rinse the inside of the pan with 1 tablespoon warm water.

Slowly whisk in the egg yolks. Return the sauce to low heat and, stirring constantly, bring the mixture to barely steaming.

Remove the sauce from the heat and mix in 2 teaspoons of the melted butter. Continue whisking butter into the sauce, about 2 teaspoons at a time, until the butter has been used and the sauce has emulsified. Salt to taste. Blend the chives and whipped cream into the sauce.

Crab

2 pounds lump or backfin crabmeat, or 2 pounds Dungeness crabmeat, cooked and shelled	3 tablespoons dry vermouth
butter	

Preheat the broiler to 450° F.

Pick over the crabmeat and put it in a lightly buttered gratin dish. Sprinkle the crab with vermouth. Spoon the mousseline over the crab and heat about 6 inches from the broiler for 5 minutes, or until the mousseline is puffed and browned. Serve immediately.

Serves 6.

Tuna with Chives and Olives

4 small new potatoes	12 to 16 oil-cured olives, pitted and halved
2 artichokes	salt and pepper to taste
3 to 4 tablespoons virgin olive oil	2 tablespoons chive vinegar, or white wine vinegar
2 medium-sized ripe tomatoes	1 small bunch chives, snipped
2-pound piece tuna fillet, cut into 4 pieces	

Slice the potatoes 3/8 inch thick crosswise and steam them 4 to 5 minutes. Remove from pan and cool to room temperature.

Trim the artichokes to the hearts. Pare and choke them. Slice them

1/4 inch thick crosswise. Saute in 1 tablespoon olive oil for 3 to 4 minutes, over medium heat. Remove to a plate.

Seed the tomatoes and cut them into a medium dice.

Rub the tuna on both sides with some olive oil. Place the tuna on a large baking sheet and surround it with the potatoes, artichokes, tomatoes, and olives. Salt and pepper the tuna and vegetables lightly. Drizzle the remaining olive oil and vinegar over everything.

Preheat the oven to 400° F.

Bake the dish for about 10 minutes, depending on the thickness of the tuna. Divide the tuna and vegetables among 4 warm dinner plates and sprinkle each with snipped chives. Serve hot.

Serves 4.

Broccoli and Millet Timbales

3/4 cup millet	1/2 teaspoon salt
1 tablespoon unsalted butter	1/4 teaspoon pepper
1 1/2 cups boiling water	2 teaspoons fresh, minced marjoram, or 1 teaspoon dried marjoram
1/2 teaspoon salt	1/4 teaspoon paprika
1 pound broccoli	3/4 cup grated Emmenthal cheese
2 cups milk	4 large eggs
1/4 cup snipped chives	

Saute the millet in the butter over low heat for 5 minutes. Add the boiling water and salt, bring to a boil, cover, and reduce the heat. Cook the millet until the water is absorbed, about 15 minutes.

Wash and trim the broccoli and cut it into flowerets. Blanch it for 30 seconds in rapidly boiling, salted water. Drain and refresh under cold water. Chop the broccoli finely and mix it in a large bowl with the millet, milk, and chives. Add the salt, pepper, marjoram, paprika, and cheese, and stir well.

In a small bowl, beat the eggs with a whisk for 60 strokes. Add them to the broccoli mixture and blend well.

Preheat the oven to 325° F.

Butter 12, 6-ounce timbale molds and fill each two-thirds full with the mixture. Put the molds in a large glass dish and fill the dish with hot water to the same level as the mixture in the molds. Bake for 20 minutes, or until a knife inserted in the center of a mold comes out clean.

Yields 12 timbales.

Cauliflower with Brown Butter and Chives

1 small cauliflower, about 1 pound	salt and freshly ground pepper to taste
4 tablespoons unsalted butter	1/4 cup snipped chives
about 2 tablespoons tarragon vinegar	1 to 2 tablespoons chopped Italian parsley

Trim and wash the cauliflower and cut a cross in the stem about 1/2 inch deep. Blanch the whole cauliflower in rapidly boiling, salted water for 8 to 10 minutes, until it is just tender.

Melt the butter over medium-low heat until it turns brown. Remove from the heat and let cool to room temperature. Stir in the vinegar, and salt and pepper the mixture lightly.

Break the cauliflower into serving pieces and reshape the head. Place it in a serving bowl and keep it warm. Stir the chives and parsley into the brown butter. Heat the butter over low heat for 1 to 2 minutes, then pour it over the cauliflower. Serve hot.

Serves 4 to 6.

Potato and Turnip Puree with Sour Cream and Chives

How many mothers have mashed turnips and potatoes together because every child knows that turnips are to be despised? Ours did and we still like the combination; with chives it is especially good.

6 large potatoes	1/3 cup chopped chives
4 medium turnips	salt and pepper to taste
4 tablespoons unsalted butter	Garnish: 1 tablespoon chopped chives
1/2 pint sour cream	

Wash the potatoes and turnips and steam them until fork tender. Remove from the heat, rinse with cold water, and peel. Mash them with a potato masher, adding the butter and sour cream. Blend well and add the chives, salt, and pepper.

Preheat the oven to 350° F.

Mound the puree in a ceramic baking dish and bake for 10 to 15 minutes. Serve hot, garnished with the chopped chives.

Serves 8.

CORIANDER LEAF

CORIANDER

Cilantro is the Spanish name,
Chinese parsley is the same;
so coriander grows in fame,
and around the world makes pleasing dishes
with meats, vegetables, fruits, and fishes.

OUR MASSED BORDER of coriander is the scene of one of our favorite summer stock productions. The drama begins when the soft, tender green leaves of the young plants form a carpet. This is the time for the first harvest. We gather these leaves gently, taking care that some remain to allow for full flowering. As the plants grow taller, the upper leaves become more fernlike and branch out. The effect of the lacy hedge reaches its height when the flowers bloom. The small white blossoms, borne on umbels, seem to float above the delicate foliage. Tiny, round green fruits gradually replace the flowers; they now have the sweetest and most intense flavor, offering the gardener a refreshing tidbit. As the pageant draws to a close, the seeds mature to a pale golden brown. We cut and carefully dry the coriander seed and store it with next year's garden props.

The character of coriander has been well considered for at least 3,000 years in the Mediterranean basin and China. It is likened in the Bible to manna and probably grew in the Hanging Gardens of Babylon. The Chinese used coriander seed to flavor sweets and drinks; they believed it conferred immortality, perhaps because their knowledge was from the Egyptians, who placed packets of it and other spices in royal tombs. English and European herbalists, while disdaining the leaf, found the seed a pleasant sedative and calmative for both the nerves and stomach. Pliny and Dioscorides cautioned against excessive use of the seed, as it produces a narcotic stupor when taken in large amounts. Coriander seed is still very popular as an important ingredient of garam masalas; it is used in pickling spices, in some sausages, in many baked goods, and as the center of jawbreakers and confits.

The aroma of the seed is a fragile combination of orange, lemon, cumin, and anise, but the aroma of the leaf is strong and pungent. We find it contains elements of cut wet grass, forest humus, and wild mushrooms. The taste is grassy, and a bit oily, with an aftertaste that combines bitter and sweet to leave a faint citron flavor on the tongue. Coriander's distinctive flavor and aroma become somewhat muted in cooking so that it gives a deeper, expansive flavor, rather than a sharp, contrasting accent, to many types of food.

Coriander is often used in dishes with many flavors and with spicy foods, although it combines harmoniously with fish and shellfish with few or no additions. It is used lavishly in curries; in Chinese cuisine, especially with seafood, chicken, and pork; in some Japanese dishes as a garnish; and, in Arabic dishes of lamb and vegetables. A particularly tasty sauce that comes from southern Russia combines fresh coriander, walnuts, yogurt, red pepper, and garlic. Farther west, it reappears in Portugal, where it is featured in many meat and fish stews. In the New World, it is used in Mexico, where it is known as *cilantro,* and throughout South America.

Coriander can be purchased almost all year long in the United States in areas that have Latin and South American, Mexican, Indian, or Chinese populations. It is commonly called Chinese or Mexican parsley. As the leaves wilt easily, bunches should be stored in the refrigerator in a glass or plastic jar covered loosely with plastic. It is most often sold with the roots, so that it can be refreshed by standing in cold water.

Coriandrum sativum is a very easy herb to grow in warm climates where a March sowing is possible; in colder climates, it should be planted after all danger of frost, as it does not take well to transplanting. The seeds should be covered with about one-half inch of fine soil, then watered and fertilized regularly. Good drainage is important for coriander, as for most herbs.

This herb may be grown in a flat or window planter indoors in a good potting mix. It requires full sun, water, and good drainage. Coriander tends to repel insects, making it an especially good companion plant, indoors or outside.

The leaves may be harvested when the plants are about five inches tall. The aroma and flavor become more pronounced as the plant reaches the seeding stage. Coriander leaves can be dried on a screen away from sunlight, individually frozen, or preserved in a light oil. When the fruits are golden brown (in about ninety days) they should be harvested for seed. If left too long, they drop to reseed very quickly. As the aroma of coriander is very fragile, it is a distinct advantage to have fresh seed. It must be stored in airtight containers and pulverized just before use.

We trust our recipes will please cilantro's fans, and convince the uninitiated of its culinary virtues.

Enchilada Sauce with Cilantro

Cilantro is the Latin-American word for fresh coriander leaves.

3 pounds ripe tomatoes	1/4 cup packed coriander leaves
4 jalapeno peppers	1/4 cup corn oil
5 large garlic cloves	salt to taste

Peel, seed, and chop the tomatoes. Put the tomatoes and juice in a saucepan. Seed and finely dice the peppers. Finely mince the garlic and chop the coriander leaves. Add the peppers, garlic, coriander, oil, and a little salt to the tomatoes. Simmer the sauce, uncovered, for about 25 minutes.

Yields about 1 1/2 quarts.

Coriander and Lemon Broth

1 large carrot	2 tablespoons coriander leaf, minced
1 medium onion	about 1 1/2 tablespoons lemon juice
2 quarts completely defatted chicken stock	salt to taste
10 parsley sprigs	Garnish: 6 coriander leaves
10 coriander seeds	

Peel the carrot and onion and cut them into quarters. Add the vegetables, parsley, and coriander seeds to the stock. Bring the broth to a boil, reduce the heat to a simmer, and cook for about 25 minutes.

Strain the broth through cheesecloth that has been rinsed and folded in thirds. Return the broth to the pot. Stir in the minced coriander, lemon juice, and salt. Simmer for about 5 minutes. Ladle into warm soup bowls and garnish each with a coriander leaf.

Serves 6.

Mushroom Soup with Coriander

1 pound fresh mushrooms	1 cup half-and-half cream
1 small onion	1/2 cup white wine, preferably a medium-dry Riesling
4 tablespoons unsalted butter	salt and freshly ground white pepper to taste
1 quart chicken or vegetable stock	Garnish: raw mushroom slices
1 tablespoon chopped coriander leaves	coriander leaves
3 tablespoons chopped parsley leaves	

Clean the mushrooms and reserve 2 for garnish. Slice the rest about 1/4 inch thick. Dice the onion finely. Sweat the mushrooms and onion in butter in a soup pot.

Add the stock and bring the soup to a simmer. Add the chopped coriander and parsley and simmer the soup about 5 minutes. Puree about three-quarters of the soup, reserving enough to have some mushroom slices.

Return the soup to the pot. Over very low heat, add the cream and wine. Season lightly and cook just below a simmer for about 15 minutes. Taste for seasoning before serving. Ladle the soup into warm soup bowls. Slice the reserved mushrooms. Garnish each bowl with mushroom slices and coriander leaves.

Serves 6 to 8.

Cheese Enchiladas

The *queso cojito* is available at Mexican food stores. If you can't find it, use Monterey Jack cheese.

1 pound queso cojito or Monterey Jack cheese	1 small red onion
1/4 cup chopped coriander leaves	24 corn tortillas
1 or 2 jalapeno peppers	1 recipe Enchilada Sauce with Cilantro (see Index)
1 small, sweet red pepper	

Grate the cheese and mix it with the coriander. Seed and finely chop the peppers. Peel and finely dice the onion. Toss the vegetables with the cheese.

Lightly oil 2 9-by-12-by-2-inch baking dishes. Warm the tortillas over a gas burner on low heat for about 15 seconds on each side, or wrap them in foil and warm them in a moderate oven for about 10 minutes. Be careful that the tortillas do not dry out.

Dip one side of each tortilla lightly in the Enchilada Sauce with Cilantro and lay them on a baking sheet, sauced side up. Fill each tortilla with about 2 tablespoons of the cheese mixture. Roll the tortillas and place them, seam side down, in the oiled baking dishes, fitting 12 tortillas in each dish.

Preheat the oven to 350° F.

Cover the tortillas with the rest of the sauce and bake them about 25 minutes. Serve immediately.

Serves 8 to 12.

Chicken Mole with Coriander

Latin-American food stores are the best places to find dried chilis, but some supermarkets carry an assortment of them also. *Pasilla* chilis give a rich, smoky flavor to the mole. A New Mexico dried chili can be used instead.

3 1/2- to 4-pound frying chicken	*3 large garlic cloves, minced*
3 tablespoons corn oil	*2 tablespoons sesame seeds*
about 3 cups chicken stock	*1/3 cup coarsely chopped natural almonds*
2 dried pasilla *chilis, or 1 New Mexico dried chili*	*1 teaspoon ground coriander seed*
3 chipotle chilis, or other small, hot dried chilis	*2 tablespoons chopped coriander leaves*
1 corn tortilla	*1 ounce Mexican chocolate, or 1 ounce semisweet chocolate and a pinch of cinnamon*

Cut the chicken into serving pieces and reserve the innards for another use. Saute the chicken in a large skillet in 2 tablespoons corn oil until it is browned, about 10 minutes. Pour in enough chicken stock to half cover the chicken. Cover the skillet and simmer for 10 to 15 minutes.

Stem and seed the pasilla and chipotle chilis. Soak them in very hot water for 10 minutes. Drain, pat dry, and chop the chilis. Cut a corn tortilla into 1-inch strips. Saute the chilis and tortilla strips in the remaining tablespoon corn oil for 5 minutes over low heat. Add the garlic and saute for another minute or two. Add the mixture to the chicken.

In a small, dry skillet over low heat, toast the sesame seeds and almonds until they are pale golden brown. Add the seeds and almonds to the chicken, along with the coriander seed. Simmer the chicken for another 10 minutes or so. Add the coriander leaves and the Mexican chocolate and stir until the chocolate dissolves, about 2 to 3 minutes. Serve the mole hot with corn tortillas.

Serves 4.

Pork Chops with Red Cabbage and Green Apples

6 loin pork chops, about 1 1/4 inches thick	1 teaspoon ground coriander seed
4 tablespoons clarified butter	1 tablespoon chopped coriander leaves
1/2 pound red cabbage	salt to taste
1 medium onion	freshly ground black pepper to taste
4 medium Granny Smith apples, or other tart green apples	Garnish: 4 to 6 coriander sprigs

Use a large nonporous skillet with a tight-fitting lid. Heat 1 tablespoon clarified butter over moderately high heat and saute the pork chops about 5 minutes, turning them until they are browned. Remove them to a platter and keep warm.

Thinly slice the red cabbage and onion. Core and thinly slice the apples. Using the same skillet, heat the remaining 3 tablespoons clarified butter over medium heat. Saute the vegetables and fruit about 5 minutes, tossing the pan to coat them evenly. Stir the coriander seed and coriander leaves into the vegetables. Salt and pepper the vegetables and chops lightly.

Place the chops under the vegetables and fruit and cover the skillet. Steam the chops about 15 minutes, until they are just done. Transfer the vegetables and fruit to a warm serving platter and put the chops on top. Garnish with coriander sprigs and serve hot.

Serves 6.

Salmon in Champagne with Coriander

Our friend Joel Butler gave us the idea for this dish. Steaming the salmon in this manner creates a wonderful perfume.

2-pound salmon fillet, skinned and boned	8 Italian parsley sprigs
salt and freshly ground white pepper to taste	1 cup champagne
18 to 20 coriander leaf sprigs	Garnish: 4 to 6 coriander leaf sprigs

Sprinkle the salmon lightly on both sides with salt and pepper. Cut an 18-by-30-inch piece of heavy foil. Put the foil on a baking sheet and fold up 3 inches along the lengths and 8 inches along the widths.

Preheat the oven to 450° F.

Strew 10 coriander sprigs and all the parsley sprigs in the center of the foil. Place the salmon on the herbs. Pour the champagne over the fish and strew 8 coriander sprigs on top. Fold the foil to make a package, sealing the ends tightly. Bake for 10 to 15 minutes, depending on the thickness of the fish.

Open the package, remove the cooked herbs, and place the salmon on a warm serving platter. Garnish with fresh coriander sprigs and serve hot.

Serves 4.

Baked Zucchini

Filling

6 green or yellow zucchini, each about 4 inches long	3 tablespoons ground hazelnuts
6 mushrooms	1 egg, lightly beaten
2 tablespoons unsalted butter	1 garlic clove, minced
1/3 cup half-and-half cream	2 tablespoons plus 1 teaspoon chopped coriander leaves
2 tablespoons freshly grated Parmesan cheese	salt and freshly ground black pepper to taste
6 tablespoons fine, dry, whole grain bread crumbs	

Trim the zucchini and steam them whole until they are just done, about 10 minutes. When cool enough to handle, halve them lengthwise and discard the seeds. Remove the pulp, leaving a 3/8-inch shell for each zucchini half. Set the zucchini cut side down. Squeeze excess liquid from the pulp.

Chop the mushrooms finely and saute them in butter for 5 minutes. Put them in a small bowl and add the cream, cheese, bread crumbs, hazelnuts, egg, and garlic. Finely chop the zucchini pulp and mix with the mushrooms. Stir in the coriander and season the mixture.

Pat the zucchini shells dry and spoon in the filling. Butter a large baking dish and arrange the shells in it.

Preheat the oven to 350° F.

Gratin Topping

3 tablespoons freshly grated Parmesan cheese	2 tablespoons fine, dry bread crumbs
3 tablespoons virgin olive oil	

Mix the ingredients together. Spread the topping equally over the stuffed zucchini. Bake for 25 minutes and serve hot.

Serves 6 or 12.

Orange, Olive, and Avocado Salad with Cilantro

Coriander has an affinity for both avocados and oranges. This salad can be arranged handsomely; we like to serve it with dishes from Mexico or Latin America.

Salad

1 small heart of escarole	juice of 1/2 lemon
about 1 cup loosely packed coriander leaves	2 small oranges
1 ripe Haas avocado	1/3 cup Moroccan oil-cured olives

Wash and trim the escarole. Arrange the leaves on a serving platter. Scatter the coriander leaves over the escarole. Cut the avocado lengthwise and peel it. Remove the pit and cut each half crosswise into 1/4-inch slices. Sprinkle a few drops of lemon juice on the avocado slices.

Peel the oranges, seed them if necessary, and cut them into 1/4-inch rounds. Arrange the avocado and orange slices on the escarole. Pit the olives and scatter them over the salad.

Dressing

1/3 cup freshly squeezed orange juice	1 small garlic clove, minced
1/3 cup light olive oil	salt and pepper to taste

Mix the orange juice, olive oil, and garlic together. Season with salt and pepper. Drizzle the dressing over the salad and let stand 5 minutes before serving.

Serves 4.

Snapper and Shellfish Salad with Coriander

2 pounds very small clams, scrubbed	reserved poaching liquid
1 cup dry white wine	juice of 1 lime
4 Italian parsley sprigs	1/4 cup virgin olive oil
2 medium garlic cloves, peeled	2 tablespoons chopped coriander leaves
1 pound very fresh snapper fillet, or other firm-fleshed, white fish fillet	salt to taste
1/2 pound medium shrimp	Garnish: coriander sprigs

Steam the clams open in the white wine with the parsley and garlic. As the clams open, remove them to a platter. When all are open, shuck them into a bowl. Rinse a cheesecloth, fold it in three layers, and place in a sieve. Strain the collected juices and pan liquid through the cheesecloth. Save the cheesecloth.

Transfer the strained liquid to a pan, bring it to a simmer, and poach the snapper for 3 to 4 minutes, until it is just done. Remove it to a plate to cool.

Poach the shrimp in the same liquid until they are just done, about 2 minutes. Remove them to cool, then shell them. Strain the poaching liquid again through the cheesecloth.

Measure 1/4 cup of the poaching liquid into a small bowl. Add the lime juice, olive oil, chopped coriander, and salt.

Carefully flake the fish and remove any bones. Toss the fish gently with the clams, shrimp, and vinaigrette. Cover and chill the salad for 2 hours. Remove from the refrigerator about 30 minutes before serving. Transfer the salad to a serving platter and garnish with coriander sprigs.

Serves 4 to 6.

Fruit Salad with Cilantro

This salad is especially good if you have a variety of fruit.

6 citrus fruits, such as mandarin and blood oranges, emerald and honey tangerines	1/2 cup loosely packed coriander leaves
1 medium-sized ripe pineapple	1 recipe Coriander Coconut Dressing (see following recipe)
2 ripe bananas	

Peel the citrus fruit and cut into slices. Remove any seeds. Peel and core the pineapple and cut it into pieces. Peel and slice the bananas. Toss the fruit in a large serving dish with 1/4 cup coriander leaves. Garnish the salad with remaining coriander leaves and serve with Coriander Coconut Dressing.

Serves 8 to 10.

Coriander Coconut Dressing

Oriental and Latin American food stores often sell cans of unsweetened coconut milk with no preservatives. If this is not available, you can make coconut milk by grating the meat of a coconut and pouring 1 cup boiling water over it. Let the mixture stand for 10 to 15 minutes. Strain it and reserve the liquid. Pour another cup of boiling water over the grated coconut and let it stand for 20 minutes. Strain the liquid into a separate bowl, and add just enough of it to the first batch of coconut milk to equal 10 fluid ounces.

10 ounces unsweetened coconut milk	1 teaspoon ground coriander seed
2 tablespoons honey	lemon juice to taste

Blend all the ingredients in a blender until the dressing is very smooth. Serve with fruit salad.

Yields about 1 1/4 cups.

CRESS

CRESS

Watery cress, Queen of the stream,
in salads fine you have no peer;
poor man's bread, rich man's cream,
all men's delight for half the year.

WE SET OUT eagerly every year at the first signs of spring to inspect our favorite cress streams. The earth is still cold and moist under foot as we follow the sound of the water to banks of fresh green growth. The tiny cress tendrils have their most subtle flavor now, a delicate balance of sweetness and spice. We are always thrilled to gather spring's first herbal bounty.

This abundance provides a welcome chance to eat cress every day in different ways. Although cress is not an aromatic herb, its peppery flavor has added interest to salads and soups for centuries. Perhaps because cress tingles the tongue so definitely, we like it best as a salad herb. It enlivens any green or vegetable salad and goes well with combination salads that include grains, potatoes, pasta, fish, or chicken. Cress is a versatile and pretty garnish; its different forms and flavors, and its availability, stimulate the cook to use it freely.

Of the several varieties of cress, watercress, *Nasturtium officinale,* is the best known and most commonly available, found in markets in fall and spring. This is the oldest known of the cresses and herblore usually refers to it. Winter cress, *Barbarea verna,* which is cultivated commercially much more today than in the past, has a flavor and color very like watercress, but its leaves are longer and more pointed. The pleasant bite of both disappears in cooking, and a different but agreeable herbal vegetable taste, with over-tones of spinach, parsley, and mustard greens, is revealed. Garden cress,

Lepidium sativum, a member of the mustard family with a flavor similar to watercress but with paler and smaller leaves, does not retain its flavor and color when heated and should be eaten raw.

When buying cress, look for deep green leaves in compact bunches; the small flowers, if any, should be closed. Store cress in the refrigerator, with the stems in water, in an ample, well-covered glass or plastic container. Cress should be used within one or two days of purchase.

The rich, holly green color of cress is a sign of the many minerals it contains. Its name, from the Greek word *grastis* meaning green fodder, indicates how long it has been valued as food. Persians steeped cress in milk and gave it to their children to increase their growth. The Greek armies of Alexander's time ate it because they believed it imparted strength during battle. From the Middle Ages through the nineteenth century, English peasants ate cress in place of bread when they had no flour. The Romans, who knew all herbs, harvested wild cress for their salads.

Because water and winter cress require very rich, marshy earth, running water, and protection from the cold, they are usually cultivated commercially. Unless you are lucky enough to have a stream running through your garden, growing watercress will be difficult. But you might try sowing the seeds in flats of wet compost in the early summer or transplanting rooted stems to a trench. Either way, the soil must be kept constantly moist, but not soggy.

Garden cress, however, can be grown easily. To sprout the seeds indoors, spread them evenly on a piece of absorbent toweling in a tray, soak them thoroughly, and cover them with waxed paper. Remove the paper when the seeds begin to sprout and keep them moist until they are four to six inches tall. Trim them about a quarter of an inch from the base and use in salads. In the garden, cover the seeds lightly with fine soil and keep them moist with a fine spray until the cress is ready to harvest. Mature garden cress can be eaten, but it has a definite bitterness.

One attraction of watercress is the pleasure of picking it free and wild. Another is the pageant of full-grown cress, its diadems of tiny white flowers alluding to the title "Queen of Herbs." In these recipes, cress contributes the crowning touch.

Cress Eggrolls

1 small green cabbage	1 cup mung bean sprouts
1/2 pound mushrooms	1 1/2 tablespoons soy sauce
2 1/4 cups peanut oil	2 cups packed cress leaves
1/2 teaspoon black mustard seeds	Optional: 2/3 cup shredded cooked chicken or cooked bay shrimp
1 large garlic clove, finely chopped	1 egg
2 teaspoons freshly grated gingerroot	24 to 30 4-inch-square eggroll skins
2 medium carrots, coarsely grated	

Finely shred enough cabbage to measure 4 cups. Coarsely chop the mushrooms.

Heat 1/4 cup oil in a wok or a large skillet over moderate heat. Add the mustard seeds, garlic, and gingerroot. When the first mustard seed pops, add the cabbage and stir fry for 3 minutes. Add the mushrooms and stir fry for 1 minute. Add the grated carrots and mung beans and stir fry for 1 minute. Remove the wok or skillet from the heat and stir in the soy sauce and cress leaves. Toss in the chicken or shrimp, if desired.

Lightly beat the egg. Fill each eggroll skin with 2 tablespoons of the cooked mixture. Fold the corners over the center and seal the top flap of each eggroll with a dab of beaten egg.

Heat the remaining 2 cups peanut oil in a wok or deep skillet until the oil is very hot, almost smoking. Fry the eggrolls, 4 at a time, for 45 seconds on each side, or until both sides are golden brown. Remove the eggrolls with a slotted spoon and drain on paper towels. Allow the oil to become very hot before frying each batch. Keep the eggrolls hot on a warm serving platter until all are cooked. Serve immediately with Chinese mustard and soy sauce for dipping. Garnish the platter with cress sprigs, if desired.

Serves 8 to 12 as appetizers.

Cress Bearnaise

1 large shallot	1 tablespoon hot water
3 tablespoons white wine	6 tablespoons unsalted butter
3 tablespoons tarragon vinegar	salt and white pepper to taste
1 egg yolk	1 tablespoon minced cress leaves

Finely mince the shallot. Combine it with the white wine and tarragon vinegar in a small, heavy saucepan. Reduce the liquid in the saucepan over moderately high heat to about 1 tablespoon.

Whisk the egg yolk with hot water. Remove the pan from the heat and whisk in the egg yolk mixture.

Cut the butter into bits. Return the sauce to a very low heat and add the butter, about one-fourth at a time, whisking vigorously and constantly. When the sauce has emulsified to a glossy, medium-thick consistency, remove from the heat. Stir in the salt and pepper, then stir in the cress leaves. Serve the sauce with Cress Crepes (see Index) or with poached or grilled fish.

Yields about 3/4 cup.

Watercress Creme Fraiche Soup

1 quart defatted chicken stock or vegetable stock	salt and white pepper to taste
2 1/2 cups packed watercress leaves	1 cup creme fraiche

Heat the stock over low heat until it barely simmers. Add the watercress, salt, and pepper and simmer for 5 minutes. Stir in the creme fraiche.

Remove the soup from the heat and puree it in batches in a blender or food processor. Return it to low heat for 2 to 3 minutes. Ladle the soup into warm soup plates and serve immediately.

Serves 4.

Cress Crepes

1 cup packed cress leaves	1/2 teaspoon salt
1 cup milk	about 1 teaspoon clarified butter
2 eggs	6 poached eggs
2/3 cup all-purpose flour	Garnish: 6 or more cress sprigs

Mince the cress leaves finely. Combine the cress, milk, eggs, flour, and salt in a bowl. Beat the batter well with a whisk and let it stand at room temperature for 1 to 4 hours.

To cook the crepes, brush a very small amount of clarified butter in a 7-inch crepe or omelette pan and heat the pan over moderately high heat. Pour 1/4 cup batter into the pan, swirling it to distribute the batter evenly. Cook the crepe for 40 seconds, or until the edges begin to curl. Turn the crepe and cook for 30 to 40 seconds on the other side. Put the crepe on a platter and hold in a 200° F. oven. Cook the rest of the crepes, stacking them and keeping them warm. Cover the crepes with a barely damp tea towel until the eggs are ready.

To poach the eggs, drop them one at a time into simmering, lightly salted, vinegared water. Baste the top of each egg with the water for 2 to 3 minutes, until the whites are set and the yolks are cooked as desired. With a slotted spoon, remove the eggs to a large pan containing plain warm water. Trim the strands of egg white before serving the crepes.

Fold the crepes in quarters and arrange 2 on each of 3 warm plates. Center a poached egg on each crepe and surround each egg with cress sprigs. Serve plain or with Cress Bearnaise (see Index).

Yields 6 crepes.

Cress Turbot Mousse

Poaching the Fish	
1 medium carrot	1 1/2 cups dry white wine
1 small white onion	about 1 teaspoon salt
10 parsley sprigs	2 pounds turbot fillets
10 peppercorns	water
1 bay leaf	

Peel the carrot and onion and quarter them. Combine the vegetables, parsley, peppercorns, bay leaf, and wine in a pan large enough to hold the fish in one layer. Add the salt and the fish. Add enough water to just cover the fish. Bring the bouillon to a simmer and cook 4 to 5 minutes, until the fish just flakes. Remove the fish from the bouillon and cool to room temperature. Gently flake the fish and remove any bones.

Preparing the Mousse

flaked fish	*2 teaspoons finely minced, fresh summer savory, or 1 teaspoon finely ground, dried summer savory*
1/2 cup whipping cream	*1 teaspoon powdered mustard*
4 tablespoons unsalted butter, melted	*1 tablespoon Dijon mustard*
3 cups packed cress leaves	*salt and white pepper to taste*

Puree the fish in batches in a blender or in a food processor. Rub the fish puree through a fine sieve into a large bowl set over ice. With a wooden spoon, work in the cream and butter a little at a time. Work the mixture at least 10 minutes, keeping it cold. Work in the cress, then the seasonings, and refrigerate the mixture over ice for 30 minutes.

Preheat the oven to 325° F.

Thickly butter a 1-quart stainless or tin-lined copper mold. Stir the mousse mixture again and put it into the mold. Put the mold in a large baking dish and add hot water to cover two-thirds of the mold. Bake the mousse for 25 minutes. Remove the mold from the water and let cool to room temperature. Carefully unmold the mousse onto a serving platter, cover, and chill for 2 to 3 hours.

Garnish: Tomato Mayonnaise (recipe follows)	*12 to 15 cress sprigs*

Blot the excess water from the platter. Mask the mousse with Tomato Mayonnaise (see following recipe) or serve it separately. Garnish the platter with sprigs of cress and serve with small, buttered croutons or unsalted crackers.

Serves 10 to 12.

Tomato Mayonnaise

1 large egg yolk	3/4 cup vegetable oil
1 teaspoon lemon juice	3 tablespoons tomato paste
pinch of salt	1 tablespoon lemon juice, or to taste

Beat the egg yolk, 1 teaspoon lemon juice, and salt in a deep bowl. Add 1/4 cup oil, a drop or two at a time, beating constantly. Drizzle the rest of the oil into the bowl in a fine stream, continuing to whisk until the mayonnaise has emulsified. Stir the tomato paste and lemon juice into the mayonnaise, blending well.

    Yields about 1 cup.

Potato Pie with Wilted Cress

This is a savory potato pie, baked to a crusty golden brown and crowned with a wreath of slightly wilted cress leaves.

3 pounds medium-sized brown potatoes	1 cup milk
1 medium, white onion	2 teaspoons salt, or to taste
about 5 tablespoons unsalted butter	1 teaspoon freshly ground white pepper
1 1/2 cups coarsely grated Gruyere or Emmenthal cheese	2 cups packed cress leaves
2 large eggs	

Boil the potatoes in their skins until they pierce easily with a fork. Drain, rinse briefly under cold water, and let cool to room temperature. Peel the potatoes and set aside.

    Finely chop the onion and saute over moderate heat in 4 tablespoons butter until it is limp and golden brown. Mash the potatoes in a large bowl, add the sauteed onion and the cheese, and blend well.

    Preheat the oven to 375° F.

    In a small bowl, beat the eggs with the milk, salt, and pepper. Add the milk mixture to the potatoes and combine well. Butter a 9 1/2-inch glass or ceramic pie dish with the remaining butter and fill with the potato mixture. Bake the pie for 45 minutes, or until the top is golden brown and crusty.

Barely wilt the cress leaves in a steamer over boiling water, about 30 seconds. Remove the pie from the oven and arrange the wilted cress leaves in a circle on top. Cut the pie into wedges and serve hot.

Serves 8.

Avocado Cress Salad

2 large, ripe California avocados	1/2 cup chopped celery
1/2 lemon	1 cup packed cress leaves
1 tablespoon lemon juice	salt to taste
1 tablespoon virgin olive oil	Garnish: 8 leaves red leaf or oak leaf lettuce
2 small, ripe tomatoes	8 to 12 cress sprigs
1/2 cup chopped red onion	

Halve the avocados and scoop out the meat, leaving about 1/4 inch next to the skin. Rub the avocado halves with the lemon half. Dice the avocado meat into 1/2-inch cubes and toss in a bowl with the lemon juice and olive oil.

Roughly chop the tomatoes. Mix the tomatoes, onion, celery, and cress leaves with the diced avocados. Season with salt.

Arrange the lettuce leaves on 4 salad plates. Fill the avocado halves with the vegetable mixture and place them on the lettuce. Garnish with cress sprigs and serve with Cress Raita (see Index).

Serves 4.

Bulgur Wheat and Cress Salad

2 cups medium bulgur wheat	1 large garlic clove, finely minced
4 cups hot vegetable or chicken stock	fresh pineapple to equal 1 cup of 1-inch chunks and juice
1 cup packed cress leaves	salt to taste
1/2 cup olive oil, or to taste	Garnish: 10 to 12 cress sprigs
juice of 1 lemon	6, 3/8-inch slices pineapple rounds, cut in half

Put the bulgur in a large bowl and pour the hot stock over it. Let stand for 3 hours. Pour into a fine sieve and drain at least 1/2 hour.

Coarsely chop the cress leaves. In a small bowl, mix the cress, olive oil, lemon juice, garlic, and pineapple chunks and juice. Pour the dressing over the drained bulgur, toss well, and season. Marinate at room temperature for 2 hours. Transfer the salad to a serving dish and garnish with cress sprigs and pineapple slices.

Serves 8.

Salmon and Pasta Salad with Cress

Poaching the Salmon

1/2 pound salmon steak or fillet	6 peppercorns
1 cup dry white wine	6 parsley sprigs
1 garlic clove, peeled	1/2 teaspoon salt
1 bay leaf	

Combine all the ingredients, except the salmon, in a pan deep enough to allow the fish to be covered by the liquid. Bring the liquid to a simmer and poach the salmon until it is just done, about 4 to 5 minutes. Remove the salmon from the pan and let cool for 30 minutes at room temperature. Strain the poaching liquid and reduce to 1/2 cup.

Cooking the Carrots and Pasta

1/2 pound fingerling carrots	1 teaspoon olive oil
1 cup water	1/2 pound tiny shell pasta
1 teaspoon salt	3 quarts boiling, salted water

Clean the carrots and cook them in 1 cup water, with the salt and olive oil, until the carrots are barely tender. Drain the carrots and rub off the skins under cold running water. Cut the carrots on the diagonal into 1/2-inch pieces and set aside.

Cook the pasta in boiling, salted water until al dente. Drain the pasta and rinse briefly with cold water. Drain again and transfer to a large bowl with the carrots.

Preparing the Vinaigrette

1/2 cup virgin olive oil	reduced poaching liquid
1 large garlic clove, minced	salt and lemon juice to taste
1 tablespoon Dijon mustard	

Mix the oil, garlic, mustard, and poaching liquid together. Taste for salt and lemon juice. Pour the vinaigrette over the pasta and carrots and toss well.

Finishing the Salad

poached salmon	1/2 cup Nicoise olives
1 cup packed cress leaves	

Flake the salmon carefully into the pasta salad, trimming away bones and skin if necessary. Add the cress leaves and olives and toss everything together gently. Cover the salad and chill for 2 hours. Serve it on 4 large shells or salad plates.

    Serves 4.

Cress Raita

1 quart good quality, unflavored yogurt	1 teaspoon ground mustard seeds
1 1/2 cups packed cress leaves	1/4 teaspoon cayenne pepper, or to taste
2 tablespoons finely chopped onion	

Finely chop the cress leaves and mix them with the yogurt, onion, mustard seeds, and pepper. Cover the raita and chill for at least 2 hours. Serve with Avocado Cress Salad (see Index), or meat or vegetable curries.

    Yields about 5 cups.

DILL

DILL

Lullaby dill, the baby calms to sleep;
Fragrant dill, the cook bakes bread;
Fruitful dill, the gardener goes to reap.

THIS IS THE herb we rub shoulders with every summer, the tall, golden brown flower heads as large as dinner plates and full of plump seeds, waiting for us to pick, dry, and enter them in the county fair. It is stalwart and accommodating all year; we use the feathery fresh leaves in green salads and the seeds for heavier foods—breads and potatoes—or as an herb salt.

Throughout its history, dill has displayed the mien of a cheerful, plain soul, ready to lighten everyday fare. Although many culinary and medicinal recipes have collected around it, sacred, poetic, or fanciful imaginations have not found dill an inspiring herb. It has remained, for the diverse populations that have used it, a comforting, pleasant herb adapted to practical roles.

Its Greek name, *anethum,* is simply a description of its essential oil; in English, its name is from the Saxon *dillan,* "to lull or soothe." Dill water has soothed babies' colic for ages in England, Europe, and Turkey. Dill wine was taken by adults as people now take bicarbonate preparations. It was probably for this calming effect on the stomach, as much as for the complementary flavors, that cooks began pickling cucumbers with dill. Every English household that cultivated herbs had dill vinegar for salads.

Although native to the Mediterranean area, dill is used sparingly in the food of that region, except in Greece and Turkey. It is popular in many eastern European cuisines—in Rumania, Bulgaria, Poland, and Russia—and in France, Germany, England, and especially Sweden. Dill (seeds, leaves, or both) is found in baked goods of all descriptions, including breads, crackers, cookies, cakes, and pies. It is very common with fish: the gravlax and marinated herring of Scandinavia; dill sauce for fresh trout in England; and, fish grilled with dill in France and Russia. Dill is used in sauces for poultry and vegetables; with meats, particularly in Russian and eastern European foods; and, as an enlivener of simple egg or potato dishes. When small amounts are used, dill combines successfully with parsley or chervil to poach chicken, fish, and early summer vegetables.

The flavor, from dill's particular camphor compound, is a mixture of anise, parsley, and celery, with a distinctive green bite on the sides of the tongue. The aroma is a clean combination of mint, citrus, and fennel, with a touch of sea air. The seeds' flavor is predominately a combination of caraway and anise.

Dill's aroma is fairly delicate and loses much in drying or cooking. We find dried dill weed to have very limited uses; fortunately, fresh dill is available most of the year in major produce areas of the United States. Dill should have no yellow or pale green color in the leaves or stems. As the bunches are usually large, freezing is a good way to preserve any that is left over. Rinse the dill and pat it thoroughly dry. Freeze six-inch lengths individually, or three to four tablespoons of snipped dill in small containers.

Dill grows in most climates with the modest requirements of fairly friable soil, light fertilization, and sun. It will not grow successfully indoors as it needs eighteen inches of taproot space and much branching room. Although it flourishes in the garden and conveniently reseeds itself with good plants coming in for many years, it languishes in confined areas. It germinates and grows quickly and can be planted after danger of frost, or year round, in suitable climates.

The seeds and leaves are harvested at different times. If you want fresh dill weed into the late fall, sow again in midsummer. Cut the leaves close to the stem about two months after planting. To harvest the seeds, allow the umbels to form on some plants and the seeds to turn pale brown. Cut the tops with about a foot of stalk and hang them upside down, with the umbels in paper bags to catch the seeds. Be sure they are completely dry before storing. Dill can be grown near vegetables for leaf harvesting, but should not be allowed to mature, especially near carrots, as it effectively slows their growth.

The recipes here accent dill's fresh fragrance and pleasing ways with many foods.

Dilled Ricotta Torte

We like serving this savory, rich torte for Sunday brunch or lunch as a change from the familiar egg and cheese dishes. It goes well with a variety of fruit and green salads and a platter of imported sliced hams. Use the natural cream cheese, without gums or chemicals, available in cheese stores and delicatessens.

2/3 cup whole natural almonds	2 tablespoons half-and-half cream
1 1/4 cups dry whole wheat bread crumbs	1/3 cup finely snipped dill leaves
1/2 cup unsalted butter, softened	1/2 teaspoon freshly grated nutmeg
about 1/4 teaspoon salt	1 teaspoon grated lemon peel
3/4 pound fresh cream cheese, softened	pinch of salt
1 cup ricotta cheese	Garnish: dill sprigs
2 eggs	

Make a medium-fine meal of the almonds in a blender or food processor. Transfer to a bowl. Grind the bread crumbs to a fine meal and combine with the almonds. Blend the softened butter well with the almonds and bread crumbs. Stir in a little salt. Press the mixture on the bottom and sides of a 9 1/2-inch springform baking pan.

With an electric mixer on medium speed, or with a food processor, combine the cream cheese, ricotta, eggs, cream, dill, nutmeg, lemon peel, and salt. Blend thoroughly.

Preheat the oven to 350° F.

Pour the mixture carefully into the prepared shell and bake for 1 hour and 10 minutes. Cool the torte to room temperature on a rack and garnish with dill sprigs. The torte can be served chilled.

Serves 8 to 12.

Eggs with Avocado Dill Sauce

6 large eggs, at room temperature	juice of 1/2 lime
1 large, ripe Haas avocado	salt and cayenne pepper to taste
1/4 cup sour cream	Garnish: several dill sprigs
2 tablespoons snipped dill leaves	

To hard-cook the eggs, cover them with warm water, bring the water to a boil, remove the pan from the heat, and let stand for 10 minutes. Rinse the eggs under cold water for 2 or 3 minutes. Shell them and drain on a tea towel.

Peel the avocado and puree it with the sour cream, dill leaves, lime juice, salt, and pepper. Put the avocado pit in the sauce to prevent discoloration, cover the sauce, and chill for 1 hour.

Slice the eggs evenly and arrange them on a serving platter. Cover them tightly and chill for 1 hour. Just before serving, spoon the sauce over the eggs and garnish with dill sprigs.

Serves 4 to 6 as an appetizer.

Dill Cracker Bread

2 cups unbleached white flour	1/2 cup warm water
1/2 cup whole wheat flour	3 tablespoons finely snipped dill leaves
1/2 cup rye flour	1 teaspoon salt
1 teaspoon salt	1 teaspoon dill seed
1/2 cup unsalted butter, softened	

Mix the flours and 1 teaspoon salt together in a large bowl. Rub the softened butter in by hand or process in a food processor to make a fine meal. With a wooden spoon, stir in the warm water and dill leaves.

Knead the dough for 5 minutes. Roll on a lightly floured surface into a 1/8-inch thick rectangle. Prick the dough well with a fork and roll the dough with a lefse roller for decoration.

Preheat the oven to 325° F.

In a mortar, grind 1 teaspoon salt and the dill seed together to make a fine powder. Sprinkle the dough with the powder. Cut the dough into crackers 3-by-1 1/2-inches and place them slightly apart on lightly buttered baking sheets. Bake for 25 minutes, turning the crackers after 15 minutes.

Yields about 40 crackers.

Dill Corn Sticks

corn oil	2 eggs
1 cup stone-ground cornmeal	1 cup cold water
1 cup unbleached white flour	1 cup fresh corn kernels, cooked and drained
1 tablespoon baking powder	5 tablespoons butter, melted
1/2 teaspoon salt	3 tablespoons finely snipped dill

Preheat the oven to 350° F.

Generously oil two corn stick molds and preheat them for 10 to 15 minutes.

Combine the cornmeal, flour, baking powder, and salt in a large bowl. In another bowl, lightly beat the eggs and combine them with the water, corn kernels, butter, and dill.

Barely combine the liquid and dry ingredients. Spoon the batter into the heated molds, filling each mold about 3/4 full. Bake for 25 to 30 minutes, until the sticks are golden brown. Serve hot.

Yields 14 sticks.

Dill Mayonnaise

1 large egg yolk	3 tablespoons snipped dill leaves
lemon juice	1 teaspoon ground mustard seed
1 teaspoon honey	1/2 teaspoon salt, or to taste
1/4 cup light olive oil	pinch of cayenne pepper
1/2 cup vegetable oil	

In a mortar or bowl, whisk the egg yolk with about 1 teaspoon lemon juice and the honey. Mix the oils together and add them to the bowl, drop by drop, stirring constantly.

When half the oil has been added, pour in the rest in a fine, steady stream, stirring constantly. When the mayonnaise has emulsified, stir in the dill, mustard seed, salt, and pepper. Adjust the seasoning with lemon juice.

Yields about 1 cup.

Fresh Tomato Soup with Dill

The flavor of this soup depends on the tomatoes; they should be completely and perfectly ripe.

3 pounds ripe tomatoes	1/2 teaspoon salt
1/4 cup snipped dill	1/4 teaspoon paprika
1 medium garlic clove, finely minced	Garnish: about 3 teaspoons snipped dill

Blanch the tomatoes in boiling water for about 10 seconds. Cool under running water, peel, and seed them.

Puree the tomatoes briefly, about 10 seconds, in a blender or food processor with the dill, garlic, salt, and paprika. Chill the soup at least 2 hours. Ladle into 6 chilled soup bowls and garnish with a little snipped dill.

Serves 6.

Baked Leg of Lamb with Yogurt Dill Marinade

3 1/2- to 4-pound leg of lamb, shank end	6 to 8 sprigs Italian parsley, stemmed and minced
1 cup plain yogurt	scant 1/2 cup minced dill leaves, loosely packed
2 to 3 tablespoons minced onion	1/2 teaspoon cayenne pepper, or to taste
1 to 2 minced garlic cloves	salt and freshly ground black pepper

Bone the leg of lamb. Remove as much fat and sinew as possible. Butterfly the lamb so that the meat is of approximately the same thickness. Secure any small pieces or thin ends with wooden skewers.

Mix the yogurt with the onion, garlic, parsley, and dill and season the mixture with cayenne pepper. Pat the marinade all over the lamb and place it in a shallow glass or ceramic casserole. Marinate the lamb at a cool room temperature for 2 to 4 hours.

Preheat the oven to 450° F.

Salt and pepper the lamb lightly on both sides. Place the lamb, cut side up, on a rack and roast it for 10 minutes.

Reduce the heat to 350° F. and roast the lamb for 15 minutes. Turn the lamb and roast it for 20 minutes. The lamb will be rare.

Remove the lamb to a serving platter and let it stand for about 5 minutes before cutting it into 3/8-inch slices.

Serves 4 to 6.

Dilled Cucumbers

If English or Japanese cucumbers are available, use them in this salad.

3 cucumbers, or 2 English or Japanese cucumbers	1/2 cup virgin olive oil
1 small red onion	about 1 1/2 tablespoons white wine vinegar
3/4 cup loosely packed dill leaves	salt and freshly ground black pepper to taste

Scrub the cucumbers. Peel them if the skins are waxy or tough; if the skins are tasty, remove 4 or 5 strips lengthwise around the cucumbers. Trim the ends and cut the cucumbers into 1/4-inch thick slices.

Halve the onion lengthwise and cut it into thin rings. Chop the dill coarsely. Mix the oil, vinegar, salt, and pepper, and stir in the dill. Toss the vinaigrette with the vegetables, cover, and marinate at least 1 hour in the refrigerator.

Serves 6 to 8.

Dilled Yellow Squash

One of our grandmothers made this dish every summer at our shore house when the squash came in season. We have added fresh dill to the recipe but we cook it, as she did, in a black iron skillet.

2 1/2 pounds yellow squash	1/3 cup finely snipped dill
1 large, yellow sweet onion	salt and freshly ground black pepper to taste
6 tablespoons butter	

Wash and trim the squash and cut it into 1/3-inch thick rings. Peel and halve the onion and cut the halves into thin rings.

Melt the butter in a heavy skillet and saute the vegetables over medium heat for 10 to 15 minutes, until they are crisp tender. Stir in the dill and season with salt and pepper. Lower the heat, cover, and cook 5 minutes longer. Serve hot.

Serves 8.

Coleslaw with Dill Mayonnaise

1 green cabbage, about 2 pounds	1 cup Dill Mayonnaise (see Index)
2 carrots	lemon juice to taste
1 small red onion	salt to taste
1/3 cup finely snipped dill	

Trim and wash the cabbage. Grate it coarsely. Finely grate the carrots and onion. Combine the vegetables in a large bowl. Add the dill and Dill Mayonnaise, and toss well. Season with lemon juice and salt.

Serves 8.

Mussel and Potato Salad with Dill

Steaming the Mussels

4 dozen mussels	2 large garlic cloves
1 cup dry white wine	

Debeard the mussels, then scrub and rinse them well. Put them in a very large pot (or cook them in 2 batches). Peel and roughly chop the garlic. Add the garlic and wine to the pot. Cover and steam the mussels over high heat until they just open, 2 to 5 minutes. Start checking for opened mussels after 2 minutes and remove them. Discard any mussels that do not open. Shuck the mussels and rinse them well.

Strain the pot liquor through a fine sieve and tripled cheesecloth. Put the mussels in a little of the strained liquor. Reduce the rest of the liquor by half over high heat. Set the reduced liquor aside.

Preparing the Vegetables

6 new potatoes, about 2 inches in diameter	1/3 cup snipped dill leaves
salt to taste	1/3 cup finely cut scallions, with some green

Scrub the potatoes. Cover them with 1 inch of cold water, salt lightly, and cook until they are just done, about 10 minutes. Drain the potatoes and cool just until they can be handled. Peel them, if necessary, and cut into 1/4-inch thick rounds. Combine them in a large bowl with the mussels, dill, and scallions.

Finishing the Salad

1/3 cup reduced mussel liquor	freshly ground black pepper to taste
about 1/3 cup extra virgin olive oil	Garnish: dill sprigs
2 to 3 tablespoons lemon juice	

Mix the mussel liquor, olive oil, lemon juice, and pepper. Taste for seasoning. Toss the vinaigrette with the mussels and potatoes while the potatoes are still warm. Let stand for about 30 minutes. Arrange the salad on a platter and garnish with dill sprigs.
    Serves 4 to 6.

Dilled Beet Salad

This and the following salad look and taste good on the same plate.

2 pounds beets, 2 to 2 1/2 inches in diameter	about 3 tablespoons lemon juice
3/4 cup sour cream	salt and freshly ground white pepper to taste
1/4 cup snipped dill leaves	Optional: 1 tablespoon freshly grated horseradish root

Trim and scrub the beets. Cover them by 1 inch with water and cook until they are just tender, about 20 minutes. Refresh them under cold water, cool, and peel. Grate them coarsely.
    Mix the sour cream, dill, lemon juice, salt, pepper, and horseradish in

a large bowl. Toss with the grated beets. Cover and chill at least 1 hour. Arrange the salad on individual plates, next to the Dilled Daikon Salad (see following recipe), or in a serving dish. Serve chilled.

Serves 4 to 6.

Dilled Daikon Salad

2 pounds daikon (oriental white radish)	2 tablespoons minced onion
1 cup plain, whole milk yogurt	salt and pepper to taste
1/4 cup snipped dill	Garnish: dill sprigs

Scrub, trim, and peel the daikon. Grate it coarsely and drain it in a colander for 1 hour. Squeeze out any excess liquid.

Mix the yogurt, dill, and onion in a large bowl and season with salt and pepper. Add the daikon and toss well. Cover and chill the salad at least 1 hour.

To serve, arrange the salad in a shallow bowl and garnish with dill sprigs.

Serves 4 to 6.

GARLIC

GARLIC

The garlic bulb is sturdy and strong,
and favors those who would live long.
Yet savoury stews with garlic styled,
are relished by the meek and mild.

IF WE WERE FACED with the unhappy predicament of banishing all herbs but one from our kitchens, we would have to choose garlic as indispensable. Clearly, we are not the only people who revel in the glories of garlic. The garlic harvest has been celebrated in Provence for centuries. Huge bowls of aioli in the center of tables laden with bread, fresh vegetables, sausages, and plenty of young red wine are shared by the communities as they pay tribute to the season's bounty. Garlic films, festivals, books, and newsletters flourish, especially in California, where the bulk of the United States crop is grown. An annual garlic festival is held in Gilroy, a small northern California town that exudes a warm and powerful aroma in midsummer. There is a competition for the best garlic recipe of the year, a bulb topping contest, and, of course, a garlic queen.

Garlic is usually associated with Mediterranean cuisine, but it circles the temperate zone of the globe, featured in Mexican, Caribbean, South American, Middle Eastern, Indian, and Chinese cooking. It speaks of the hot sun even in the winter, adding pungency and warmth to the dishes prepared with it. The culinary use of garlic is ancient; recipes were recorded in Egypt, Babylonia, and China 2,000 and 3,000 years before Christ.

Allium sativum has inspired more magical, religious, and medicinal lore than any other herb. The Hebrews and Egyptians held it sacred; the Greeks used it in temple purification ceremonies. In some Hebrew sects, the groom wore a clove in his wedding costume to symbolize a happy marriage. Roman charioteers ate garlic for strength. Even today, Greek peasants find the strength for their hard lives on a basic diet of bread, garlic, and olives.

Garlic has long been used as a disinfectant, as a folk remedy for colds and flus, and as an antidote for poison, as well as to ward off the plague. Its antiseptic and digestive properties have been well documented in this century. It has sustained a reputation for conferring long life on its users and for protecting them from evil.

We are sure that much of the prejudice against garlic would vanish if more people sampled fresh, sweet, crisp-tender garlic, rather than the old, yellow, limp, or moldy bulbs packed in little boxes. Even further from the true taste are garlic salt, powder, flakes, and chips, and chopped garlic preserved in oil. These preparations detract from a cook's efforts to prepare honest dishes by leaving bitter, metallic, and off flavors that linger long after the other ingredients are forgotten.

For some, garlic's odor is a deterrent to its enjoyment, but there are many ways to render it inoffensive. The aroma is less noticeable when the meal is accompanied by salad greens (unless, of course, the salad dressing has garlic in it). Fresh parsley neutralizes garlic odor in the breath most effectively. A whole head of garlic may have a mild flavor, especially if it is baked. Using whole cloves, peeled or unpeeled, makes the taste less pungent. The odor of garlic can be removed from the hands by sprinkling them with salt and rinsing with cold water.

Cooking transmutes garlic's rough and simple essence to the piquant and subtle. It is still popular with peasants and gourmets from Europe to Asia. Bean and game dishes seem to lack savor without garlic. The Chinese use garlic with fish and shellfish. French chefs use it in many ways, from brushing a wooden spoon with it and stirring a delicate sauce, to the whole cloves in aioli.

Garlic is easy to grow outdoors. In cold climates, plant it in November after the first frost in well-mulched soil. In temperate climates, plant it in January during a period when the soil is relatively dry. Garlic wants full sun and a soil that is well drained to prevent rotting. Buy bulbs for planting at the market, or from a good seed supplier, using the same selection criteria as for cooking: well-formed, large cloves; a bulb with the firmness of an apple; and no rotted cloves or mold on the paper-like skin.

Two different varieties, good for experimentation, are elephant garlic and Mexican red or purple garlic. They are as simple to grow as white garlic. Elephant garlic is about twice as large as white garlic; it usually has four cloves and a mild flavor. Mexican red or purple garlic is so called because its outer skin is reddish purple and much of it is cultivated in Mexico. It is often the first garlic available at the beginning of the season.

Garlic is a good companion herb to hardy, above-ground vegetables and makes a good border plant. We have seldom found rotting or diseased cloves in garlic grown in home gardens. Plant the individual cloves about two inches deep and six to eight inches apart with the pointed end up. Do not overwater or fertilize during the last month in the ground (July or August depending on the climate). When the garlic forms a flower and the leaves begin to turn yellow and wither, bend the leaves completely over about an inch above ground level.

Harvest when the leaves are completely dry. Dig the bulbs and shake them free of excess dirt. Lay them on a screen in a sunny place with good air circulation. Two or three days of full sun should be sufficient to dry the garlic. The outside skins should be moisture-free before storing. The tops can be cut off and the bulbs stored in mesh onion bags or in a box in a cool place away from light. Or the tops can be left on and the garlic braided.

In the recipes that follow, garlic has many guises.

Fettunta

Good bread, preferably Tuscan-style with whole wheat flour and little salt, makes this dish one of our favorite appetizers. We like to toast the bread over an open fire and make a little hearth ceremony of rubbing it with garlic and anointing it with a fine olive oil before serving it to friends.

4 large garlic cloves	*1/2 teaspoon salt*
1/2 cup extra virgin olive oil	*12, 1/2-inch thick slices Italian bread*

Peel the garlic and cut each clove in half. Mix the olive oil and salt in a small dish. Toast the bread over an open flame or under the broiler until it is golden brown on both sides. Rub the toast on both sides with the cut garlic, then dip one side of each slice lightly in the olive oil. Eat the fettunta immediately.

Serves 6.

Garlic and Herb Cheese

This cheese is simple to make, tastes better, and is less expensive than prepackaged herb cheeses. It lends itself to experimentation with different herb combinations.

1 pound natural cream cheese, at room temperature	*4 to 5 summer savory sprigs*
2 to 3 tablespoons half-and-half cream	*2 medium garlic cloves*
10 parsley sprigs	*about 1/4 teaspoon salt*
4 to 5 marjoram sprigs	

Cream the cheese, adding half-and-half cream if the cheese is dry. Stem the parsley, marjoram, and summer savory and mince. Peel the garlic and mince it finely. Add the herbs, garlic, and salt to the cream cheese. Blend the mixture well, cover tightly with plastic wrap, and refrigerate at least 2 hours before serving.

The cheese improves in flavor after a day and can be kept for 2 to 3 days, if covered tightly and refrigerated.

Yields about 2 1/2 cups.

Roasted Nuts with Garlic and Soy Sauce

5 cups assorted, unroasted nuts	*4 medium garlic cloves, crushed*
1/3 cup tamari soy sauce	*1 teaspoon cayenne pepper*
1/4 cup water	

Soak the nuts in the soy sauce, water, garlic, and pepper for 1 hour, stirring occasionally.

Preheat the oven to 350° F.

Drain the liquid from the nuts and spread them on a large baking sheet. Place the baking sheet in the oven and bake for 20 minutes, stirring the nuts two or three times. Let the nuts cool to room temperature before packing them in an airtight container.

Yields about 5 cups.

Garlic Parmesan Twists

1/2 cup unsalted butter	1 large egg, lightly beaten
3 cups unbleached white flour	1/2 cup lukewarm water
1 teaspoon salt	3 medium garlic cloves, finely minced
1 tablespoon baking powder	2 tablespoons poppy seeds
1 cup freshly grated Parmesan cheese	

Melt the butter over low heat and let cool.

Preheat the oven to 375° F.

Sift the flour with the salt and baking powder into a large mixing bowl. Stir in the cheese. Make a well in the flour mixture and add the egg, water, garlic, and butter. Stir with a wooden spoon until the liquids are incorporated. Knead the dough on a smooth surface for 5 minutes.

On a pastry cloth or floured sheet of waxed paper, roll the dough into a 10-by-12-inch rectangle, 3/8 inch thick. Cut into 1/2-inch strips and twist two strips together. Cut these twists into 4-inch lengths and pinch the ends together.

Spread the poppy seeds on waxed paper and roll the twists lightly in the seeds. Place the twists on buttered and floured baking sheets, about 1 1/2 inches apart, and bake for 25 minutes.

Yields 26 twists.

Creamy Mushroom Garlic Sauce

1/4 pound mushrooms, sliced	1/2 cup finely minced parsley
3 medium garlic cloves, crushed	1 cup freshly grated Parmesan cheese
6 tablespoons unsalted butter	salt and freshly ground black pepper to taste
1/2 pint heavy cream	

Saute the mushrooms and garlic in the butter, over low heat, for 10 minutes. Add the cream and parsley and bring to a simmer. Stir in the cheese. Season with salt and pepper. Serve over hot, drained pasta.

Serves 4.

Garlic Honey Lemon Dressing

1/4 teaspoon salt	3 tablespoons walnut oil
juice of 2 lemons	3 garlic cloves, minced
3/4 cup good quality olive oil	1 tablespoon honey

Dissolve the salt in the lemon juice. Pour into a blender with the olive oil, walnut oil, garlic, and honey. Blend at high speed for 1 minute.

Yields 1 1/2 cups dressing for spinach, rice, or green salad.

Tomato Cream Sauce

This is a sauce for the day you want a quick, easy, elegant, and satisfying pasta dinner.

1/4 cup tomato paste	1/2 teaspoon salt
2 tablespoons finely chopped, fresh basil, or 1 scant teaspoon dried, crumbled basil	1 pint light cream
1 large garlic clove, minced	Garnish: 1/2 cup freshly grated Parmesan cheese

Carefully mix all of the ingredients, except the cheese, in a saucepan over low heat. Barely simmer over very low heat for 8 to 10 minutes. Serve over hot pasta and sprinkle with ample cheese.

Yields enough sauce to dress 4 to 6 servings of pasta.

Roasted Eggplant and Garlic Soup

1 1/2 pound eggplant	salt and white pepper to taste
3 cups chicken or vegetable stock	Optional garnish: 1 tablespoon white wine vinegar
3 large garlic cloves	4 sprigs minced tarragon
3 tablespoons olive oil	1 teaspoon cracked black pepper

Preheat the oven to 375° F.

Cut the eggplant in half lengthwise and place it, cut side down, on a baking sheet lined with aluminum foil. Bake it for 30 minutes.

Remove the eggplant pulp from the skin. Puree the pulp with 1/2 cup stock. Transfer to a soup pot.

Mince the garlic finely and saute it in the olive oil for 2 minutes. Add this and the rest of the stock to the soup pot. Stir well and heat over low heat. Season with salt and pepper.

Mix the garnish ingredients together. Ladle the soup into heated bowls and put 1 teaspoonful of garnish on top of each bowl. Serve hot.

Serves 4.

Ravioli di Zucca

A superb way to eat pumpkin—blended with Parmesan cheese and garlic, wrapped in tender pasta, and napped in a velvety cream sauce—this is a perfect dish for an autumn evening.

Filling

1 shallot	1/4 cup freshly grated Parmesan cheese
4 garlic cloves	1/4 cup fine, dry bread crumbs
2 tablespoons unsalted butter	salt and pepper to taste
1 cup fresh pumpkin puree, or winter squash puree	

Finely mince the shallot with the garlic and saute them in the butter, over low heat, until limp and golden. Add the pumpkin puree and simmer about 2 minutes. Remove from the heat, add the cheese and bread crumbs, and blend well. Season to taste. Set aside and prepare the pasta.

Pasta

1 recipe Egg Pasta (see index)

Prepare the Egg Pasta as directed in the Paglia e Fieno recipe. After the pasta has been rolled through the narrowest setting, cut it into 6-inch lengths and set it on a lightly floured surface so that the pieces do not touch.

Place the pasta, one sheet at a time, in a ravioli press. Fill each indentation with 1 level teaspoon of filling, cover with another sheet of pasta, and press. To make ravioli without a press, evenly space 8 level teaspoons of filling (in mounds) on a 6-inch piece of pasta. With a pastry brush lightly moistened with water, outline the filling on all sides to divide it into 8 equal ravioli. Place another piece of pasta over the filling and press down well around each mound. Trim all edges and cut the ravioli with a crimped edge pastry cutter. (At this point, the ravioli can be kept on floured baking sheets, covered with a lightly floured cotton towel, for 4 to 6 hours. The ravioli should be placed so that they do not touch.)

Cooking the Ravioli

4 quarts water	2 tablespoons butter
1/4 cup salt	

Bring the water, salt, and 1 tablespoon of butter to a rolling boil. Butter a serving dish with the remaining butter. Drop the ravioli, 10 at a time, into the boiling water and stir with a wooden spoon for 30 seconds. Cook each batch for about 1 minute after the ravioli have risen to the top, or until they are al dente. Remove with a strainer and place on the buttered serving dish. Keep the ravioli warm while cooking the next batch.

When all the ravioli are cooked, pour Tomato Cream Sauce (see Index) over them and serve immediately.

Yields about 40 ravioli, which serves 4 to 6.

Indonesian Chicken with Garlic and Peanut Butter Sauce

Sambal oeulek is a very piquant Indonesian condiment made from red peppers.

3- to 4-pound frying chicken	juice of 1/2 lemon
2 tablespoons peanut oil	2 teaspoons sambal oeulek
1 small onion	1 cup warm water
3 large garlic cloves	1/2 cup smooth, natural peanut butter
1 tablespoon soy sauce	

Cut the chicken into serving pieces. Saute it in a large skillet, in the oil, over moderately high heat for 15 minutes, turning frequently. Remove the skillet from the heat and transfer the chicken to a platter.

Finally mince the onion and garlic and saute them in the chicken skillet, over low heat, for 5 minutes. Add the soy sauce, lemon juice, and sambal to the skillet. Stir well and cook for 5 minutes. Add the water and peanut butter to the skillet and stir well to make a smooth sauce.

Return the chicken to the skillet and cook, covered, over moderately low heat for 20 to 30 minutes. Stir occasionally to prevent the sauce from sticking. Transfer to a heated serving platter and serve immediately.

Serves 4.

Moroccan Lentils

When we were in Morocco, we became friends with the manager of the little hotel where we spent a winter. Abdelkader, who had once worked as a cook on a Spanish ship, taught us how to make many Moroccan and Spanish-style foods. This is one of which we are particularly fond.

2 cups brown lentils	1/4 cup olive oil
1 large onion	1 large bay leaf
4 cups water	4 large garlic cloves, finely minced
1 teaspoon salt	1/2 cup finely chopped parsley
3 tablespoons olive oil	1 teaspoon cayenne pepper
2 cups roughly chopped tomatoes	

Wash and pick over the lentils, and put them in a heavy 3-quart saucepan that has a tight-fitting lid. Coarsely chop the onion and add it to the saucepan with the water, salt, and 3 tablespoons olive oil. Bring to a boil, reduce the heat, and simmer for 30 minutes, or until most of the liquid has been absorbed.

Add the tomatoes, remaining olive oil, bay leaf, garlic, parsley, and pepper. Simmer for 20 minutes, stirring occasionally. Transfer to a heated serving dish and serve hot.

Serves 6.

Cabbage, Mushroom, and Walnut Gratin

1 pound green cabbage	1/4 cup parsley leaves, finely chopped
1/2 pound mushrooms	1 tablespoon thyme leaves, finely minced
1 small onion	pinch of cayenne pepper
4 tablespoons unsalted butter	freshly grated nutmeg to taste
3 medium garlic cloves	1/2 cup freshly grated Parmesan cheese
3 tablespoons all-purpose flour	1 cup coarsely chopped walnuts
2 cups half-and-half cream, at room temperature	1 cup soft whole grain bread crumbs
1 tablespoon soy sauce	

Wash the cabbage and slice into thin wedges. Steam it until barely tender, about 7 minutes. Spread half the cabbage in a lightly oiled, 2-quart gratin or souffle dish.

Preheat the oven to 350° F. Slice the mushrooms and finely chop the onion. Soften the vegetables in butter over moderately low heat. Mince the garlic and stir into the vegetables. Cook about 5 minutes, then increase the heat to medium.

Add the flour all at once, stirring constantly. When the flour and butter begin to bubble, stir in 1 cup cream. Stir well. Add the remaining cream and the soy sauce.

Add the parsley, thyme, pepper, and nutmeg. Gradually stir in the cheese. Cook the sauce over low heat for 5 minutes, then add the chopped walnuts. Pour half the sauce over the cabbage, layer the rest of the cabbage, and cover with the remaining sauce. Sprinkle bread crumbs over the gratin and bake for 25 to 30 minutes. Serve hot.

Serves 6 to 8.

Zucchini Marinati

1 1/2 pounds zucchini, no longer than 4 inches	1 tablespoon finely chopped oregano leaves
1/2 cup virgin olive oil	about 1/2 teaspoon salt
juice of 1 lemon, or to taste	Garnish: 4 to 6 ounces oil-cured black olives
3 medium garlic cloves, finely chopped	freshly ground black pepper

Wash the zucchini and trim them. Cut them into eighths lengthwise. In a small bowl, make the marinade with olive oil, lemon juice, garlic, oregano, and salt to taste.

Spread the zucchini on a platter and pour the marinade over them. Cover and marinate at least 2 hours at a cool room temperature or in the refrigerator. (If you refrigerate the zucchini, remove 1 hour before serving.) Garnish the zucchini with pitted and halved olives and freshly ground pepper.

Serves 6 to 8.

LEMON BALM

LEMON BALM

Balmy summer days will bring
quiet cheer to gardens all
and fragrant kitchens will recall
Melissa's promise of the spring.

LEMON BALM evokes high summer scenes: the soft hum of bees in still air, the sun at the height of its languor-producing power, and balm's sweet scent reviving heat-weary palates and spirits. Our Balmy Sunset, a rosy and refreshing drink, is an ideal reflection of summer evenings. The fragrances of the most perfect lemon and the sweetest honey mingle in lemon balm's leaves in a way that both soothes and excites the sense of smell as no other herb does.

Balm's perfume, however, is not the only important feature in the herb's two thousand year history. Its botanical name, *Melissa officinalis,* derived from the Greek word for bee, denotes its extreme attractiveness to bees. Our balm patch is abuzz with activity all summer, especially when the plants are in bloom.

Like garlic, balm has always been associated with longevity. Tea with balm and honey was a popular drink in ages when long life offered the possibility of wisdom and the calm reflective joys. Balm wine or tea was recommended to scholars for sharp memories and clearheadedness and, somewhat contradictorily, to insomniacs for its alleged sleep-inducing properties.

The culinary uses of lemon balm tend to group around light foods: green salads, fruit salads, and macerated fruits. The crushed, fresh leaves steeped with Ceylon or Assam tea, and then iced, make a wonderful hot weather beverage. If you live in a cold climate, it is worth drying balm to make this hot tea in the winter, although the herb will have lost some of its aroma. Balm is seldom used in cooked dishes, but we find it contributes a subtly sweet, grassy flavor and a hint of lemon to a variety of foods. We like it especially with vegetables, light grains, and baked fish and chicken, and in desserts. Lemon balm should be added very near the end of cooking, as its volatile oils are dissipated by heat. The fragrance of balm keeps fairly well in baked goods because it is captured by the surrounding medium.

Lemon balm is an unfussy herb to grow, especially in the garden. It can be grown from seed or rooted cuttings, or by root division. The seeds germinate best if soaked in water for twenty-four hours before planting. The light, fine soil should be fairly fertile, well balanced, and well drained. Balm thrives in full sun but can be grown in partially shaded areas as well. The hardy root system will survive the coldest winters if the plants are well mulched.

Balm is a member of the mint family and looks and grows much like mint, although it does not send runners as several of the mints do. It grows from two to two and one-half feet tall, bushing out laterally, so that each plant should be given two feet all around. Trimming during growth helps it to keep a handsome bushy appearance. Indoors, it needs at least four hours of sun daily, good drainage, and plenty of water.

Sweet Melissa charms us every year with its clean, honeyed–lemon scent and bountiful, bright green foliage. Lemon balm imparts its unique fragrance and delicate flavor to the recipes that follow.

Balmy Sunset

This drink goes down especially well at the end of a long, hot summer day spent wrestling with weeds.

1 1/2 cups unsweetened pineapple juice	*1 1/2 teaspoons grenadine*
1 cup freshly squeezed orange juice	*4 or 5 5-inch lemon balm sprigs*
3/4 cup light rum	*Garnish: lemon balm leaves*

Mix the juices, rum, and grenadine in a glass pitcher. Add the lemon balm sprigs, bruising them slightly. Steep the punch in the refrigerator at least 3 hours, preferably all day.

Remove the lemon balm springs. Rub the rims of 4 chilled glasses with a lemon balm leaf. Serve the punch on the rocks or over crushed ice.

Yields 4 drinks.

Anchovy Balm Butter

5 tablespoons unsalted butter, softened	1/4 teaspoon lemon juice, or to taste
2 salt-pack anchovy fillets, minced	salt to taste
1 tablespoon finely minced lemon balm leaves	

Cream the butter with the minced anchovies. Add the balm, lemon juice, and salt. Serve with radish or cucumber sandwiches.

Yields about 1/2 cup.

Lemon Balm and Chive Butter

6 tablespoons unsalted butter, softened	1 tablespoon finely snipped chives
2 tablespoons finely minced lemon balm	salt to taste
1 tablespoon finely minced parsley	

Combine the butter and herbs. Season, cover, and chill overnight to ripen the flavors. Serve with blanched or steamed vegetables, or with poached or grilled fish.

Yields about 1 cup.

Lemon Balm Broth

1 large potato	2 quarts water
1 medium-large turnip	1 teaspoon salt
1 large yellow onion	6 large parsley sprigs
2 celery ribs	8 6-inch lemon balm sprigs
2 large carrots	

Wash and quarter the potato, turnip, and onion, leaving skins on. Scrub the celery and carrots well, trim, and cut into sixths. Put the vegetables in a large soup pot and cover with the water. Add the salt, parsley, and balm. Simmer the broth, uncovered, for 25 minutes.

Garnish

1 small potato	2 garlic cloves, minced
1 small turnip	6 to 8 lemon balm leaves
1 small carrot	

Peel and julienne the potato, turnip, and carrot. Remove the broth from the heat and strain it through a large sieve lined with rinsed, tripled cheesecloth. Return the broth to low heat and bring it to a simmer. Add the minced garlic and julienned vegetables, and cook for 7 to 10 minutes, until the vegetables are just done. Cut the balm leaves in a chiffonade. Serve the broth in warm soup bowls and garnish with the balm.

    Serves 4 to 6.

Baked Snapper with Onions and Balm

2 medium, yellow onions	1/2 teaspoon freshly ground white pepper
2 tablespoons unsalted butter	12 8-inch lemon balm sprigs
1 1/2 pounds fillet of snapper, rock cod, or sea bass	1/2 cup medium-dry white wine
1 teaspoon sea salt	Garnish: lemon balm leaves

Thinly slice the onions and saute them in butter over medium heat for 5 minutes. Set the onions aside. Pat the fish dry and rub the fillets on both sides with the mixed salt and pepper. Lightly butter a 9-by-12-inch baking dish and line it with 6 lemon balm sprigs. Lay the fish on the balm and spread the onions over the fish.

    Preheat the oven to 450° F.

    Cover the onions with the remaining lemon balm sprigs. Pour the wine into the dish and bake for 7 to 9 minutes, until the fish just flakes. Remove the cooked lemon balm. Put the fish and onions on a serving platter and garnish with fresh lemon balm leaves.

    Serves 4 to 6.

Chicken Roasted with Lemon Balm

4-pound chicken, preferably a small roaster	1-inch piece peeled gingerroot
1 teaspoon salt	16 6-inch lemon balm sprigs
3 tablespoons lemon juice	Garnish: fresh lemon balm sprigs

Preheat the oven to 375° F.

Rinse the chicken and pat it dry, reserving the innards for another use. Dissolve the salt in the lemon juice and rub the chicken inside and out with the mixture. Rub the chicken with gingerroot. Stuff the chicken with 8 balm sprigs and the gingerroot.

Place the chicken in a lightly oiled, small roasting pan, breast up, and cover it with remaining balm sprigs. Roast the chicken for 50 to 60 minutes. Place the chicken on a platter and remove the outside lemon balm. Let the chicken stand for 5 to 10 minutes before carving. Transfer the chicken pieces to a serving platter and garnish with fresh balm sprigs.

Serves 4 to 6.

Herbed Rice

1 1/4 cups short grain white rice, preferably Italian Arborio	salt and pepper to taste
1 tablespoon unsalted butter, melted	3 tablespoons minced lemon balm leaves
1 tablespoon virgin olive oil	1 tablespoon minced parsley
1 quart hot chicken or vegetable stock	1 tablespoon minced fennel leaves or dill weed

Saute the rice in the butter and olive oil over medium heat for 5 minutes, stirring constantly. Reduce the heat to low and add 1 cup of stock, stirring well. Season lightly.

Cook the rice, uncovered, over low heat for 18 to 20 minutes, adding 1/2 cup stock at a time, and stirring well every 5 minutes. When done, the rice should be al dente and slightly creamy. It may not be necessary to add all the stock. Remove the rice from the heat and stir in the herbs.

Serves 4.

Jerusalem Artichokes with Peas and Lemon Balm

1/2 pound Jerusalem artichokes	1 tablespoon unsalted butter
2 cups cold water	2 medium shallots, minced
1 tablespoon lemon juice	salt to taste
1 pound unshelled peas	2 tablespoons minced lemon balm leaves

Clean and peel the Jerusalem artichokes and cut them into 1/4-inch julienne. Soak the artichokes in cold water and lemon juice for about 10 minutes.

Shell the peas. Drain the artichokes and pat them dry. Saute the artichokes in butter over medium heat for 2 minutes. Add the peas and shallots, cover, and cook for 4 minutes. Season and toss with the lemon balm. Serve immediately.

Serves 4 to 6.

Vegetable Balm Vinaigrette

4 small turnips	1 pound broccoli
5 small carrots	

Wash and peel the turnips and carrots. Slice the carrots into 1/2-inch thick pieces on the diagonal, and the turnips into 1/4-inch rounds. Wash and trim the broccoli into flowerets. Break the flowerets into 1-inch pieces.

Blanch the vegetables separately until they are crisp-tender. Refresh them under cold water, drain, and pat dry.

Vinaigrette

1 cup light sesame oil	2 small garlic cloves, minced
1 cup roughly chopped lemon balm leaves	about 1/2 teaspoon salt
2 tablespoons lemon juice, or to taste	freshly ground white pepper to taste

In a blender or food processor, combine the vinaigrette ingredients and blend well. Arrange the vegetables on a platter, pour the vinaigrette over, and chill 1 hour before serving.

Serves 6 to 8.

Lemon Balm Custard Sauce

3/4 cup milk	1/2 cup sugar
5 5-inch lemon balm sprigs	2 egg yolks
1 1/2 teaspoons arrowroot	1 teaspoon rum

Scald the milk with the lemon balm in a small pan. Remove from the heat and bruise the balm against the side of the pan with a wooden spoon. Steep the mixture for 1 hour.

Remove the balm from the pan and whisk in the arrowroot. Add the sugar and cook the mixture over low heat, stirring occasionally, until the sugar is dissolved.

Lightly beat the egg yolks in a small bowl and whisk in about 1/2 cup of the hot milk. Pour the egg yolk mixture into the pan and cook the custard over low heat, stirring constantly, until it is thick enough to coat a wooden spoon. Remove from the heat and stir in the rum. Cover and cool to room temperature. Serve with Lemon Cake or over fresh fruit.

Yields about 1 1/2 cups.

Lemon Cake

7 tablespoons unsalted butter	1 cup flour
3 large eggs	1/4 teaspoon salt
1 egg yolk	grated rind of 1 lemon
2/3 cup sugar	

Preheat the oven to 375° F.

Melt the butter over low heat and set aside to cool. Beat the eggs and egg yolk with the sugar until the mixture becomes pale yellow, thick, and fluffy, about 5 minutes.

Sift the flour 3 times with the salt. Very slowly fold the flour, in thirds, into the egg mixture. Carefully fold in the melted butter in thirds. When the batter is thoroughly blended, fold in the lemon rind.

Pour the batter into a buttered and floured 8-inch square pan, spreading it evenly. Bake for 20 minutes. The cake is done when the top is pale golden brown, the edges pull away slightly, and a cake tester comes out clean. Cool on a rack to room temperature before cutting into squares.

Serves 8 to 10.

Pineapple Balm Sorbet

1/2 cup sugar	*1 large, ripe pineapple*
1 cup boiling water	*1/2 cup packed balm leaves*

Dissolve the sugar in the boiling water and set aside to cool. Clean and core the pineapple. Cut it into chunks and measure 5 cups. In a food processor, or in batches in the blender, puree the pineapple with the balm leaves. Stir the sugar syrup into the puree and blend well.

Pour the mixture into a stainless steel bowl and freeze for 40 to 60 minutes, until very firm. Remove from the freezer, break the sorbet into 1-inch chunks with a spoon, and stir well. Return to the freezer for 1 hour, or as long as desired.

Ten minutes before serving, break up the sorbet and blend or process to a smooth consistency. Transfer to chilled serving glasses and return to the freezer for 5 minutes.

Serves 10.

Lime Balm Tart

This tart is lighter, yet more satisfying, than an ordinary lemon meringue pie; the tang of the limes and the honey-like sweetness of the lemon balm strike a fine balance.

Pastry

1/2 cup unsalted butter, well chilled	*1 1/2 to 2 tablespoons water*
1 cup all-purpose flour	*1 egg white*
1 tablespoon sugar	

Cut the butter into bits. Mix the flour and sugar. Cut the butter into the flour by hand, or in a food processor with the steel blade, to make a medium meal. Add just enough water to bind the dough, and gather the pastry to form a flattened round, about 3/4 inch thick. Cover the round with plastic wrap and chill at least 30 minutes.

Preheat the oven to 375° F.

Press the dough into a 9-inch tart pan with a removable bottom. Cover and chill at least another 30 minutes. Bake the shell for 25 minutes, until golden brown. Cool to room temperature on a cake rack.

Beat the egg white lightly and brush it gently over the tart shell. Bake the shell for 3 minutes and cool to room temperature.

Custard

1/4 cup milk	4 4-inch lemon balm sprigs
1 teaspoon arrowroot	1/4 cup lime juice
4 egg yolks	4 tablespoons unsalted butter
1/2 cup sugar	grated rind of 1 lime
pinch of salt	1/2 cup minced lemon balm leaves

Dissolve the arrowroot in the milk. Beat the egg yolks and sugar thoroughly in a small, heavy saucepan. Add the milk, salt, lemon balm sprigs, and lime juice. Bruise the balm against the inside of the pan with a wooden spoon. Put the pan over low heat and stir the mixture.

Cut the butter into bits and add it to the custard along with the lime rind. Stir for 5 to 10 minutes, until the custard coats a spoon. Remove the cooked balm sprigs and squeeze the excess liquid from them. Remove the pan from the heat and stir in the minced balm leaves. Cover the custard and cool to room temperature.

Baking the tart

4 egg whites	Garnish: 1 lime
3 tablespoons sugar	12 to 16 small lemon balm leaves
pinch of cream of tartar	

Preheat the oven to 400° F.

Beat the egg whites together with the sugar and cream of tartar until they are glossy and form peaks.

Pour the cooled custard into the cooled shell and cover it with the beaten egg whites. Bake for 5 minutes, or until the meringue is golden brown. Cool the tart to room temperature.

Slice the lime thinly and cut the slices in half. Garnish the tart with lime slices and lemon balm leaves.

Serves 8.

MARJORAM AND OREGANO

MARJORAM AND OREGANO

Marjoram sings of sweet earth's flowers,
while oregano summons the spicy powers.

ELIGHTFUL MYTHS and lovely uses surround sweet marjoram, while herbal remedies and hearty dishes are associated with oregano, its close cousin. Marjoram has long been one of the most popular culinary herbs. Its cultivation in the Mediterranean has been recorded for twelve centuries, spreading from its native Portugal to central Europe. Recipes dating from the Renaissance call for marjoram in salads, in egg dishes, with rice, and with every variety of meat and fish. It was used to flavor beer before hops, and as a tea in England before Eastern teas were imported.

Sweet marjoram has almost as much mythology linking it with love as basil does. The Romans began circulating the story that it had been touched by Venus, who left its perfume to remind mortals of her beauty. Marjoram was used in love potions and bridal bouquets in France, Italy, Greece, Spain, Portugal, and England during the period from the Renaissance to the nineteenth century, when herbs were known and used by peasants, witches, and royalty. Italians gave nosegays of it to banish sadness. East Indians knew it well, but did not use it in cooking as it was a plant sacred to Vishnu.

Oregano was named by the Greeks from *oros*, "mountain," and *ganos*, "joy." Its history, thirteen hundred years longer than marjoram's, is mainly medicinal, with the relief of ailments from toothaches to opium addiction claimed by a long list of herbalists. American Indians have known oregano for generations and have used it as a medicinal tea and as a flavoring for meats. During the Renaissance, the Spanish began recording its use for cooking, especially in meat and vegetable stews and with shellfish. Since World War II, when spice merchants began promoting and importing it in quantities, oregano has moved from obscurity to being one of the most popular dried herbs in the United States.

Marjoram's fragrance is still prized by perfume and soap makers, as well as by cooks. We share with the bees the enjoyment of marjoram's blossoms at the end of the summer. While we are drying the clusters of small purple flowers, we anticipate the further pleasure of our herb and flower potpourri. The Romans, who recognized and chronicled the sensual delights of many plants, made sachets of marjoram, oregano, rosemary, and lavender to perfume linens and baths. The sweetness of marjoram's aroma, and the spiciness of oregano's, complement one another equally well in the kitchen.

The use of marjoram and oregano together and the similarity of their appearance and growing habits have caused problems with identification for cooks and herbalists alike. Sweet marjoram is sometimes classified as *Origanum majorana* and sometimes as *Majorana hortensis*. Oregano for culinary use is either *Origanum vulgare* or *Origanum heracleoticum*. This confusion is compounded by the common names of wild marjoram for *Origanum vulgare* and winter marjoram for *Origanum heracleoticum*.

The characteristics that identify fresh marjoram are a perfume reminiscent of sweet broom and mint, pale green leaves with faint, silvery shadows, and a slightly bitter, resinous flavor. When dried, marjoram retains its sweet aroma, and its color becomes a pale gray green.

Fresh oregano has a spicier fragrance than marjoram, with hints of clove and balsam. *Origanum vulgare,* which is commonly cultivated in the United States, Mexico, and Spain, has a more pronounced sharpness to its aroma and bitterness to its flavor than does *Origanum heracleoticum,* which is used in its native Greece, as well as in Italy and France. The fresh leaves of both oreganos are green with a yellowish tinge. *O. vulgare* has smoother and larger leaves than does *O. heracleoticum* and may have flowers ranging from white to pink and purple. Both of the oreganos' leaves are more oval and pointed, and larger than marjoram's. They dry to a lighter color and their flavor becomes very pungent, rather like a blend of peppermint, pine, and clove oils. *O. heracleoticum,* imported from Greece, is usually sold as oregano by United States' purveyors; *O. vulgare* is also sold as oregano, especially in Hispanic markets. As freshly cut oregano and marjoram are difficult to buy in American markets, it is worth the small effort to cultivate them yourself.

O. *vulgare* is a hardy perennial that will survive northern winters if well mulched. O. *heracleoticum* and marjoram are perennials only in mild, Mediterranean-like climates, but both do well in indoor window boxes for the winter.

The Origanum family likes good drainage and prefers to be kept free of weeds. The plants need plenty of room for their fine branching, lateral roots. They do best if fertilized about once a month. Indoors, oregano and marjoram grow easily, especially in a well-drained container. They are fairly unfussy plants but should be pinched back before they flower. They can be trimmed severely and will profit from this treatment, giving handsome, bushy little plants and many savoury dishes. Both of the herbs dry well if the stems are cut, tied in bunches, and hung upside down in a warm, dry place.

The sunny temperaments of marjoram and oregano shine here.

Spanakopita

1 pound fresh spinach	freshly grated nutmeg to taste
1 medium onion	salt and pepper to taste
3 tablespoons unsalted butter	1/2 pound fresh phyllo
1 tablespoon fresh oregano leaves, or 1 scant teaspoon dried, crumbled oregano	1/2 cup unsalted butter
10 ounces feta cheese	

Clean and stem the spinach. Using only the water that clings to the leaves, steam the spinach in a covered pot, over moderate heat, for 3 minutes. Remove from the heat, drain, chop coarsely, and transfer to a large bowl.

Finely chop the onion and saute it in 3 tablespoons butter, over moderate heat, for 10 minutes. Finely mince the oregano leaves and add them and the onion to the spinach. Crumble the cheese, add it to the vegetables, and stir the mixture well. Season with nutmeg, salt, and pepper.

Preheat the oven to 375° F.

Have ready 18 sheets of phyllo. Melt the 1/2 cup butter and keep it warm. Working carefully with 3 phyllo sheets, brush each sheet on one side with butter. Layer the sheets in a buttered 9-by-12-inch, shallow baking dish. Spread one-fifth of the filling over the phyllo. Continue buttering 3 sheets at a time and spread each layer with filling. The last layer will be phyllo.

Bake for 30 minutes, or until the spanakopita is golden brown. Cut into triangles or diamond shapes and serve hot.

Serves 10 as an appetizer, or 6 as a main course.

Stuffed Mushrooms with Oregano

12 large mushrooms	1/3 cup fine whole grain bread crumbs
3 tablespoons olive oil	1/4 cup freshly grated Parmesan cheese
1 large garlic clove, finely minced	salt and pepper to taste
1/3 cup finely chopped parsley	1/2 cup dry white wine
1 tablespoon finely chopped, fresh oregano, or 1 scant teaspoon dried, crumbled oregano	

Carefully wipe the mushrooms clean. Remove and mince the stems. Heat the olive oil in a small skillet and saute the stems with the garlic, over moderate heat, for about 3 minutes.

Remove the mixture from the heat and add the parsley, oregano, bread crumbs, cheese, salt, and pepper, blending well.

Preheat the oven to 350° F.

Divide the stuffing among the mushroom caps, packing it and mounding it. Arrange the mushrooms in a lightly buttered, 11-by-8-inch gratin dish. Add the wine to the dish and bake for 10 minutes.

Place the dish under a preheated broiler, about 2 inches from the heat, for about 1 minute, or until the tops are golden brown. With a slotted spatula, transfer the mushrooms to a heated platter.

Yields 12 hors d'oeuvre.

Marjoram Corn Bread

1 1/2 cups cornmeal, preferably stone-ground	1/2 cup wheat germ
1 1/2 cups whole wheat flour	2 tablespoons minced, fresh marjoram leaves, or 1 1/2 teaspoons crumbled, dried marjoram
1 teaspoon baking powder	2 cups milk
1 teaspoon baking soda	2 eggs
3/4 teaspoon salt	1/4 cup vegetable oil or melted butter

Sift the cornmeal, whole wheat flour, baking powder, baking soda, and salt into a large bowl. Add the wheat germ and marjoram and mix the ingredients lightly.

In a small bowl, combine the liquid ingredients and whisk them for 1 minute.

Preheat the oven to 350° F.

Add the liquid ingredients to the dry ingredients and blend well. Pour the batter into a buttered, 12-inch pie plate and bake for 30 minutes, or until a cake tester inserted in the center comes out clean. Let the corn bread cool in the plate, on a rack, for 10 minutes before cutting.

Serves 8.

Salsa Semplice

2 pounds tomatoes, peeled, seeded, and chopped, or 1 28-ounce can plum tomatoes	*1 medium, red onion, finely minced*
1 tablespoon plus 1 teaspoon finely minced, fresh oregano leaves, or 1 teaspoon crumbled, dried oregano	*1/2 teaspoon salt, or to taste*
2 teaspoons finely minced, fresh marjoram leaves, or 1/2 teaspoon crumbled, dried marjoram	*1/4 cup olive oil*

In a stainless steel or enameled saucepan, combine the tomatoes, oregano, marjoram, onion, salt, and olive oil. Bring to a boil and simmer the mixture over moderate heat for 20 minutes, stirring occasionally. Serve the sauce with pasta.

Yields about 4 cups.

Antipasto di Pomodoro e Basilico

Genoa Green Basil

Minted Tomatoes Gratinee

Italian Parsley

Tarragon

Steamed Vegetables
with Tarragon Vinaigrette

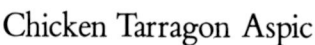
Chicken Tarragon Aspic

Salmon in Champagne with Coriander

Coriander in Bloom

Lemon Balm

Lime Balm Tart

Thyme in Bloom

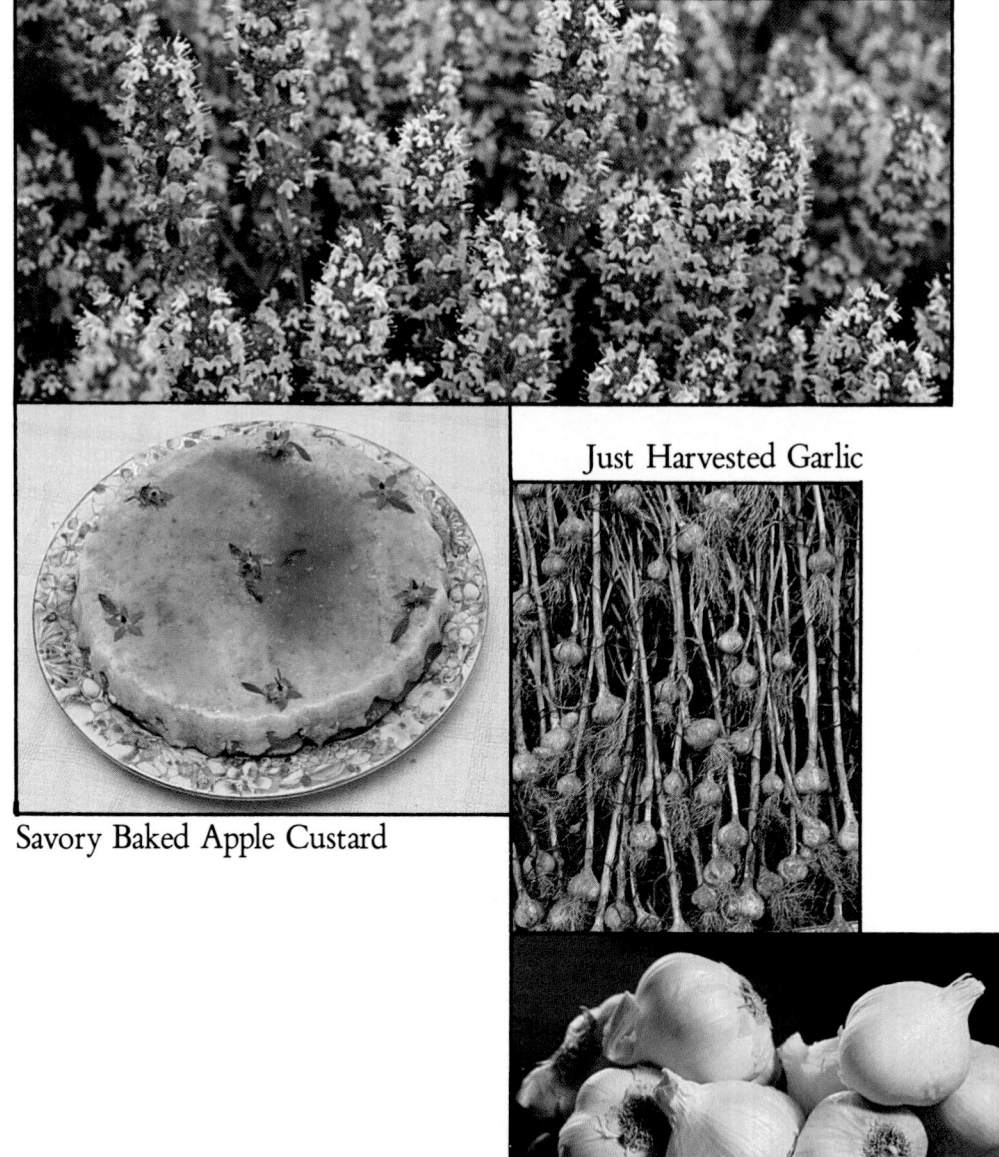

Just Harvested Garlic

Savory Baked Apple Custard

Garlic Bulbs

Sage Tea

Chervil with Ladybug

Sage

Dilled Ricotta Torte

Dilled Summer Squash

Potato Pesto Pizza

Dill Seed Umbels

Watercress by the Stream

Eggrolls with Watercress

Bay Hot Cross Buns

Bay Laurel Tree

Rosemary in Bloom

Sushi with Rice, Ginger, and Sorrel

Sorrel Sushi Style

Hearty Minestrone

A minestrone should be individual and variable. Use vegetables that are fresh and appealing. Onions, carrots, garlic, and some greens are necessary; but try minestrone without tomato, add sausage, use rice instead of pasta, and experiment with basil.

2 stalks celery	1/4 pound green beans
2 large carrots	1 pound chard
1 large potato	1 cup cooked cranberry beans
1 large red onion	1 cup pastine pasta
1/4 cup olive oil	1 tablespoon freshly chopped marjoram, or 1 teaspoon crumbled, dried marjoram
14-ounce can Italian tomatoes	1 tablespoon freshly chopped oregano, or 1 teaspoon crumbled, dried oregano
1 1/2 quarts vegetable or chicken stock	salt and pepper to taste
3 garlic cloves, chopped	Garnish: freshly grated Parmesan cheese
1 medium zucchini	

Wash and coarsely chop the celery, carrots, potato, and onion. Saute in olive oil in a very large soup pot, over medium heat, for about 7 minutes. Add the tomatoes, stock, and garlic, and cook for about 25 minutes.

Wash the zucchini, green beans, and chard. Thinly slice the zucchini, french cut the beans into 1-inch lengths, and chop the stems from the chard into 1-inch pieces. Add to the soup and cook 5 minutes more.

Coarsely chop the chard tops and add to the soup, along with cranberry beans, pasta, marjoram, oregano, salt, and pepper. Cook 10 minutes longer. Let stand for 10 minutes. Serve hot, garnished with cheese.

Serves 8 to 10.

Herbed Leek and Prosciutto Tartlets

Pastry

10 tablespoons hard, unsalted butter	8 tablespoons ice water
2 1/4 cups unbleached white flour	1 egg white
1/4 teaspoon salt	

Cut the butter into 20 pieces. Mix the flour and salt together in a bowl. Add the butter and work it into the flour with a pastry cutter, or the fingers, until the mixture has a coarse texture and the butter pieces are the size of large peas.

Add the ice water, sprinkling in 2 tablespoons at a time, to moisten the flour while lifting the mixture with a fork. Use just enough water to hold the dough together. Form the dough into a ball, wrap loosely with plastic wrap, and flatten it into a rough round about 1 1/2 inches thick. Chill the dough at least 30 minutes before rolling out.

Roll the dough 1/8 inch thick on a floured surface. Cut 8 rounds with a 5-inch cutter or with a sharp knife. Fit each round into a 3-by-3/4-inch tartlet tin and crimp the edges decoratively. Prick the bottoms of the shells lightly with a fork and chill them at least 30 minutes.

Preheat the oven to 425° F.

Place the shells on a baking sheet and bake them in the lower third of the oven for 10 minutes.

Lightly beat the egg white and brush the bottom and sides of the shells. Bake the shells 5 to 10 minutes longer, until they are golden. Let the shells cool in the tins, on a rack, for 5 minutes. Carefully turn them out onto the rack and cool completely.

Filling

2 small leeks	1/2 cup half-and-half cream
2 tablespoons unsalted butter	1 tablespoon minced, fresh oregano leaves, or 1/2 teaspoon crumbled, dried oregano
1/4 pound prosciutto, thinly sliced	1 tablespoon minced, fresh marjoram leaves, or 1 teaspoon crumbled, dried marjoram
2 large eggs	salt and pepper to taste

Wash the leeks well and chop the white part in a fine dice. Cook the chopped leeks in butter over medium-low heat about 10 minutes. Cut the prosciutto in a medium-fine dice.

Preheat the oven to 350° F.

Arrange the shells on a baking sheet and divide the leeks among them. Cover the leeks with the prosciutto. Beat the 2 eggs lightly with the cream. Stir in the herbs, salt, and pepper.

Fill the shells with the egg mixture and bake for 15 minutes, or until a cake tester comes out clean from the centers. Transfer the tartlets to a platter and serve them warm or at room temperature.

Serves 8 as a first course.

Lasagna Casalinga

This is a homey and light, yet filling, lasagna. We made this kind of lasagna frequently when we lived in the country in Italy.

Pasta

1 recipe Egg Pasta (see Index)

Make the pasta and let it rest while you prepare the filling.

Chicken Filling

2 1/2- to 3-pound chicken, poached (see Index)	*1 tablespoon chopped, fresh marjoram leaves, or 1 teaspoon dried, crumbled marjoram*
1 medium onion	*1 tablespoon chopped, fresh oregano leaves, or 1 teaspoon dried, crumbled oregano*
3 tablespoons virgin olive oil	*1/4 teaspoon cayenne pepper*
28-ounce can of plum tomatoes	*salt and freshly ground pepper to taste*
4 large garlic cloves	

Poach the chicken and let it cool. Skin and bone it and cut the meat into 1/2-inch dice.

Dice the onion and soften it over medium-low heat in the olive oil. Add the tomatoes and break them up with a wooden spoon. Mince the garlic and add it to the sauce. Stir in the herbs, cayenne pepper, salt, and pepper. Simmer the sauce about 20 minutes, then stir in the diced chicken. Let the sauce cool to room temperature.

Cheese Filling

1 pound whole milk ricotta cheese	1 cup freshly grated Parmesan cheese
2 large eggs	freshly grated nutmeg to taste
1/3 cup chopped Italian parsley leaves	salt and pepper to taste
1 tablespoon chopped, fresh marjoram leaves	

Mix all the filling ingredients together in a bowl, seasoning lightly with nutmeg, salt, and pepper.

Assembling the Lasagna

Bring a large pot of well-salted water to a boil. Put 3 quarts of cold water and 3 tablespoons of salad oil in a separate pot.

Roll the pasta through the thinnest setting of the pasta machine. Cut into 4-inch lengths and lay out the pasta so that it does not touch.

When the water is boiling rapidly, drop the pasta squares, 4 at a time, into the pot. Cook for 10 seconds and remove them to the cold water, using a large strainer or slotted spoon. Repeat until all the pasta is parcooked. Drain the water from the cold water pot and add fresh cold water. Spread the parcooked pasta on tea towels.

Preheat the oven to 375° F.

Butter a 13-by-9-by-2-inch lasagna pan. Line the pan sides with pasta, allowing 1 1/2 inches to drape over the outside of the pan all around. Cover the bottom of the pan with 1 or 2 pasta squares. Spoon about 2/3 cup chicken filling over the pasta. Cover with pasta squares and spread these with about 2/3 cup cheese filling. Repeat the layering until all the filling is used. Cover the last layer of filling with pasta. Fold the outside edges over the top. Drizzle the top with a little olive oil.

Bake about 25 minutes. The edges and top should be light golden brown and crunchy. Let the lasagna stand about 10 minutes before cutting and serving.

Serves 8 to 10.

Chiles Rellenos

This is a variation of the traditional relleno, which has a very fluffy egg batter. Ours has a cornmeal and whole wheat flour batter, which gives it more substance and makes it decidedly the best we have ever eaten.

8 Anaheim chili peppers, about 5 inches long	1/3 cup cornmeal, preferably stone-ground
1/2 pound Monterey Jack cheese	1/3 cup whole wheat pastry flour
2 large eggs	salt and pepper to taste
2 tablespoons water	vegetable oil
1 tablespoon minced, fresh oregano leaves, or 1 teaspoon crumbled, dried oregano	

Preheat the broiler.

Arrange the chili peppers on a broiler pan rack. Broil them about 6 inches from the heat, turning them frequently, for 5 to 7 minutes, or until the skins are blistered and charred. Put the peppers in a paper bag, close the bag, and let stand until the peppers are cool enough to handle.

Starting with the stem end, remove the pepper skins. Make a lengthwise slit in the peppers, remove the seeds and ribs, but leave the stems intact. Do not rinse the peppers but pat them dry.

Cut the cheese into 8 sticks to fit the peppers and stuff each pepper with a piece of cheese.

In a small bowl, beat together the eggs, water, and oregano. Stir in the cornmeal, flour, salt, and pepper. Thin the batter, if necessary, to a coating consistency, using 1 to 2 tablespoons more water.

In a deep skillet, heat 3/4 inch of oil to 375° F. Dip the stuffed peppers into the batter and add 4 to the skillet. Fry for about 1 minute on each side or until they are golden. Transfer the chiles rellenos with a slotted spoon to paper towels to drain. Fry the second batch of 4 and drain. Arrange on a heated platter and serve with Oregano Hot Sauce (see Index).

Serves 4.

Cima alla Genovese

The tastiness and handsome appearance of a cima more than compensate for the work of sewing it together.

4 1/2- to 5-pound breast of veal	*1 large bunch spinach*
2 carrots	*6 to 8 sprigs fresh marjoram, or 1 tablespoon dried marjoram*
1 onion	*6 ounces each ground pork and ground veal, or 4 ounces each ground pork and ground veal and 4 ounces cleaned and trimmed sweetbreads*
1 large celery rib	*1/2 cup freshly grated Parmesan cheese*
10 black peppercorns	*1/2 cup shelled pistachios*
1 bay leaf	*about 1 1/2 teaspoons salt*
2 teaspoons coarse salt	*freshly ground black pepper to taste*
8 eggs	*freshly grated nutmeg to taste*

Carefully bone the breast of veal, leaving the meat in one piece. Trim the veal of extra fat. Place the boned veal on a board, fell side up, and pound it into an evenly shaped rectangle. Cover the meat.

Divide the bones into sections of 2 and put them in a stockpot large enough to hold the rolled breast. Peel the carrots and onion and chop them roughly along with the celery. Add them to the stockpot with the peppercorns, bay leaf, and coarse salt.

Hard cook 4 eggs, then cool and shell them.

Clean and stem the spinach and chop it fine. Mince the fresh marjoram or crumble the dried marjoram. If using the sweetbreads, cut them into 1/4-inch dice. Put the spinach, marjoram, ground pork and veal, sweetbreads, cheese, pistachios, and 4 raw eggs in a large bowl. Add the salt, pepper, and nutmeg. Mix everything together well with the hands. Season the mixture well or it will be too bland.

Spread the stuffing lengthwise along the breast and bury the hard-cooked eggs in the stuffing, spacing them evenly. Beginning at one end, wrap the meat around the stuffing, and sew the meat carefully.

Wrap the cima in a 30-by-12-inch piece of muslin or tripled cheesecloth. Tuck the ends of the cloth under and tie it securely around the cima. Place the cima in the stockpot, cover it with 1 inch of water, and bring to a boil. Reduce to a simmer and cook, uncovered, for 1 hour, skimming occasionally. Cover the pot and simmer 1 1/2 hours longer.

Remove the pot from the heat and let cool for 1 hour. Remove the cima from the stock and place in a shallow baking dish or deep platter. Weight the top of the cima. Strain the stock and reserve for another use. Leave the cima at room temperature for 3 to 4 hours. Then remove the weight and refrigerate at least 24 hours before serving.

To serve, unwrap the cloth and remove the thread. Let the cima stand at room temperature for 1 hour. Slice into 3/8-inch slices on a slight diagonal.

Serves 12 to 14 as an antipasto, or 6 to 8 as a main course.

Note: Unsliced, the cima keeps well for 5 to 6 days in the refrigerator. Once it has been cut, it will keep 3 to 4 days if refrigerated.

Roasted Red Pepper and Fennel Vinaigrette

2 large red peppers	*2 bulbs Florence fennel*

Roast the peppers under a broiler or over a high gas flame until they are completely blackened. Place in a brown paper bag for about 5 minutes or until they are cool enough to handle. Peel completely, cut in half, and remove the seeds. Slice into 3/4-inch slices.

Trim and clean the fennel and cut it lengthwise into 1/4-inch slices. Blanch in abundant, boiling, lightly salted water for about 1 minute. Cool to room temperature.

Place the vegetables in a flat-bottomed, shallow dish.

Vinaigrette

about 1/2 cup virgin olive oil	*1 tablespoon fresh marjoram leaves, minced*
2 to 3 tablespoons balsamic vinegar or good quality red wine vinegar	*1 tablespoon fresh Italian parsley, minced*
1 large clove garlic, minced	*salt and freshly ground black pepper to taste*

Combine all the ingredients for the vinaigrette and pour it over the vegetables. Let the vegetables marinate for 1 hour before serving. Arrange vegetables on a serving plate.

Serves 4 as a salad and 6 as an appetizer.

Oregano Hot Sauce

4 large jalapeno peppers	1 tablespoon fresh oregano leaves
2 pounds ripe tomatoes, peeled, seeded, and finely diced, or 1-pound can plum tomatoes, finely diced	salt and pepper to taste
1 small white onion	

Wearing rubber gloves, remove and discard the seeds and ribs from the peppers. Mince the peppers.

In a bowl, combine the peppers and tomatoes. Mince the onion and oregano leaves and add to the bowl. Season with salt and pepper.

This sauce is best if allowed to stand at room temperature for 1 hour.

Yields about 2 cups.

MINT SPRIG

THE MINTS

Balsam and pepper, apple and ginger,
many tastes their names have lent,
while spear describes the leafy finger.
In such a bunch of jolly herbs
why is none named merriment?

PROFUSION, INFUSION, and confusion characterize the mint family. Its growing habits and many members explain the first attribute; its long history as a medicinal and social tea, the second; and the large number of varieties, the third. We have carefully rooted through our mint beds to offer some clarification of the kinds of mints and some inspiration for their uses.

The nature of mints, with their many types and tendencies to cross-breed, makes the marketing and buying of mint seem capricious. Even herbal experts do not always describe the same species in the same way. Of course, the advantage of such a large and varied family is that there are mints to whet the appetite of almost everyone.

The mints in this chapter are ones that we have grown and used. The best way for you to choose them is to select flavors and appearances that appeal to you. To assure the closest true species selection, buy from a good herb grower. Sniff and, if possible, taste the leaves. Remember, leaves from a greenhouse plant will be milder than those from a garden mint.

Once you have brought home your mints, think carefully about where to place them. Plant different varieties away from one another to retain individuality. Especially for small gardens, we strongly advise confining mint in tubs or pots, either buried in beds or left to stand as handsome container plants. Mints are strong propagators through runners and can change from a pleasurable little bed to a nuisance in one season. Rather than bemoan their habits, plan for them. Water, good drainage, and a well-fertilized soil are their only growing requirements. They prefer sun but will grow in partial shade.

Mint can be snipped freely for kitchen use throughout the season. Larger plantings for dried herbs can be cut back three times. Early and midsummer cuttings should be taken two to three inches above the ground. Fall harvesting should take place just before flowering or when the lower leaves yellow, whichever comes first. Cut the plants back to the ground at this time and cover with well-rotted compost for the winter. Large harvests call for hanging bunches of mint upside down in a shady, dry, and warm place. To dry small amounts, strip the leaves from the stems and dry them on a screen under the same conditions as above.

Peppermints have the strongest flavor and offer great versatility for those who love mint. One of the small joys of growing herbs is to work in the garden with a tingly peppermint leaf under the tongue. Blue Balsam (a variety of *Mentha piperita*) has the most intense taste, in fact balsamic. It is excellent for cooked dishes and refreshing in summer drinks. Blue Balsam mint has a deep purplish blue cast to the stem and the leaves and somewhat larger rounder leaves than peppermint. It tends to branch lower and grows about two and one-half feet tall.

Peppermint (*M. piperita*) does have a hint of pepper and is good in cooked dishes, especially in jellies and mint sauces. The plant will grow erect to about three feet, and the leaves may be slightly fuzzy. Both of these plants have medicinal and stomach-soothing uses and make wonderful teas. They are therefore good herbs to grow in abundance and to dry.

Spearmints (*Mentha spicata* and *M. viridis*) are milder and sweeter than peppermints and are good in salads or wherever a lighter flavor is desired. These are the most famous mints, the ones people associate with mint juleps, fresh mint teas, sauces, and jellies. Sipping a glass of hot, sweet spearmint tea always weaves the fabric of memory, and we are once again sitting at an outdoor cafe in Morocco. The scent of garden mint just after a rain entwines yet another thread, and we are children in Arizona, playing in the shady mint patch that flourishes under the outdoor water cooler. Desert places or northern latitudes, mint accommodates itself to a wide range of climates. Forms and variations in this group are great. We have grown rounded, fuzzy-leaved spearmints and pointed, sharply serrated-leaved varieties. The plants range from one and one-half to three and one-half feet tall.

Pineapple mint (*Mentha suaveolens v.*) is a sweetly citrus-flavored mint, which we like to use in confections, for candying, and for punches because of its aroma and small leaves. It has pleasantly variegated and slightly fuzzy leaves and grows to about two and one-half feet tall.

Orange mint (*Mentha citrata*) is also called bergamot mint but should not be confused with the Bee Balm Bergamot plant (*Monarda didyma*). It is highly perfumed with a strong citrus flavor that we enjoy in iced drinks. The delightful fragrance is exceptional in fruit preserves and butters, or as part of a bouquet. We grow a lot of it to dry for use in tea blends.

The long and colorful history of mint has been recorded in Greek mythology, the Bible, and herbals of all times. Romans used it to flavor many kinds of food and drink and adorned their halls with it in preparation for feasts so that the smell would stimulate the guests. Pliny appreciated the properties of mint when he stated "the smell of mint stirs up the mind and appetite to a greedy desire for food." The herb symbolized strength to the Greeks, who used it in their athletic ceremonies.

In Elizabethan times, it was used not only as a strewing herb but also as a bath herb, to strengthen the nerves and stomach, and as a whitener for the teeth. Mint is used in many of these same ways today—from air fresheners and bath oils to toothpastes and stomach preparations. Nicholas Culpeper, writing in the mid-seventeenth century, listed forty ailments for which mint was a cure. It is especially good for the digestive system, as it has stomach-soothing properties.

As one of the herbs that has kept its reputation throughout the world, both culinarily and medicinally, mint is an important part of our kitchens and gardens. In the following recipes, the suggested mints can be replaced with any you might prefer.

Mint Daiquiri

We think this drink is best with Blue Balsam mint; other peppermints are also very good.

6 limes	*7 ounces light rum*
1/3 to 1/2 cup sugar	*1 ounce clear creme de menthe*
about 4 cups water	*Garnish: 8 small mint sprigs*
5 large peppermint sprigs	

Squeeze enough limes to yield 1/2 cup juice. Dissolve the sugar in the lime juice and add the water. Adjust the taste with more juice or sugar. Soak the large mint sprigs in the limeade, bruising the leaves a bit against the side of the pitcher. Add the rum and creme de menthe. Chill the mixture for 30 minutes. Serve the daiquiris on the rocks and garnish with a small sprig of fresh mint.

Yields 8 drinks.

Moroccan Mint Tea

To prepare the traditional Moroccan tea, keep the following essentials in mind. The tea must be green, with a mild flavor. The mint must be fresh (absolutely not dried), and it must be spearmint. The tea is traditionally very sweet; there is always sugar in the bottom of the glasses in Morocco. The tea should be served in small glasses with several fresh mint sprigs in each glass.

1 heaping tablespoon green tea, such as Dragonwell or Gunpowder	1/4 to 1/2 cup sugar
about 20 4-inch spearmint sprigs	boiling water

Rinse a teapot with boiling water and pour the water out. Add the green tea and enough spearmint to loosely fill the pot about three-quarters full. Add at least 1/4 cup sugar and fill the pot with boiling water. Steep for 5 minutes. Put 2 or 3 mint sprigs in each glass and pour the tea. Sip slowly.

Yields enough tea for 6 small glasses.

Minted Eggplant Croquettes

This is a fine, unusual appetizer, inspired by the Italian dish *Mozzarella in Carozza*. In our opinion, eggplant is one of the few vegetables that really benefits by deep frying.

6 Italian or Japanese eggplants, each 4 to 6 inches long	1 cup fine, dry bread crumbs
kosher or sea salt	3 eggs
1/2 pound Bel Paese cheese	1 teaspoon salt
20 to 30 Blue Balsam or peppermint leaves	about 1 quart of peanut oil
about 1 cup unbleached white flour	

Trim the eggplants and slice them crosswise into 1/4-inch slices. Layer the slices on a baking sheet, sprinkling each layer lightly with coarse salt. Weight the slices and let drain about 30 minutes. Rinse them and pat very dry.

Slice the cheese into 1/4-inch slices. Trim the cheese so that it fits the eggplant rounds. Layer 1 cheese slice and 1 mint leaf between 2 eggplant rounds. Continue until the eggplant, cheese, and mint have been used.

Spread the flour thickly on a sheet of waxed paper. Spread the bread crumbs on another sheet of waxed paper. Beat the eggs lightly with 1 teaspoon salt in a shallow dish. Pat the croquettes all over with flour. Dip them into the beaten egg, then into the bread crumbs, covering them completely. Lay the croquettes on waxed paper on a baking sheet. Chill at least 30 minutes.

Bring the oil to 375° F. in a deep fat fryer. Fry the croquettes, 6 to 8 at a time, about 3 minutes on each side. They should be a rich golden brown. To prepare the croquettes without deep frying, fry them in a skillet in about 1 inch of very hot peanut oil, about 3 minutes on each side.

Serves 6 to 8.

Minted Pea Soup

1 1/2 pounds fresh peas, shelled	*3 tablespoons unsalted butter*
3 tablespoons chopped spearmint leaves	*1 1/2 cups half-and-half cream*
2 shallots	*salt and freshly ground white pepper to taste*

Put the peas and mint in a pan and barely cover with water. Cover and cook over low heat until the peas are just tender, about 5 minutes.

Dice the shallots finely and saute them in butter in a small pan, over medium-low heat, until they are soft and golden.

Puree the peas and shallots together. Return them to the pan and add the cream, salt, and white pepper. Heat over low heat until the soup is very hot, but do not allow it to boil.

Serves 6.

Minted Lamb, Moroccan-Style

1 1/2 pounds boned leg of lamb	2 garlic cloves, minced
2 large onions	salt and pepper to taste
3 tablespoons unsalted butter	3 tablespoons minced mint
1 cup lamb stock or water	1 tablespoon minced marjoram
4 tablespoons honey	

Cut the lamb into 1 1/2-inch pieces. Peel the onions and slice them thinly. Saute the onions in butter over low heat for 10 minutes. Push the onions to the side of the pan and increase the heat to medium. Saute the lamb until it is browned. Add the stock, honey, garlic, salt, and pepper. Cover and cook over low heat about 45 minutes.

Remove from the heat and stir in the mint and marjoram. Cover and let stand for 10 minutes. Serve hot over couscous or rice.

Serves 4.

Roast Duck with Gooseberry Mint Sauce

4- to 5-pound duck	about 20 Blue Balsam mint sprigs
salt and pepper	1/2 cup gooseberry jam or jelly
1 celery rib	1/4 cup minced mint leaves
1 carrot	Garnish: 8 to 10 mint sprigs
1 onion	

Preheat the oven to 450° F.

Wash the duck and pat it dry. Prick the skin all over, especially the fatty deposits covering the legs. Salt and pepper it lightly inside and out. Place the duck, breast up, on a rack set on a baking sheet and roast for 20 minutes.

Prepare the vegetables by peeling and trimming them, and cutting them into a medium dice. Remove the duck from the oven and stuff it with the mint sprigs and vegetables. Pour off the accumulated fat and reduce the oven temperature to 350° F. Bake for 40 to 60 minutes, depending on the desired doneness.

Remove the duck to a heatproof serving platter. Carefully pour the fat from the baking sheet and put the cooking juices in a small saucepan. Stir in the gooseberry jam and minced mint. Simmer 1 to 2 minutes over low heat.

Increase the oven temperature to 450° F.

Brush the duck lightly with the sauce and return to the oven for 3 to 4 minutes, until the duck is glazed. Remove and let stand for 5 minutes. Mix the accumulated juices with the remaining sauce and serve separately. Garnish the platter with mint sprigs if desired.

Serves 2 to 4.

Minted Tomatoes Gratine

Fried tomatoes were a treat that Carolyn's father, Robert Dille, used to prepare for the family. The meltingly sweet flavor still appeals to us.

3 medium-sized, firm-ripe tomatoes	5 tablespoons fine, dry bread crumbs
3 tablespoons unsalted butter	3 tablespoons freshly grated Parmesan cheese
2 tablespoons roughly chopped, fresh spearmint leaves	2 tablespoons finely chopped, fresh spearmint leaves

Slice the tomatoes into 1/2-inch slices. Melt the butter with the roughly chopped spearmint over medium-low heat. Saute the tomatoes in the butter about 1 minute on each side.

Place the tomatoes on a heatproof serving dish or baking sheet. Combine the butter and mint from the pan with the bread crumbs, cheese, and finely chopped mint. Divide the mixture evenly over the tomato slices. Place them under a preheated broiler until the gratin is golden brown. Serve the tomatoes and their juices in a warm dish.

Serves 3 to 4.

New Potatoes with Mint

18 to 20 new potatoes, about 1 1/2 inches in diameter, or 6 to 8 new potatoes, about 2 1/2 inches in diameter	1 tablespoon chopped mint leaves
3 tablespoons unsalted butter	salt and freshly ground black pepper to taste

Scrub the potatoes and peel if desired. Steam the small potatoes whole for about 3 minutes, or quarter the larger potatoes and steam them for about 5 minutes.

Heat the butter in a large skillet over moderate heat and add the potatoes and mint. Cook for about 3 to 5 minutes over lively heat, until the potatoes are just done. Shake the pan constantly while the potatoes are cooking.

Transfer to a hot platter and sprinkle lightly with salt and plenty of pepper. Serve immediately.

Serves 6 to 8.

Carrot, Green Bean, and Red Onion Salad with Mint Dressing

We were inspired to create this recipe because our friend Gina Thomson's mint dressing was so tasty. The dressing also goes well with green salads that use bitter or sour greens and herbs, such as curly and Belgian endive, chicory, dandelion greens, and sorrel.

2 large carrots	*2 small red onions*
1/4 pound green beans	*1 small head butter or red leaf lettuce*

Peel the carrots and grate them coarsely. Slice the green beans into tiny rings and steam them for about 1 minute, or until just tender. Cut the onions in half lengthwise and slice each half into very thin rings. Wash and dry the lettuce, and arrange it on a platter.

Dressing

1 cup light sesame oil	*about 1/4 cup minced peppermint or spearmint leaves*
2 1/2 tablespoons white wine vinegar, or to taste	*salt and pepper to taste*
1 1/2 tablespoons honey, or to taste	

Combine the dressing ingredients in a blender and puree just until smooth. Arrange the carrots, green beans, and onions on the lettuce. Just before serving, whisk the dressing and pour over the salad.

Serves 4 to 6.

Cucumber Mint Raita

This is a cooling condiment to serve with spicy foods. It is especially good with curries or as a sauce for falafels.

2 medium or 1 large cucumber	3 tablespoons finely chopped mint
2 cups plain yogurt	scant 1/2 teaspoon salt
2 tablespoons finely chopped onion	2 to 3 cardamom seeds, finely ground, or 1/2 teaspoon ground cardamom

Peel the cucumbers if the skins are bitter. Seed the cucumbers and cut into medium-fine dice. You should have about 1 1/2 cups diced cucumber. Combine the cucumber and the remaining ingredients in a bowl. Cover and chill for 1 hour or longer.

Yields about 4 cups.

Grape Mint Jelly

The jelly is especially fragrant and flavorful when made with bergamot mint.

2 1/2 pounds purple grapes	1 cup light honey
28 fresh mint leaves	2 6-inch mint sprigs
2 cups sugar	6 small mint sprigs

Wash the grapes and layer them in a large enameled or stainless steel pan, mashing each layer as it is added. Add 20 of the fresh mint leaves and stir. Bring to a simmer over low heat and cook for 20 minutes.

Pour the hot mixture through a jelly bag, or a large sieve lined with fine cloth, straining it into a bowl. Squeeze the cloth to extract all the juice. Return the pulp to a saucepan and just cover it with water. Add 8 more mint leaves and bring to a simmer. Cook 15 minutes and repeat the straining process, squeezing to get all the juice. There should be 4 cups of juice; if necessary, add a little water to equal this amount.

Reheat the juice in a clean enameled or stainless steel pan with the sugar and honey. Add the 6-inch mint sprigs and stir well. Simmer and continue stirring until the jelly just sheets from a metal spoon, or reaches 220° F. on a jelly thermometer. Remove the mint sprigs.

Have ready 6 sterilized, hot half-pint jelly jars. Place a clean, small mint sprig in each jar. Ladle the hot jelly into the jars immediately and seal.

Yields 6 half-pints.

Buttermint Cookies

12 tablespoons unsalted butter, softened	1/2 teaspoon peppermint extract
2/3 cup sugar	2 cups unbleached white flour, sifted
1 large egg	1 tablespoon minced peppermint leaves
1/2 teaspoon vanilla extract	pinch of salt

Cream the butter and sugar. Beat in the egg and extracts. Gradually mix in the flour. Stir in the minced peppermint and salt. The dough will be soft.

Divide the dough into 3 parts. Using plastic wrap to shape the dough, roll each part into a cylinder about 1 1/4 inches in diameter. Chill the rolls for 1 to 2 hours.

Preheat the oven to 350° F.

Remove the plastic wrap and slice the dough into 1/4-inch rounds. Place the cookies on ungreased baking sheets and bake about 10 minutes, until the cookies are a light golden brown. Remove the cookies from the baking sheets while they are hot and cool on racks.

Yields about 4 dozen.

Mint Ice Cream in Chocolate Mint Cups

1 1/2 cups half-and-half cream	2 large, fresh spearmint sprigs
4 egg yolks	1/2 pint whipping cream
1/2 cup sugar	1 tablespoon creme de menthe

Scald the half-and-half cream. Remove from the heat and pour into a double boiler over simmering water. Beat in the egg yolks and sugar. Add the mint sprigs. Cook the mixture, stirring frequently, until it coats a spoon, 10 to 15 minutes. Do not allow the custard to boil.

Remove from the heat and take out the mint sprigs. Pour the mixture into a stainless steel bowl, cover with foil, and let it come to room temperature. Freeze the custard for 30 minutes. Remove it from the freezer and beat with a whisk. Return to the freezer and repeat this process twice.

Beat the whipping cream until stiff. After the last whisking, fold the whipped cream and creme de menthe into the custard until well blended.

Return to the freezer for at least 3 hours before serving. Serve in Chocolate Mint Cups (see following recipe).

Yields enough ice cream for 16 cups.

Chocolate Mint Cups

9 ounces semisweet chocolate, preferably Lindt Excellence	*16 small, fresh peppermint leaves*
2 teaspoons vegetable oil	*about 1 tablespoon creme de menthe*

Have ready 16 paper baking cups, each 2 inches wide and about 1 1/2 inches tall. Break the chocolate into bits. Melt the chocolate with the vegetable oil in a double boiler over simmering water. When completely melted, spread it evenly into the paper cups.

Put the cups on a baking sheet and freeze for 15 minutes. After they have hardened a bit, remove them from the freezer and place 1 mint leaf in the bottom of each cup. Sprinkle each leaf with 2 or 3 drops creme de menthe. Keep in the freezer until ready to use.

To serve, remove the paper carefully, fill the cups with ice cream, and garnish with mint leaves. Serve immediately.

Yields 16 cups.

YOUNG ITALIAN PARSLEY

PARSLEY

The last to leave, yet rises early,
it floats in pots, and lies on plates.
Whether its shape is flat or curly,
it's a character with pleasing traits.

A GOOD THEATER production has one understudy who can play any part. Parsley fills this role in the kitchen with accommodating ease and versatility. The cook can direct it with confidence to star or support, as needed. It requires little prompting, and its fresh, green taste does not quarrel with other cast members.

A bite of fresh parsley reveals its faint peppery tang and green apple aftertaste. The brilliance of its emerald green leaves and its mild yet piquant flavor have made it a standard garnish; it is a pleasant counterpoint to most vegetables, fish, and meats. Parsley is the sine qua non of bouquets garnis and fines herbes; for soups and stews, certainly, it is difficult to overuse this herb. So familiar that it seems perhaps plain, its use adorns all manner of dishes, from fresh salads to long-simmered ragouts.

This clean and delicate taste has a long history of being appreciated. To cleanse and refresh the palate, the Romans served parsley at feasts. They were the first people to eat parsley, but the Greeks, a thousand years before, made wreaths of it for weddings and athletic games and fed it to their horses before battle to insure valor. The word *parsley* is anglicized from the Greek *petros,* "rock," referring to its rocky, wild habitat. Once its use and cultivation were recorded, parsley became one of the most popular culinary herbs. The Renaissance herbalists of England had a wealth of medicinal uses for it, as well as lore on when and how to plant it.

Curled parsley, *Petroselinum crispum,* is the one fresh herb that is a staple in United States' markets. Italian parsley, *P. crispum neapolitanum,* sometimes found in produce or specialty markets, has much broader, flat leaves. It is the variety we prefer for its dark, handsome, celery-like foliage and fuller flavor. Parsley is as rich in vitamins and minerals as its sprightly leaves suggest, chiefly iron and vitamins A and C.

Parsley's slow germination has stimulated some fanciful theories: that it goes to the devil nine times and back before it sprouts, or that a pregnant womn planting it speeds germination. Today, we soak the seeds in warm water for one or two days before putting them in the soil. The flat-leaved Italian parsley is well worth cultivating for its special taste and because it is more difficult to find. Outdoors, it is very hardy and can be used well into winter, even when the leaves have frozen. In the summer, too, when other herbs are blooming or have gone to seed, parsley is in the wings, a seasoned standby. Although it is a biennial and will reseed itself, we sow parsley every year to have a plentiful crop. The herb will grow well in full sun, but some shade helps to develop a deeper green color.

Harvest parsley by cutting it about an inch above ground level. The stems of tender parsley can be used as well as the leaves. We follow the practice of many cooks and save the stems for stocks. So much of the real flavor is lost in drying the leaves that we always preserve parsley by freezing.

Parsley's great fame is as a companionable herb, enhancing or lending subtlety to many of the stronger herbs.

Parsley Cheese Spread

This mixture may sound a bit strange, but it makes a tasty sandwich filling, stuffing for tomatoes, or cracker spread.

1 pint ricotta or cottage cheese	1 cup finely chopped parsley
1/4 cup old-fashioned, chunky peanut butter	2 stalks celery, finely chopped
3 tablespoons mayonnaise	1 small onion, finely chopped
1 teaspoon Dijon mustard	1/2 teaspoon freshly ground celery seed
1 tablespoon olive oil	1/2 teaspoon paprika
1/4 cup grated Parmesan cheese	Optional: 1/2 small green pepper
1 tablespoon prepared hot sauce	salt to taste
1 jalapeno pepper, finely chopped	

In a bowl, blend together the ricotta cheese and peanut butter. Add the mayonnaise, mustard, olive oil, Parmesan, hot sauce, jalapeno pepper, and parsley and blend well. Add the celery and onion to the mixture with the celery seed and paprika. If desired, finely chop the green pepper and add it. Mix well and season.

Yields about 3 cups, enough for 6 sandwiches or 6 tomatoes.

Parsley Chickpea Pate

1 cup dried chickpeas	1/2 teaspoon freshly ground cumin seed
1/2 cup tahini	1/2 to 1 teaspoon cayenne pepper
juice of 1 lemon	salt and pepper to taste
1/4 cup olive oil	Garnish: red pepper strips
1/4 cup reserved chickpea stock	oil-cured black olives
1 cup packed parsley leaves	parsley sprigs
3 medium garlic cloves	

Wash and pick over the chickpeas. In a large saucepan, cover them with 4 cups cold water and soak overnight. Pour off the water, add fresh water to cover the chickpeas by 1 inch, and cook them for 1 to 1 1/2 hours, or until they are tender. Drain the chickpeas, reserving 1/4 cup of the liquid.

Puree the chickpeas with the reserved liquid in a food processor or through a food mill. Combine the puree, tahini, lemon juice, and olive oil in a bowl, blending well. Finely mince the parsley and garlic and add to the chickpea mixture. Add the cumin seed and cayenne, and season with salt and pepper. The mixture should be thick.

Pat the pate into a dome shape on a serving dish, or pack it into a 1-quart terrine, and chill it, covered, at least 1 hour. Garnish with red pepper strips, black olives, and parsley. Serve with toast points or pita bread.

Serves 8 to 12 as an hors d'oeuvre.

Pecan Parsley Dip

1 pint sour cream	3/4 cup pecans, lightly toasted
1/2 cup chopped parsley	1/2 teaspoon paprika
1 garlic clove, pressed	dash of cayenne pepper
1 small cucumber	salt to taste

In a glass bowl, combine the sour cream, parsley, and garlic. Peel and finely chop the cucumber and add it to the sour cream mixture. Chop the pecans medium-fine and stir them into the mixture along with the paprika and cayenne. Add the salt and blend the ingredients well.

Cover the dip and chill at least 2 hours before serving. Serve with crackers, fresh vegetable sticks, and scored rounds of cucumber.

Yields 3 cups.

Green Goodness Dressing

We developed this recipe while working in a restaurant and could barely make enough of it. We like it so much that we have to restrain ourselves from eating it on bread. Try adding one of your favorite herbs for a different flavor.

2 cups packed parsley leaves	1 teaspoon Dijon mustard
juice of 1 lime	1/2 teaspoon salt
1 tablespoon white wine vinegar	1 cup virgin olive oil
2 medium garlic cloves, finely minced	

In a blender, blend all the ingredients at low speed for 1 minute and at high speed for 30 seconds, or until the mixture is bright green. This dressing keeps, covered and chilled, for 1 week. Stir the dressing before using and serve it at room temperature with green salads or vegetables.

Yields about 1 1/2 cups.

Parsley Bread

1 tablespoon honey	2 tablespoons light oil
1/2 cup lukewarm water	1 1/2 teaspoons salt
2 tablespoons dry yeast	3 cups whole wheat flour
1 1/2 cups very hot water	1 cup unbleached white flour
1 cup stone-ground cornmeal	1 cup finely minced parsley

In a small bowl, combine the honey, lukewarm water, and yeast.

In a large bowl, combine the hot water, cornmeal, oil, and salt. When this mixture has cooled to warm, add the yeast mixture. Add the flours, 1 cup at a time, stirring well after each addition. Stir the parsley into the batter.

Leave the bowl in a warm place, covered with a damp towel, until the batter triples in size. Beat the batter down with a wooden spoon and turn it into a standard size, oiled loaf pan. Let rise for 15 minutes.

Preheat the oven to 450° F.

Bake the loaf for 10 minutes. Reduce the oven to 350° F. and bake for 50 minutes, or until the top is a rich brown.

Cream of Parsley Soup

6 tablespoons unsalted butter	2 cups finely minced parsley
6 tablespoons flour	salt to taste
3 cups hot chicken or vegetable stock	freshly grated nutmeg to taste
2 teaspoons finely minced, fresh summer savory, or 1 scant teaspoon finely crumbled, dried summer savory	Garnish: 6 parsley sprigs
3 cups half-and-half cream	freshly grated pecorino or Romano cheese

In a large saucepan, melt the butter over moderately low heat. Stir in the flour and cook the roux, stirring, for 3 minutes.

Remove the pan from the heat. Add the stock in a stream, whisking vigorously, and whisk the mixture until it is thickened and smooth. Add the savory and simmer the mixture, stirring occasionally, for 10 minutes.

Add the cream, minced parsley, salt, and nutmeg and heat the soup over moderately low heat, stirring, until it is hot. Do not let it boil.

Ladle the soup into heated bowls. Garnish each with a parsley sprig and serve with freshly grated cheese.

Serves 6.

Fettuccine with Scallops and Parsley Sauce

3/4 pound sea scallops	1/2 cup heavy cream
4 tablespoons unsalted butter	1 cup half-and-half cream
1 shallot, minced	1 cup freshly grated Parmesan cheese
1/2 cup finely minced parsley	freshly grated nutmeg to taste
1/2 cup dry white wine	1 recipe Spinach or Egg Fettuccine (see Index)

Cut the scallops into bite-sized pieces. Melt the butter in a large skillet over medium-low heat. When it foams, add the shallot and 1/4 cup of the parsley. Saute gently for 5 minutes.

Add the wine, increase the heat, and reduce the liquid to about 6 tablespoons. Reduce the heat, add the scallops, and saute gently for 2 minutes. Add the creams and heat for 2 minutes. Add the cheese and remaining parsley.

Remove from the heat and grate 3 or 4 dashes of nutmeg over the sauce. Serve immediately over hot, drained fettuccine on a heated platter.

Serves 4.

Fillet of Sole with Parsley

4 tablespoons unsalted butter	2 pounds sole fillets
3 eggs	1 cup flour
1/2 teaspoon salt	Garnish: parsley sprigs
1/2 cup packed parsley leaves	lemon wedges

In a large skillet, melt the butter over low heat. Beat the eggs with the salt in a flat bowl until they are homogenous. Finely mince the parsley leaves.

Dredge the fillets in the flour, shaking off the excess. Leave the fillets on a lightly floured surface and return the butter to medium heat. Dip the fillets into the egg, covering both sides, and saute 2 minutes, or until pale golden brown on one side. Turn the fillets, sprinkle the minced parsley over them, and cook for 2 minutes. Serve on a heated platter and garnish with parsley sprigs and lemon wedges.

Serves 4.

Braised Artichokes with Parsley

6 medium artichokes	1 teaspoon salt
1/2 lemon	1/2 cup dry white wine
1 cup packed parsley leaves	1/2 cup water
2 garlic cloves	1/2 cup olive oil

Cut the stem ends of the artichokes flush with the bases. Snap off the lower outer leaves and cut the center thorny tips about 1 1/2 inches from the top. Trim the thorns from the remaining leaves with scissors. Rub all cut surfaces with the lemon.

Mince the parsley and garlic. Mix them with the salt. Spread the artichoke leaves from the center out and stuff the parsley mixture between the leaves.

Choose a terracotta casserole, or heavy nonaluminum and nonporous pan, large enough to hold the artichokes loosely. The lid must fit tightly.

Pour the wine and water into the pan and add the 1/2 lemon. Put the artichokes in the pan and pour the olive oil between the leaves, dividing it evenly among the artichokes. Cover the pan and bring the liquid to a simmer over medium heat. Reduce the heat slightly and cook the artichokes for 20 to 30 minutes, or until an inside leaf detaches easily.

Transfer the artichokes to a serving dish, pouring some pan juices over each artichoke. These can be served hot as a vegetable course or at room temperature as an appetizer.

Serves 6.

Brown Rice and Walnut Casserole

4 cups cooked brown rice	1/2 cup grated, sharp cheddar cheese
1 cup whole grain bread crumbs	2 cloves finely minced garlic
1 cup coarsely chopped parsley	1/4 cup vegetable stock or water
2 eggs, lightly beaten	6 to 8 sage leaves, finely chopped, or 1/2 teaspoon crumbled, dried sage
1 1/2 cups chopped walnuts, or other nuts	1/2 teaspoon freshly ground celery seed
1 onion	1/4 teaspoon cayenne pepper
3 tablespoons olive oil	salt to taste
1/2 cup freshly grated Parmesan cheese	

In a large bowl, combine the rice, bread crumbs, parsley, eggs, and nuts.

Finely chop the onion and soften it in the olive oil over medium-low heat for about 5 minutes. Mix the onion into the rice. Stir in the cheeses and the garlic.

Toss the mixture with the stock, sage, celery seed, and cayenne. Salt lightly and turn the mixture into an oiled casserole.

Preheat the oven to 350° F.

Topping

1/4 cup grated, sharp cheddar cheese	1/4 cup whole grain bread crumbs

Mix the cheese with the bread crumbs and spread over the casserole. Bake for 35 to 40 minutes, until the casserole is a rich golden brown.

Serves 4 as a main course or 8 as a side dish.

Sweet Potato and Parsley Salad

People who do not like the usual sugary sweet potato concoctions will appreciate the way they are prepared in this recipe. Both the dark orange-colored (often sold as yams) or the light yellow sweet potatoes can be used. Bake or steam them in their jackets, as you prefer, but do not overcook them.

6 cooked sweet potatoes	2 teaspoons soy sauce
1 small onion	1/2 cup coarsely chopped parsley
1 medium celery rib	4 to 5 marjoram sprigs or 1 teaspoon dried marjoram
1/3 cup virgin olive oil	salt and freshly ground pepper to taste
juice of 1 lemon, or to taste	Garnish: 1/2 cup cashew nuts, freshly toasted

Peel the sweet potatoes and cut them into 1/2-inch dice. Finely dice the onion and celery. Put the vegetables in a large bowl.

Mix the olive oil, lemon juice, and soy sauce in a small bowl. Stir in the chopped parsley. Stem and chop the fresh marjoram or crumble the dried leaves. Add to the olive oil and season the dressing lightly. Toss the dressing with the vegetables.

Just before serving, sprinkle the salad with the cashew nuts. The salad can be served warm or at room temperature.

Serves 6.

ROSEMARY

ROSEMARY

In the rocky cliffs,
Hanging o'er the sea,
Forgotten not by sun and dew,
Blooms sweet rosemary.

W E CANNOT CLAIM positively that any herb lightens doldrums or depression, but we are always cheered when we brush rosemary leaves through our fingers to release its refreshing scent. Its quintessential fragrance of a seacoast with pines affects us like an offshore breeze at early evening. The drears and dulls are blown away, even if we are miles from the sea and enduring the freezing days of February.

Rosemary is an herb of diverse and strong symbols, the great majority of which are beneficent. Popularized in Ophelia's plea, "Rosemary's for remembrance, pray you love, remember," it was also the emblem of loyalty and friendship. Where basil symbolized the quickening of love, rosemary tokened its lastingness and was woven into bridal wreaths as early as the Roman Republic. It was put under nuptial mattresses to encourage faithfulness, as well as to keep away insects and mildew.

The plant's beautiful form and flowers gave rise to some legends full of symbolic meaning. One of the oldest is that a beautiful young woman from Sicily was changed into a rosemary bush. At the time of this transformation, Sicily was under the domination of Circe, who caused violent volcanoes to erupt and plants to wither and die. She also enchanted the inhabitants so that they would throw themselves into the sea. The blue-eyed woman who had become rosemary clung to the cliffs to remind men of the ever-renewing power of good in the world.

The Romans transplanted rosemary to England, where the sea-saturated climate of the south was mild enough to favor it. The name is from the Latin *ros marinus,* "dew of the sea." It flourished through Medieval and Renaissance periods, every garden having a single bush or several, often pruned in fanciful or symmetrical shapes. Some favorite uses of the essential oil, or the leaves and flowers, were in refreshing baths, as an insect and moth repellent, as a mouthwash, and in liniments.

Incensier, a French term for rosemary, comes from its use as incense in church ceremonies. Its pleasing scent was not the only reason for this tradition; rosemary's reputation against evil was well established. It was put in sachets under pillows to prevent nightmares; and it was carried to funerals to be placed on graves, in the belief that dark spirits would not disturb departed souls under the protection of light-loving rosemary.

Rosemary has fallen somewhat out of favor as a culinary herb except in Italy, where it is still much loved. A sprig of rosemary (and sometimes a branch of sage as well) are commonly included with purchases at butcher shops in northern Italy. Italians consider it excellent with roast meats, poultry, and fish. Branches of rosemary are usually put on the coals when lamb and kid are roasted. It is also used in bean dishes, with potatoes, and in certain sweets. It is served finely chopped with Pecorino cheese and Tuscan olive oil in country *trattorie.*

Rosemary's aroma is a combination of fir, balsam, and ocean air. Its components of tannin and camphor give it a moderate bitterness and pepperiness, which are especially good with foods rich in fat or with bland foods, such as potatoes or legumes. For some, the flavor of rosemary is very strong, but its champions like the warmth and richness it gives to hearty dishes and its spiciness with more delicate fare. Dried rosemary generally can be used for fresh, except with cheeses. Rosemary must be dried in the whole needle to preserve its oils, but it should be ground or tied in cheesecloth to prevent the sensation of chewing on pine needles. The strength of the dried herb varies greatly, but commonly the amount used is one-quarter that of fresh.

Although rosemary is a true Mediterranean plant and will not survive extremely cold winters, it can be grown indoors with the following care. Keep the plants in appropriately sized containers, transplanting as necessary. When transplanting, allow plenty of room for the roots. Use a mix of perlite or large-grained, sterile sand, humus, and potting soil for good drainage and aeration. Set the plants outdoors in the summer, taking care to water them well. About one month before the first frost is expected, bring the plants to a protected area near the house. Move them into the house in two weeks, before the heat is turned on, so that they have time to adjust to the temperature difference. Rosemary loves light, and this need must be met in the house or garden.

A cutting is the best way to start rosemary, as seed germination is slow. Rooted cuttings are generally available from herb or nursery suppliers. *Rosmarinus officinalis* is the herb to buy for culinary use and is the easiest to grow. (See the chapter "Working with Herbs" for more detailed information on rooting rosemary and other plants.) Growth can be slow, but once rosemary takes hold it is a plant for generations. It can be trimmed to make a fine dwarf plant.

Water and mist rosemary regularly and fertilize at least once a month, both outside and inside. Reduced sunlight and lower daytime temperatures in the house lessen the need for water; let the plants dry between waterings.

In temperate gardens, rosemary does very well against brick or stone. We have seen some magnificent plants growing against walls and barns in Italy, where the plant was apparently spread by layering. It grows nicely as a freestanding shrub but requires more attention to avoid a straggly look. It is frequently used as a hedge in the coastal areas of northern California, where Italian familes settled.

Rosmarinus prostratus makes a fine ground cover, as it grows ten to twelve inches tall and spreads easily.

Rosemary lends its clean aroma and piney tang to the following dishes.

Mulled Rosemary Wine and Black Tea

1 bottle claret wine	2 oranges, thinly sliced and seeded
1 quart black tea (Assam type)	1 3-inch cinnamon stick
1/4 cup mild honey	6 whole cloves
1/3 cup sugar, or to taste	2 3-inch fresh rosemary sprigs

Pour the steeped tea into a 3-quart saucepan along with the wine. Add the honey, sugar, oranges, spices, and rosemary, and heat over low heat until barely steaming. Stir to make sure that the honey is dissolved. Cover and let stand for 30 minutes or longer. Heat to just steaming and serve hot.

Yields about 2 quarts.

Dolmades with Rosemary

Our version of dolmades is more lavish than the usual lemon-soaked dabs of rice thickly wrapped in grape leaves. We think this recipe has just the right balance of flavors.

2 cups short grain white rice	*2 tablespoons finely chopped, fresh rosemary, or 2 teaspoons dried rosemary, finely crumbled*
3 cups water	*1/4 cup fresh chopped parsley*
1 teaspoon salt	*1/2 teaspoon salt*
2 large shallots, minced	*2 tablespoons lemon juice*
4 tablespoons olive oil	*4 tablespoons olive oil*
1/2 cup currants	*1 8-ounce jar grape leaves*
1/2 cup pine nuts	

In a saucepan, combine the rice, water, and salt. Cover, bring to a boil, and reduce the heat. Cook the rice until tender, about 25 minutes.

Saute the shallots in 4 tablespoons olive oil in a small frying pan for about 5 minutes. Add them to the cooked rice with the currants, pine nuts, rosemary, and parsley.

Dissolve the salt in the lemon juice and add the remaining 4 tablespoons olive oil. Add to the rice mixture and toss so that all ingredients are mixed well.

Remove the grape leaves from the jar and trim the stems. Blanch the leaves in unsalted, boiling water for 2 minutes. Refresh under cold water and pat them dry.

Put 1 heaping tablespoon of rice mixture on the large leaves and 1 level tablespoon of mixture on the smaller leaves. Roll them up and place them on a lightly oiled tray. These can be made in advance and chilled up to 24 hours.

Cook the dolmades in a steamer/spaghetti cooker. Add enough water to barely touch the bottom of the steamer. Gently pile the dolmades in the steamer and weight them with a small plate. Steam for 20 minutes. If they have been refrigerated, they will take a bit longer. Serve hot or cold.

Yields about 40 dolmades.

Rosemary Scones

2 cups whole wheat flour	1 tablespoon raw sugar
2 cups unbleached white flour	4 tablespoons unsalted butter
1/2 teaspoon salt	2 tablespoons finely chopped, fresh rosemary, or 2 teaspoons dried rosemary, finely crumbled
2 teaspoons baking powder	1 1/2 cups milk
1 teaspoon baking soda	

In a large bowl, sift the flours, salt, baking powder, baking soda, and sugar. Cut the butter into the dry ingredients to make pea-sized lumps. Add the rosemary and milk and mix together to form a soft dough.

Preheat the oven to 400° F.

Roll the dough out 1/2 inch thick on a lightly floured board. Cut into 1 1/2-inch squares and place close together on a greased and floured baking sheet. Bake for 20 minutes.

Yields about 30 scones.

Country Pea Soup with Rosemary

Rosemary really does something wonderful for split pea soup. For a warming herbal dinner, serve the soup with Light Whole Wheat Sage Muffins (see Index).

1 1/2 pounds split peas	1 small onion
3-inch rosemary sprig	1/4 cup olive oil
1 bay leaf	1 teaspoon salt
2 carrots	3 garlic cloves, minced
1 large potato	2 tablespoons finely chopped, fresh rosemary, or 2 teaspoons dried, crumbled rosemary
3 stalks celery	

Soak the peas overnight. Wash the peas, put them in a large soup pot, and cover them by 2 inches with water. Add the rosemary sprig and bay leaf. Cover and bring to a boil, reduce the heat, and simmer for 20 minutes.

Chop the carrots, potato, celery, and onion and saute them in a small pan in olive oil for 10 minutes. Add them to the peas with the salt, garlic,

and remaining rosemary. Cook over low heat for 25 minutes, stirring occasionally. Salt to taste. This soup improves in flavor when made in advance.
Serves 8.

Calzone al Ramerino

1 recipe pizza dough (see Index)	2 tablespoons olive oil
1/2 pound mozzarella cheese	2 garlic cloves
1/2 pound Fontina cheese	1/4 cup parsley leaves
1 medium onion	6 ounces thinly sliced, julienned prosciutto
6 3-inch fresh rosemary sprigs	salt to taste

Make the pizza dough. Coarsely grate the cheeses.

Finely chop the onion and rosemary. Saute the onion and rosemary in olive oil over moderate heat for 5 minutes. Remove to a bowl. Mince the garlic and parsley and add to the bowl.

When the dough has doubled in bulk, punch it down and divide it into 4 equal portions. Roll or pat the dough into 6-inch circles.

Preheat the oven to 400° F.

Combine the cheese, herbs, onions, and prosciutto and mix well. Divide the mixture equally between the circles, heaping it on half of each circle about 1/2 inch from the edge. Sprinkle lightly with salt. Fold the dough over the filling and crimp well. Bake on a lightly oiled baking sheet for 15 minutes. The calzone should be a rich golden brown. Serve immediately.

Yields 4 calzone.

Chickpea Tagine

This recipe is a variation of a traditional dish that we savored many times in northern Morocco.

1 cup dry garbanzos (chickpeas)	1 large onion
5 tablespoons olive oil	2 garlic cloves, minced
3 tablespoons chopped, fresh rosemary, or 2 1/2 teaspoons crumbled, dried rosemary	1/4 teaspoon cayenne pepper, or to taste
1 teaspoon turmeric	1/4 cup currants, soaked and drained
1/2 teaspoon curry powder, or to taste	Garnish: rosemary sprigs

Soak the garbanzo beans overnight. Drain off the water, put the beans in a medium saucepan, and cover with water to 3 inches above the beans. Cover and cook about 1 hour, or until the beans are just tender.

Puree half the cooked beans and all of the cooking liquid in a blender, with the olive oil, 2 tablespoons fresh rosemary, or about two-thirds of the dried rosemary, the turmeric, and the curry powder. Combine the puree with the remaining garbanzo beans in a saucepan and reheat over low heat.

Slice the onion into very thin rings. Saute them in a large, heavy skillet in 1 tablespoon olive oil until they are golden brown. Add the remaining rosemary, and the garlic and cayenne pepper. Cook together for 2 minutes. Add the bean mixture and currants, stir well, cover, and let stand for about 5 minutes.

This tagine should be accompanied by couscous or rice. To serve, place the couscous in a mound on a large, warm serving dish and pour the tagine over it. Garnish with rosemary sprigs.

Serves 6.

Rosemary Ragout

1 pound beef stew meat	1-pound can plum tomatoes
1 pound beef heart	3 garlic cloves
1/2 cup flour	1 large carrot
1 teaspoon salt	1 large red onion
6 tablespoons olive oil	1 large celery stalk
1 bottle full-bodied, good quality red wine	8 parsley sprigs
4 3-inch rosemary sprigs, or 1 1/2 teaspoons dried, crumbled rosemary	

Cut the stew meat and heart into 1-inch cubes. Flour the cubes lightly by shaking them in the flour and salt. Heat 4 tablespoons olive oil in a large, heavy casserole until very hot. Sear the meat for 10 minutes, stirring occasionally with a wooden spoon. Add the wine and simmer, covered, for 1 hour.

Add 3 rosemary sprigs, or all the dried rosemary, the tomatoes, and garlic cloves. Season with salt. Simmer uncovered for 1 hour.

Finely chop the carrot, onion, and celery. Saute the vegetables in the remaining olive oil over moderate heat for 10 minutes. Add them to the meat. Simmer uncovered for 20 minutes, stirring occasionally.

Add the parsley sprigs and remaining rosemary sprig and simmer for 15 minutes. Discard the rosemary, parsley, and garlic and transfer the ragout to a warm serving platter. Serve hot with boiled or riced potatoes.

Serves 6.

Rosemary Roasted Chicken

4-pound frying chicken	1 tablespoon olive oil
1/2 lemon	1/2 teaspoon salt
1 medium white onion	2 pieces lemon peel, each about 1 inch long
1 large garlic clove	1/2 cup chicken stock
10 3-inch rosemary sprigs	

Rinse the chicken and pat it dry. Reserve the gizzard, liver, and neck for another use. Rub the chicken inside and out with the lemon half. Peel the onion and garlic. Place them in the cavity with 6 rosemary sprigs and the salt.

Using the olive oil, oil the bottom of a baking dish large enough to hold the chicken. Place the remaining rosemary sprigs between the wings and breast and the thighs and back, then truss the chicken. Put the chicken in the baking dish and squeeze the rest of the lemon juice over it. Sprinkle lightly with salt. Place the lemon peel in the bottom of the dish.

Preheat the oven to 375° F.

Bake the chicken, breast up, for 45 minutes, or until done. Remove from the oven and let rest on a carving board for 10 minutes. Transfer the pan juices and chicken stock in a large skillet and simmer for 5 minutes. Remove the skillet from the heat.

Carve the chicken into serving pieces and heat it in the sauce over moderate heat for 5 minutes. Transfer the chicken to a warm serving platter and nap with the sauce. Serve hot.

Serves 4.

Trout Baked in Parchment with Fennel and Rosemary

2 1-pound trout	6 3-inch fresh rosemary sprigs
1/2 pound Florence fennel	salt and pepper to taste
1 shallot	2 tablespoons dry vermouth
1 tablespoon olive oil	

Clean and scale the trout, leaving the heads on. Cut 2 18-inch rounds of parchment paper. (Or cut 2 18-inch rounds of heavy brown paper and soak them in 1/2 cup olive oil for 5 minutes.)

Trim and discard the outer leaves from the fennel and slice it thinly lengthwise. Finely mince the shallot and cook it with the fennel in the olive oil over low heat for 10 minutes. Remove from the heat and set aside.

Salt the inside of each trout lightly and place 2 rosemary sprigs inside each cavity. Place each trout on a separate piece of parchment, centering the fish on the lower half. Divide the vegetables over the fish. Sprinkle each with salt, pepper, and vermouth and place a rosemary sprig on top.

Preheat the oven to 450° F.

Fold the paper over the fish, crimping the edges and folding them over twice. Place the parchments on a baking sheet and bake for 10 minutes. Remove to heated dinner plates and, with scissors, cut the crimped edges of the paper around to the fold. Unfold and serve immediately.

Serves 2.

Herbed Green Beans

2 pounds fresh green beans	2 teaspoons fresh sage, or a heaping 1/2 teaspoon crumbled, dried sage
1/3 cup olive oil	1 large garlic clove, crushed
juice of 1 lemon	1/2 teaspoon salt
2 tablespoons fresh rosemary, or 2 teaspoons crumbled, dried rosemary	

Wash the beans and trim the ends. French cut the beans into 1 1/2-inch pieces and steam until barely tender.

Finely mince the rosemary and sage. In a glass measuring cup, combine the olive oil, lemon juice, rosemary, sage, garlic, and salt.

Put the beans in a bowl and pour the marinade over them while they are still hot. Toss well to coat the beans and marinate for 2 hours. Serve at room temperature.

Serves 6.

Oven-Fried Rosemary Potatoes

2 pounds medium russet potatoes	1 1/2 teaspoons salt
1/2 cup olive oil	3 tablespoons fresh rosemary leaves, or 2 teaspoons dried, crumbled rosemary

Scrub the potatoes well and cut them in half lengthwise. Cut each half lengthwise into 1/8-inch slices. Coat the potatoes with the olive oil and salt. Place the potatoes and oil in a lightly oiled, 9-by-12-inch baking dish. Strew the rosemary over the potatoes.

Preheat the oven to 350° F.

Cover and bake the potatoes for 30 minutes. Remove the cover, turn the potatoes, and bake 20 minutes longer, or until the potatoes are tender and golden brown. Serve hot.

Serves 6.

Rosemary Apple Jelly

We use filtered, clear apple juice for a pretty jelly. You may want to substitute 2 cups of clear cranberry juice for 2 cups of the apple juice for a more tart jelly.

4 cups apple juice	*3 cups sugar*
3 4-inch rosemary sprigs	*4 2-inch rosemary sprigs*
2 ounces powdered pectin	

In a large stainless steel or enameled saucepan, combine the apple juice and 3 rosemary sprigs and bring to a boil. Remove the pan from the heat and let the mixture stand, covered, for 1 hour.

Remove the rosemary sprigs and stir in the pectin. Bring the juice to a boil, and stir at the boiling point for 1 minute. Add the sugar all at once and stir well. Bring to a boil that cannot be stirred down and boil for 1 minute.

Remove from the heat and skim the froth. Place a 2-inch rosemary sprig in each of the sterilized, half-pint canning jars and pour in the jelly. Wipe the rims of the jars and seal.

Yields about 4 half-pints.

Castagnaccio

This unusual, rustic sweet bread is a Tuscan specialty. Italian delicatessens often sell chestnut flour.

1/4 cup currants	*2 tablespoons honey*
1 pound chestnut flour	*1/3 cup coarsely chopped, untoasted almonds*
4 cups cold water	*1/2 teaspoon salt*
1 tablespoon roughly chopped, fresh rosemary leaves	*Garnish: 1 tablespoon plus 1 teaspoon fresh rosemary leaves*
4 tablespoons olive oil	

Soak the currants in warm water for 15 minutes, then squeeze them dry. In a large bowl, mix the chestnut flour and cold water, breaking up any lumps with a wooden spoon. Add the currants, chopped rosemary, 2 tablespoons olive oil, honey, almonds, and salt. Mix well and divide the batter between 2, 9-inch glass or ceramic pie dishes, each oiled with 1 tablespoon olive oil.

Preheat the oven to 375° F.

Sprinkle each *castagnaccio* with half of the remaining rosemary leaves. Bake on the middle oven shelf for 1 hour and 15 minutes. The top of the castagnaccio should be cracked and crisp. Remove and let cool for 30 minutes.

Cut each castagnaccio into 6 pieces and remove carefully with a spatula. Serve warm or at room temperature.

Yields 12 pieces.

SAGE

SAGE

Sage soothes both youth and age,
and brings the cook pleasing praise.

THE ASSOCIATIONS of the meanings of sage and its homonym are linked in Latin as in English. The herb's name is from *salvere*, "to be well," "to save," and the word relating to wisdom is from *sapere*, "to taste," "to know." It is certainly wise to know sage well because, in addition to its traditional uses in sausages and with poultry, game, and liver, sage can add a rich and graceful note to vegetables, breads, and sweets.

Sage graces the garden as well, with its soft grey-green foliage providing a pleasing contrast to the bright hues of most other culinary herbs. The two sages marking two corners of our herb garden show handsomely throughout the season, especially when the bloom-laden spikes are in full purple flower.

Sage's culinary use with rich dishes probably came from its reputation as a digestive. It was highly regarded as a medicinal plant by the Greeks and Romans. Its principal use was as a calmative for the stomach and nerves. Regular use of sage tea was said to confer an even disposition to excitable natures and a healthy old age to everyone. Sage was especially recommended to older persons as it was believed to restore ailing memory and banish melancholy and depression. Swiss peasants and American Indians used sage as a dentifrice, first chewing a few leaves, then brushing the gums with the twig. In England, tea made with the leaves of clary sage, *Salvia sclarea*, was the common beverage until Chinese tea began to be imported. The English, in turn, introduced sage tea to the Chinese, who would exchange up to five bushels of Chinese tea for one bushel of sage. This tea is still drunk in China today.

Sage is much respected culinarily in England and Italy, where most country gardens have a sage bush, often fifteen years or older. The flavor from good sage stock does not deteriorate with age, but sage varies in flavor as much as some of the more delicate herbs, depending on its soil and weather conditions. Dalmation sage from Yugoslavia is esteemed because the camphor odor is less pronounced than in sage grown in different climates. This aroma is also milder in the fresh leaf. The flavor of fresh sage has decided lemon rind tones over resin. The lemon flavor recedes and the camphor, and a pleasant muskiness similar to silage, comes forward when sage is dried.

The superior culinary sage is *Salvia officinalis*. This sage keeps its aroma and flavor through cooking and drying, which pineapple sage, lavender sage, mint-leaved sage, and others do not. These sages are named after their fresh aromas, which suggest other plants or herbs.

Sage will grow to a bush four feet in diameter in mild climates, keeping a well-rounded shape with little pruning. It should have well-drained or gravelly soil and some added calcium where it is lacking in the soil. Sage needs full sun and will survive the cold of winter if well mulched. It should be trimmed back severely in the fall to encourage full growth in the spring.

Sage is an excellent herb for tub planting, as the calcium and sunlight requirements can be controlled. Its shape is well suited to large planters. Once sage is established it needs little care; pruning and occasional watering are enough for its hardy nature. Sage can be kept to manageable proportions in a window box by harvesting the leaves and trimming back the woody stems in winter.

Like most herbs, sage should be dried in a warm, dry place away from sun. Once the leaves are completely dry, they should be stored in airtight containers. Sage should be crumbled (never ground) for cooking as grinding completely destroys the delicate lemony perfume, leaving the harsher resinous flavors.

In the following recipes, sage's resonant timbre counterpoints a variety of flavors.

Sage Tea

This is a comforting tea, suited to quiet, cold evenings.

1 quart spring water	*3 tablespoons sage honey*
1/2 cup packed fresh sage leaves	*juice of 1 lemon or lime*

Bring the water just to a boil and pour it over the sage leaves. Stir in the honey and juice. Steep the tea for about 20 minutes. Bring it to a boil, then strain it into a warm teapot.

Yields 4 cups.

Goat Cheese Marinated with Fresh Sage and Garlic

1 10-ounce Montrachet goat cheese, or other fresh, mild goat cheese	*12 to 15 black peppercorns, cracked*
16 to 20 large, fresh sage leaves	*3/4 cup virgin olive oil*
2 garlic cloves	

Slice the cheese into 3/8-inch rounds or slices. Scatter half the sage leaves on a serving dish just large enough to hold the cheese. Peel the garlic and slice it thinly. Scatter half the garlic slices over the sage leaves. Sprinkle half the cracked pepper over the herbs. Place the cheese on the herbs. Cover the cheese with the remaining sage leaves, garlic, and cracked pepper. Pour the olive oil over the cheese and herbs.

Marinate the cheese for 24 hours at cool room temperature, or covered in the refrigerator.

If the cheese was marinated in the refrigerator, remove it 3 to 4 hours before serving. Serve with croutons made from baguettes or with thinly sliced Tuscan bread.

Serves 6 to 8 as an appetizer.

Pizza con Pancetta

Pancetta is Italian bacon, not smoked, and rolled in a round. Like salt pork, it varies in saltiness. Use the least salty pancetta or salt pork available.

Pizza Dough

1 tablespoon dry yeast	1 cup whole wheat flour
1/4 cup warm water	2/3 cup warm water
pinch of sugar	1 tablespoon olive oil
1 1/4 cups unbleached white flour	1/2 teaspoon salt

Dissolve the yeast in 1/4 cup warm water with the sugar. Mix the flours and make a well. When the yeast is active, add it to the well. Let the sponge rise for 10 minutes or so.

Gradually add 2/3 cup warm water. About half way through adding the water, stir in the olive oil and salt. Incorporate as much flour as the sponge will take and still be a bit sticky, though very lively. Knead the dough lightly for 10 minutes. Let the dough rise for 45 minutes to 1 1/2 hours, until doubled in bulk. Punch the dough down and let rest for 15 minutes before forming into pizza shapes.

Pizza Topping

6 ounces pancetta or salt pork	5 or 6 Italian parsley sprigs
6 ounces whole milk mozzarella cheese	1 small onion
2 pounds firm, ripe tomatoes, or 28-ounce can plum tomatoes	2 to 3 tablespoons olive oil
3 or 4 garlic cloves	salt and pepper
5 or 6 sage sprigs	Garnish: freshly grated Parmesan cheese

Unroll the pancetta and cut it into 1/4-inch dice. Render the pancetta in a heavy skillet over low heat for about 15 minutes. Remove with a slotted spoon when it is golden brown. Grate the mozzarella and set aside.

Seed and dice the fresh tomatoes or drain, seed, and dice the canned tomatoes. Peel and mince the garlic. Stem and chop the sage and parsley medium-fine. Cut the onion in half lengthwise and cut each half into thin rings.

Place a baker's tile on the bottom oven shelf and preheat at 500° F. for 15 minutes. Divide the pizza dough into two equal parts. Form one piece of dough into a 9- or 10-inch round on a lightly floured pizza paddle. Brush the dough lightly with olive oil. Sprinkle 1/2 the garlic and 1/3 of the herbs on the pizza. Scatter half the pancetta over the herbs. Arrange half the onion rings over the pancetta. Cover with half of the diced tomatoes and salt and pepper lightly.

Slide the pizza onto the baker's tile and bake it for 3 to 4 minutes. Slide the pizza out of the oven and cover it with half the mozzarella. Bake the pizza another 3 to 4 minutes, until the crust is puffed around the edges and light golden brown. The cheese should bubble and just begin to color.

Remove the pizza to a cutting board and sprinkle it with some chopped herbs. Cut into 8 pieces and serve immediately. Make the other pizza in the same manner.

Serves 3 to 4 as an appetizer.

Light Whole Wheat Sage Muffins

8 to 10 large, fresh sage leaves, or 1 teaspoon crumbled, dried sage	2 tablespoons unsalted butter, melted
3/4 cup whole wheat pastry flour	scant 1/2 teaspoon salt
1/2 cup unbleached white flour	3 eggs
1 cup milk	

Preheat the oven to 450° F.

Butter and flour an iron muffin or popover tin. Mince the sage leaves finely (there should be about a tablespoon of minced leaves).

In a bowl, combine the flours. Stir in the milk, butter, salt, and minced sage. Beat the batter until smooth. Add the eggs one at a time, beating lightly but well after each addition.

Fill the muffin tin two-thirds full and place in the oven. After 15 minutes, lower the heat to 350° F. and bake 15 minutes longer.

Yields 10 muffins.

Pasta e Fagioli

1 pound white beans	2 tablespoons chopped fresh sage, or 2 teaspoons dried, crumbled sage
6 tablespoons olive oil	2 tablespoons chopped Italian parsley
1 teaspoon salt	salt to taste
1 small onion	Garnish: 6 sage leaves
5 or 6 garlic cloves	6 parsley sprigs
5 ounces small, dried pasta	olive oil
3 cups vegetable stock or water	freshly grated Parmesan or Pecorino cheese
1/4 cup tomato paste	

Soak the beans overnight. Pour off the water and transfer the beans to a large saucepan. Cover the beans with water to 1 inch above the beans and add 3 tablespoons olive oil. Cook the beans until they are tender, about 1 hour, adding the salt at the end of the cooking time.

While the beans are cooking, chop the onion and finely mince the garlic. Cook them over medium-low heat in the remaining olive oil for about 8 minutes.

Bring 4 quarts of water with a heaping teaspoon of salt to a boil. Cook the pasta until just barely al dente and drain.

Stir the pasta, onion, and garlic into the beans. Add the vegetable stock and tomato paste and simmer over low heat for about 5 minutes.

Add the chopped sage and parsley to the pasta e fagioli. Cook over low heat for 10 minutes. Taste for salt.

Mince the sage sprigs and parsley leaves together for garnish. Ladle the soup into warm bowls, and garnish each with a teaspoon of olive oil and a sprinkling of the chopped herbs. Serve hot and pass the grated cheese.

Serves 6 to 8.

Chicken Stuffed under the Skin with Cornbread, Pecan, and Sage Stuffing

4- to 5-pound roasting chicken or fryer	3 or 4 sage leaves, or 1/4 teaspoon dried, crumbled sage
salt and pepper	1 rosemary sprig, or 1/4 teaspoon dried, crumbled rosemary
4 tablespoons unsalted butter	1 or 2 thyme sprigs, or 1/4 teaspoon dried, crumbled thyme
1 medium onion	2/3 cup pecans, lightly toasted
2 celery ribs	1 small apple
1 1/2 cups crumbled cornbread, very dry	about 1/3 cup half-and-half cream
1 1/2 cups whole wheat bread cubes, very dry	about 1/2 cup chicken stock

Remove the innards and chop them medium-fine. Reserve the neck for another use. Loosen the skin of the chicken, starting at the neck and working over the breast, thighs, and drumsticks. The skin is elastic and easy to work loose, but do not tear it. Repair any tears with a needle and thread. Salt and pepper the cavity of the chicken lightly.

Melt the butter over low heat. Dice the onion and celery finely and cook them, with the chopped innards, in the butter until they are softened, about 7 minutes. Remove to a large bowl.

Mince the herbs and chop the pecans medium-fine. Core the apple and chop it medium-fine. Add the cornbread and whole wheat bread to the onions and celery. Stir in the minced herbs, pecans, and apple. Season with salt and pepper. Toss the stuffing with the cream and stock, gently but thoroughly. The mixture should be somewhat moist; it will absorb more moisture from the chicken. Taste for seasoning, adding more salt, pepper, or herbs as necessary.

Preheat the oven to 375° F.

Work the stuffing under the skin in small handfuls. Reserve about half the stuffing for the cavity. Bake the chicken for 1 hour, or until done to taste. Baste at 15-minute intervals with the pan drippings and a little chicken stock. If the chicken browns too rapidly, cover it loosely with foil and finish baking.

Serves 4 to 6.

Fegato alla Toscana

1 1/2 pounds calves' liver	2 tablespoons lemon juice
4 tablespoons light olive oil	freshly ground black pepper
1 garlic clove	Garnish: 4 small sage sprigs
6 large, fresh sage leaves	1 lemon, cut into thin wedges
1/2 teaspoon salt	

Trim the calves' liver and cut it into 3/8-inch thick strips. The liver should be cut to the same thickness to cook evenly; the width and length of the strips may vary.

Heat the olive oil in a large, heavy skillet over moderate heat. Peel the garlic and cut it in half. Add the garlic and sage leaves to the skillet. When the oil is hot, add the liver and saute it for 2 to 3 minutes, stirring or moving the pan constantly.

Dissolve the salt in the lemon juice and add it to the pan, stirring the juice for about 30 seconds. Season with pepper. Transfer the liver to a warm serving platter and pour the pan juices over it. Garnish the platter with sage sprigs and lemon wedges. Serve immediately.

Serves 4.

Chestnuts and Apples with Sage

1 pound chestnuts	1 large Granny Smith apple, or 2 small Pippin apples
about 2 cups milk	4 tablespoons unsalted butter
2 celery ribs	6 large, fresh sage leaves
1 medium red onion	salt

Roast and peel the chestnuts. Put them in a 1-quart saucepan and add enough milk to barely cover them. Cook over very low heat for about 20 minutes, until they are just tender.

Meanwhile, trim the celery and onion and core the apple. Coarsely chop the vegetables and fruit. Saute the celery and onion in butter over moderate heat. Drain the chestnuts and chop them coarsely. Add them along with the apple to the pan. Reduce the heat to medium-low. Mince the sage leaves and stir them into the pan. Salt the mixture lightly and cook for about 10 minutes. Serve with baked or broiled poultry.

Serves 4 to 6.

Eggplant Gratin with Sage

1 1/2 pounds eggplant, preferably the long, slender Italian or Japanese eggplant	2 garlic cloves
4 tablespoons light olive oil	1/4 cup chopped parsley
3 tablespoons unsalted butter	3/4 cup freshly grated Parmesan cheese
3 tablespoons all-purpose flour	pinch of cayenne pepper
2 cups half-and-half cream, at room temperature	salt and pepper to taste
14 to 16 large, fresh sage leaves	

Wash and trim the eggplants. Cut the Italian or Japanese eggplants crosswise into 1/3-inch slices. Cut larger eggplants in half lengthwise, then cut the halves crosswise in 1/3-inch slices. Sprinkle the eggplant lightly with salt and let it drain in a colander for about 30 minutes. Rinse it well and pat very dry.

Heat the olive oil in a large skillet over medium heat. Saute the eggplant for about 5 minutes, tossing well to coat it evenly with oil. Layer half the sauteed eggplant in a 2-quart casserole.

Make a roux with the butter and flour. Cook the roux for 5 minutes over low heat and add the cream. Stir it well with a wooden spoon or a whisk to make a smooth bechamel.

Mince the sage leaves (there should be 2 tablespoons). Mince the garlic and add it with the sage to the bechamel. Cook the sauce for 10 minutes over very low heat. Stir in 1/2 cup of cheese and the chopped parsley. Remove the sauce from the heat and season with cayenne, salt, and pepper.

Preheat the oven to 350° F.

Pour half of the sauce over the eggplant in the casserole and layer the rest of the eggplant over it. Pour the rest of the sauce over the eggplant and sprinkle the top with the remaining cheese. Bake the gratin for 35 to 45 minutes, until the sauce is bubbling and the crust is golden brown.

Serves 6 to 8.

Kohlrabi with Sage Cream

2 pounds kohlrabi bulbs, each about 2 inches in diameter	1/2 teaspoon salt
1 cup creme fraiche or sour cream	1/2 teaspoon white pepper
about 1 teaspoon freshly grated horseradish root, or 1 tablespoon prepared horseradish	10 to 12 large, fresh sage leaves

Scrub and trim the kohlrabi. Drop them whole into abundant boiling, lightly salted water. Cook them over moderate heat for about 30 minutes, until they are just tender. Drain the kohlrabi and refresh them under cold water. When cool enough to handle, peel them and cut into 1/8-inch julienne. Pat the kohlrabi very dry.

Mix the creme fraiche with the horseradish, salt, and pepper. Mince the sage leaves finely (there should be 1 1/2 tablespoons minced sage). Stir the sage into the cream. Toss the kohlrabi with the cream and marinate, covered, in the refrigerator for at least 2 hours. Remove from the refrigerator 15 minutes before serving and taste for seasoning.

Serves 6.

Sage Applecake

2 cups unbleached white flour	2 large eggs
1 teaspoon baking soda	6 to 8 large, fresh sage leaves
1 teaspoon baking powder	1 cup MacIntosh Applesauce (recipe follows)
1/2 teaspoon salt	1 large MacIntosh apple, or other good cooking apple
1/2 teaspoon cinnamon	1 tablespoon lemon juice
1 cup packed brown sugar	about 2 tablespoons unsalted butter
12 tablespoons unsalted butter, at room temperature	3 tablespoons brown sugar

Sift the flour with the baking soda, baking powder, salt, and cinnamon. Cream 1 cup brown sugar with 12 tablespoons softened butter. Beat the eggs into the creamed sugar and butter.

Finely mince enough sage leaves to equal 1 tablespoon. Combine the sage with the MacIntosh Applesauce and add to the butter mixture, beating well.

Core and thinly slice the apple and sprinkle with lemon juice. Butter the bottom and sides of a 9 1/2-inch springform bundt pan heavily with the remaining 2 tablespoons butter. Sprinkle the bottom and sides of the pan with 3 tablespoons brown sugar. Arrange the apple slices around the bottom and sides of the pan.

Preheat the oven to 350° F.

Gradually add the flour mixture to the applesauce mixture, blending well. Pour the batter carefully into the prepared pan. Bake for 50 to 60 minutes, until the top is a deep golden brown and a cake tester comes out clean. Cool the cake at room temperature for 1 hour before removing it from the baking pan.

To serve the cake, loosen the sides of the pan. Invert the cake on a serving platter.

Serves 8 to 10.

MacIntosh Applesauce

Good, fresh MacIntosh apples make excellent applesauce. You can find these if you live in the Pacific Northwest or Canada. If really firm MacIntoshes are not available, use your favorite cooking apple.

6 large MacIntosh apples	1 to 2 tablespoons lemon juice
1/3 cup sage honey	

Core the apples and chop them roughly. Put them in a heavy saucepan and stir in the honey and lemon juice. Cover and cook over low heat for 30 to 40 minutes, until the apples have softened completely. Puree through a food mill or in a food processor.

Yields about 2 cups.

YOUNG SORREL

SORREL

Sorrel's point is well taken;
with it the cook can wax symphonic.
Without it salmon seems forsaken
and garden salads too laconic.
It favors the palate to awaken,
and orchestrates each spring tonic.

NOT ONLY DO the French bring us haute couture each spring, they have also devised one of the most elegant means to fashion a spring tonic—cream of sorrel soup. It is traditional to eat much of the herb during this season to quicken the blood and enliven the appetite.

This is something we can understand, as we enjoy sorrel most in the spring and early summer. Its slightly sour flavor with a lemony zest sparks our palates and salads as no other herb does. We like to see it so early too—the first green to grace our herb garden and thaw our frosted spirits with the reminder of spring to come. Although it tends to look like a weed, we think it a noble plant with inimitable flavor.

Sorrel's culinary foundation rests on two French classics: sorrel soup and sorrel sauce. It has not been adopted by many other cuisines, although occasional recipes using it appear in English, Swiss, and German cookbooks. The tender-leaved and distinctive herb has great versatility if we approach it with imagination and remember the English habit of eating it in salads. We find it good with eggs and vegetables, and in sauces or mayonnaise. Cooked dishes will need less salt when sorrel is used. To keep the bright green color in soups and sauces, pay careful attention to the cooking time. We add young leaves by the handful to enliven simple salads. Moreover, salads will need less vinegar or lemon juice, or none at all, when made with sorrel.

Many of the old herbals mention sorrel, mainly as a pot or salad herb.

It did not gather a list of ailments to cure, but it did acquire a reputation for preventing scurvy and "cooling inflammation and heat of the blood." Gerard and Evelyn were extravagant in their praise of sorrel, one saying, "it is the best of sauces not only in virtue, but in pleasantness of taste"; and the other, that it "renders not plants and herbs only, but men themselves, pleasant and agreeable."

Sorrel (*Rumex acetosa* and *Rumex scutatus*) is a hardy perennial that is frost resistant. It grows best in full sun, in a rich, well-drained soil, but it will do moderately well in partial shade. The leaves appear in dense clusters on tall stems about 18 to 24 inches high. They should be cut back so they can be harvested throughout the season. In temperate climates the herb will stay green all winter, although growth is limited. If you have an abundance of sorrel, it can be frozen. Sorrel does not dry well.

Hot weather can cause the leaves to taste a little bitter, so the plants should be well mulched to retain moisture. Leaves under six inches are best in salads; larger leaves are better cooked or combined with other foods. This herb has a deep root system that can be divided in spring or fall. Our original patch of sorrel, grown easily from seed, has been divided and moved numerous times and has provided friends and family with their own crops. Sorrel does not thrive indoors, but ambitious gardeners might experiment with a grow light or nurture it in a greenhouse.

When we enjoy a salad of tender young sorrel leaves we can't help but agree with Evelyn's advice that it adds "so grateful a quickness to salad that it should never be left out." We hope you will be stimulated to include sorrel in your gardens and kitchens and to relish its clear, sour accent in many dishes.

Shrimp Paste with Sorrel

1/2 pound shelled and deveined shrimp, lightly steamed	2 salt-packed anchovy fillets
1 cup loosely packed sorrel leaves	1 teaspoon lemon juice, or to taste
1 medium garlic clove	salt and pepper to taste
1/2 cup loosely packed parsley leaves	25 to 30 slices day-old baguette

Pound the shrimp, sorrel, garlic, parsley, and anchovies together in a mortar, or make a paste in a food processor. Season with lemon juice, salt, and pepper.

Preheat the oven to 350° F. and toast the bread lightly for 5 to 7 minutes. Spread the paste on the croutons and heat them under the broiler for 1 to 2 minutes, until they just begin to brown.

Yields 25 to 30 toasts.

Sorrel Cheese Spread

6 ounces Armenian string cheese	1 garlic clove, finely minced
1 pound ricotta cheese	cayenne pepper to taste
1/2 cup coarsely chopped sorrel leaves	salt and pepper to taste

Shred the string cheese very finely. Mix it with the ricotta, sorrel, and garlic. Season with cayenne, salt, and pepper. Let the cheese stand at least 1 hour at a cool room temperature. Serve with unsalted crackers or croutons.

Yields about 2 1/2 cups.

Sorrel Sushi-Style

Although these sushi are not traditional, the laver and sorrel taste exceptionally good together.

Cooking the Rice

1 cup sweet oriental rice, or short grain oriental rice	1/2 teaspoon salt
1 1/2 cups water	

Put the rice, water, and salt in a pan and bring the water to a boil. Cover, reduce the heat to a simmer, and cook for 25 minutes. Remove from the heat and spread the rice in a shallow dish.

Flavoring the Rice

2 1/2 tablespoons rice wine vinegar	1 teaspoon oriental sesame oil
1 1/2 teaspoons sugar	

When the rice has cooled to medium-warm, mix in the vinegar, sugar, and oil.

Rolling the Sushi

4 sheets nori (laver) seaweed	12 to 18 strips pickled ginger, about 2 1/2 inches long, and about 1/8 inch thick and wide.
24 to 30 small sorrel leaves, under 4 inches long	12 to 18 strips cucumber, cut the same size as the ginger

Toast the seaweed by passing the glossy side over a medium flame. Lay one sheet of seaweed on a bamboo mat, glossy side down, with a short side of the seaweed and mat facing you. Arrange 6 to 8 sorrel leaves with the stems facing you on the lower half of the seaweed. Spread almost one-quarter of the rice across the center of the sorrel leaves. Arrange half of the pickled ginger strips in the center of the rice. Cover the ginger with 2 to 3 table-spoons of rice.

Begin rolling by bringing the edge of the seaweed closest to you over the rice, using the mat to guide the roll. Continue until the roll is complete. Hold the mat in place from 30 to 60 seconds in order to set the sushi.

Complete the next roll in the same way, using pickled ginger. Make the remaining two rolls using cucumber in place of the ginger. Cut each roll with a sharp knife into 1-inch slices.

Yields about 32 sushi.

Celery Sorrel Soup

6 large celery ribs	1 cup half-and-half cream
1 small onion	1/2 cup packed sorrel leaves
2 tablespoons unsalted butter	salt and pepper to taste
3 cups light chicken stock, or vegetable stock	

Chop the celery and onion roughly. Sweat the vegetables in butter over medium-low heat for 10 minutes. Meanwhile, heat the stock to simmering and heat the cream in a separate pan.

Puree the vegetables and sorrel with a little of the hot stock. Stir in the remaining stock and the cream and season the soup. Serve immediately.

Serves 4 to 6.

Vegetable Stock

A flavorful vegetable stock is especially good for delicate soups. The stock can be made with vegetables you have on hand; the essentials are carrots, onions, and celery. Other vegetables can add depth of flavor, depending on how you plan to use the stock. The bouquet garni can be varied also, but should not be too dominant.

2 carrots	*4 to 5 mushrooms*
1 medium onion	*Optional: 1 ripe tomato*
1 potato	*3 quarts water*
1 turnip	*salt*
1 medium celery rib	*bouquet garni (1 bay leaf; 4 or 5 thyme sprigs or 1 teaspoon dried thyme; 6 to 8 parsley sprigs; 1 large garlic clove; 6 to 8 peppercorns)*

Scrub the vegetables well and peel them. Chop them roughly and place in a stockpot. Add the water and salt the stock lightly. Make the bouquet garni and add to the pot.

Bring the stock to a boil. Reduce to a simmer and cook for 30 minutes, skimming the stock occasionally. Cool for 1 hour in the pan, then strain.

Yields about 2 1/2 quarts.

Sorrel Spinach Souffle

Bechamel

2 tablespoons unsalted butter	*1 cup milk, at room temperature*
1 1/2 tablespoons all-purpose flour	*salt and pepper*

Melt the butter over medium-low heat. Stir in the flour all at once and cook over low heat for 2 to 3 minutes. Add the milk all at once, stirring vigorously. Cook the bechamel very slowly about 15 minutes. Season lightly. Remove from the heat, cover, and cool to room temperature.

Souffle

1 1/2 cups tender spinach leaves	about 1 tablespoon butter
1 cup tender sorrel leaves	about 3 tablespoons freshly grated Parmesan cheese
3 egg yolks	4 egg whites
3 ounces St. Andre Triple Creme cheese, or other buttery cheese, at room temperature	

Wash the spinach and sorrel thoroughly. Put them in a pan, using only the water that clings to the leaves, and wilt for 15 seconds over medium heat. Transfer immediately to a bowl.

Stir the egg yolks and cheese into the bechamel. When the spinach and sorrel have cooled for about 5 minutes, stir them into the bechamel. Butter a shallow, 9-inch gratin dish or pie plate and dust it with the Parmesan cheese.

Preheat the oven to 400° F.

Beat the egg whites until they are stiff but not dry. Stir a little of the beaten whites into the bechamel mixture. Fold the rest of the whites into the bechamel in three parts.

Carefully pour the souffle mixture into the prepared dish and bake for about 20 minutes, until the souffle is a rich golden brown on top and still a little soft in the center.

Serves 4.

Creamed Eggs Sorrel in Croustades

Croustades

12 slices of fresh, good quality white bread	about 1/4 pound unsalted butter

Preheat the oven to 350° F.

Trim the crusts from the bread. Melt the butter and let it cool slightly. Brush a slice of bread liberally with melted butter, on both sides, and mold it in a small custard cup or muffin tin. Repeat with the rest of the bread. Bake the croustades for 10 to 15 minutes, until they are light golden brown and crisp. Remove from the oven and turn onto a cake rack.

Egg and Sorrel Sauce

12 eggs	1 1/2 cups half-and-half cream
2 cups packed, shredded sorrel leaves	salt and white pepper to taste
3 tablespoons unsalted butter	

Poach the eggs. Trim them into neat shapes and hold in warm water.

Melt the butter over low heat. Stir in the sorrel and cook for 10 seconds. Add the cream and season to taste. Keep the sauce warm over very low heat.

Carefully drain the eggs on a tea towel, then place one in each croustade. Arrange the croustades on a warm platter and spoon some sauce over each. Serve immediately.

Serves 12 as a first course.

Salmon with Sorrel Butter

2-pound piece salmon fillet	1 1/2 cups finely chopped sorrel leaves
about 1/4 cup clarified butter	6 tablespoons unsalted butter
1 shallot	salt and pepper
1/3 cup dry white wine	

Prepare a medium-hot charcoal fire. Brush the inside of the salmon with clarified butter.

Mince the shallot and place in a heavy stainless steel or enameled saucepan with the wine and a little salt and pepper. Reduce the liquid to about 2 tablespoons.

In another stainless or enameled pan, wilt the sorrel for about 15 seconds. Pound the sorrel with 6 tablespoons butter in a mortar.

Salt the salmon lightly and grill about 4 minutes on each side. As soon as the salmon is done, put the shallot and wine glaze over low heat and stir in the sorrel butter for about 30 seconds, just enough to heat it through. Season and remove from the heat.

Cut the salmon into 4 pieces. Reserve about 3 tablespoons of the sorrel butter. Divide the rest among 4 warm serving plates and put a piece of salmon on each. Spoon the reserved butter over the salmon.

Serves 4.

Chicken and Cantaloupe Salad with Sorrel Mayonnaise

Poaching the Chicken

3- to 3 1/2-pound chicken	1 celery rib
1 carrot	bouquet garni (6 to 8 parsley sprigs; 3 or 4 thyme sprigs; 1 bay leaf; 1 teaspoon fennel seed; 6 to 8 peppercorns)
1 onion	salt

Reserve the innards for another use. Trim the chicken of excess fat. Peel the carrot and onion and roughly chop the vegetables. Make the bouquet garni.

Put the vegetables, chicken, and bouquet garni in a stock pot and add enough water to just cover the chicken. Remove the chicken and bring the stock to a boil. Reduce the heat and simmer for 15 minutes. Add the chicken and poach it, at a simmer, for 40 to 50 minutes. Remove the chicken, drain, and cool on a rack.

Sorrel Mayonnaise

1 1/2 cups tender sorrel leaves	3/4 cup light olive oil
6 Italian parsley sprigs	1 to 2 tablespoons lime juice
1 egg yolk, at room temperature	salt and pepper to taste

Shred the sorrel leaves. Stem and roughly chop the parsley leaves. Put the leaves in a large mortar and pound them to a rough paste.

Stir the egg yolk into the mortar. Add the olive oil, a few drops at a time, while stirring with the pestle. Gradually increase the amount of olive oil added to a fine stream. When the oil has been used, season the mayonnaise with lime juice, salt, and pepper.

Finishing the Salad

poached and cooled chicken	lettuce or sorrel leaves
2 small or 1 large cantaloupe	lime juice, salt, and pepper to taste
sorrel mayonnaise	

Skin and bone the chicken, and cut it into 1/2-inch dice. Remove the meat from the cantaloupe with a melon baller (you should have 3 cups of cantaloupe). Toss the chicken and cantaloupe with the mayonnaise. Cover and chill the salad for 2 to 3 hours.

Arrange lettuce or sorrel leaves on 6 chilled salad plates. Taste the salad for seasoning and adjust if necessary. Divide the salad among the plates and serve chilled.

Serves 6.

Lentil Salad with Sorrel

1 1/2 cups lentils (the small, green French lentils are best)	about 1/3 cup virgin olive oil
1 small onion	3 ounces fresh, mild goat cheese
2 or 3 medium-sized ripe tomatoes	juice of 1/2 lemon, or to taste
2 or 3 cooked new potatoes	salt and pepper
2 garlic cloves, finely minced	1 cup coarsely chopped sorrel leaves

Rinse and pick over the lentils. Put them in a pan with water to cover by 1/2 inch. Bring to a boil. Reduce the heat, cover, and simmer until they are just tender, from 20 to 30 minutes. Meanwhile, cut the onion in a fine dice and the tomatoes and potatoes in a medium dice.

When the lentils are done, spread them on a baking sheet and toss with olive oil. Let them cool slightly. Stir in the onion, tomatoes, and potatoes. Season with lemon juice, salt, and pepper.

When the lentils are at room temperature, stir in the sorrel leaves and crumble in the goat cheese. The flavor improves if the salad is refrigerated for 3 to 4 hours, then brought to a cool room temperature before serving.

Serves 6 to 8.

A Simple Salad with Sorrel

There is nothing so appetizing for us as a salad with garden herbs and lettuce. Such a salad always reaffirms our belief that in simplicity lies the cook's highest art.

To make the salad, you need handfuls of just-picked garden lettuce and sorrel; about 1 handful of greens for each person is good measure unless you are serving salad lovers. We like the proportions of 4 parts lettuce to 1 part sorrel. It is good to include a variety of lettuces; lamb's lettuce, oak leaf, and red leaf, and other sweet varieties taste good with sorrel. The sorrel leaves should be quite young and tender, about 2 inches long.

To complete the salad, dress it with a fine extra virgin olive oil, a few drops of lemon juice, and a little salt and pepper. Simple garnishes, such as hard-cooked eggs and garlic croutons made from baguettes, complement the freshness of the salad and look pretty, too.

Warm Potato and Turnip Salad with Sorrel

8 to 10 new potatoes, about 1 1/2 pounds	3 tablespoons light olive oil
3 turnips, each about 2 inches in diameter	about 1 teaspoon white wine vinegar
3 ounces pancetta or salt pork	salt and pepper to taste
1 garlic clove, finely minced	1 cup shredded sorrel leaves

Scrub the potatoes and turnips and cook them in water to cover by 1 inch until they are just tender. Drain and let stand until they are just cool enough to peel.

Cut the pancetta into 1/2-inch dice and saute over medium heat until golden brown. Skim the pancetta from the pan. Add the garlic and olive oil to the rendered fat.

Peel and cut the vegetables into 1-inch dice. Add them to the pan and sprinkle the vinegar, salt, and pepper over them. Heat over medium heat, shaking the pan frequently. When the vegetables are heated through, remove to a bowl and toss with the sorrel leaves and pancetta. Serve immediately.

Serves 6.

Sorrel Grape Tart

Pastry

2 cups all-purpose, unbleached white flour	12 tablespoons unsalted butter, very cold
3 tablespoons sugar	4 to 6 tablespoons ice water
pinch of salt	

Mix the flour with the sugar and salt. Cut the butter into bits with a sharp knife. Cut the bits into the flour with a pastry blender or with butter knives until the pieces are about the size of very small peas. Mix 3 tablespoons of ice water quickly into the flour with a fork. Add enough ice water so that the dough just holds together when pressed lightly.

Gather the dough into a ball and flatten to about 1 inch thick. Wrap the dough loosely with plastic wrap. Chill for 1 hour. Roll the dough to fit a 9 1/2-inch tart pan with a removable bottom. Transfer the dough to the pan and pat into place. Trim the excess dough, leaving 1/2 inch all around. Turn the overlap under and flute the rim of the crust. Cover and chill for 1 hour.

Preheat the oven to 425° F.

Prick the crust lightly and bake on the bottom oven shelf for 15 minutes. Reduce the heat to 400° F. and bake 10 to 15 minutes longer, until the crust is a rich golden brown. Cover the rim loosely with foil if it is browning too much during the last few minutes.

Remove the tart shell from the oven and cool to room temperature on a rack. Prepare the filling while the crust is baking and cooling.

Filling

about 1 quart loosely packed, fresh sorrel leaves	2 tablespoons Grand Marnier
1 pound fresh cream cheese, at room temperature	zest of 1/2 small lemon
1/2 cup sour cream	1 1/2 cups green grapes, split
1/3 cup mild honey	

Rinse the sorrel and wilt it for 30 to 60 seconds in a stainless steel or enameled pan. Spread the sorrel to cool and drain. Mince the sorrel finely and blend well with the cream cheese, sour cream, honey, Grand Marnier, and lemon zest in a large bowl.

Pour the filling into the cooled tart shell and garnish with grape halves. Chill for 2 hours or longer before serving.

Serves 8 to 10.

WINTER
SAVORY

SUMMER
SAVORY

SUMMER AND WINTER SAVORY

Winter, summer, spring, and fall,
Savory flavors over all.

THE SAVORIES are some of the most amenable and useful herbs in our garden. We have found them as adaptable in their growing requirements as in the dishes they flavor. Summer savory, especially, is one of our favorite blending herbs, contributing its mildly piquant taste to mixtures with parsley, bay, basil, marjoram and oregano, rosemary, and thyme. Both savories are famous for their affinity with beans; we agree they add much to bean dishes but do not restrict our use to them. We find these herbs excellent with cabbage and brussels sprouts, very good with meats, especially pork and veal, and wonderful with corn. They offer tomatoes a refreshing change from basil and marjoram or oregano, and potatoes a rest from parsley and chives.

Without changing the nature of a bouquet garni, either savory can be used to strengthen mild herbs or to provide a softening effect to the more robust herbs. In fact, summer savory has a flavor reminiscent of aromatic marjoram and thyme together, a blend of sweet and spicy tastes. In winter savory, peppery and resinous tones dominate, giving it a heartier character.

Although treasured mainly for their culinary excellence, the savories were also respected for their medicinal properties. We have tried the old remedy of rubbing a bruised sprig on a bee sting and found that it really does relieve the pain. In Elizabethan times, the leaves were crushed into poultices for the treatment of colds and chest ailments. Savory teas were given for colic and flatulence. Perhaps this use influenced German cooks always to add savory, which they call *Bohnenkraut,* the bean herb, to bean dishes. But the savories offer even more virtues to the cook: versatility, ease of combining with other herbs, good flavor when dried, and the bonus of being easy to grow.

Both winter and summer savory (*Satureia montana* and *Satureia hortensia,* respectively) have a modest but pleasant appearance. Winter savory is a perennial, growing about 10 to 12 inches tall with thickly set, glossy deep green leaves. It is well shaped and decorates our permanent garden, especially when covered with small blossoms that the bees hover over for hours. Summer savory must be seeded every year. This annual can grow up to two feet tall on tender, reddish purple stems that have a tendency to droop. The leaves are green, often lightly tinged with red, and are spaced widely apart. The flowers of both plants are delicate, ranging in color from white through pale pink and lavender blue.

Summer savory can be started from seed in flats and transplanted when the weather is quite warm and the plants are about four to six inches tall. The seeds can be sown directly in the ground in late spring or when there is no danger of cold temperatures. The summer variety germinates and grows quickly but is not resistant to cold. It flourishes in full sun with moderate water and can use light fertilization.

Winter savory, on the other hand, is hardy and will grow almost anywhere. A place in full sun will produce fine winter savory if the roots are kept moist and the leaves dry. This bushy plant grows fairly slowly and will bear fewer leaves after two or three seasons. Root division or layering (covering part of a stem with about an inch of soil) are the best ways to keep a healthy supply of winter savory.

The savories dry very well, keeping much of their essential oils. We dry some of each variety in the same way, hanging several stems together upside down in a dry place away from sunlight. Summer savory is best when the first harvest is taken before the plants flower. The whole plant can be pulled up and dried in late summer. Winter savory can be cut back throughout the summer but, again, it is best harvested just before flowering.

The savories' nature, so sweet in the garden, becomes positively fierce as the sharply pointed leaves are carefully stripped from the stems. Inevitably you get pricked, but this is soon forgotten once the jars of dried savory are on the shelf to provide a winter's worth of flavor.

Savory Swiss Crackers

Winter savory can be used in place of summer savory but, since the flavor is stronger, less winter savory is required.

1 cup unbleached white flour	8 tablespoons unsalted butter, softened
3/4 cup whole wheat pastry flour	1/2 cup finely grated Gruyere or other Swiss cheese
1 teaspoon baking powder	3 tablespoons finely minced summer savory, or 1 1/2 teaspoons dried, crumbled savory
1/2 teaspoon salt	6 tablespoons ice water

Sift together the flours, baking powder, and salt. Cut in the butter. Add the cheese and savory and stir together. Add the ice water, 1 tablespoon at a time, until the dough is medium stiff. Roll the dough about 3/16 inch thick on a floured surface and cut into 2-inch diamond shapes.

Preheat the oven to 375° F.

Prick the crackers lightly with a fork and place on baking sheets. Bake for 15 minutes or until the crackers are a medium golden brown. Cool on racks and store in a tightly covered tin.

Yields about 3 1/2 dozen.

Black and White Bean Soup with Savory

This is a festive and flavorful soup that is really delicious with fresh cornbread. Nasturtium blossoms, although not necessary, are a perfect garnish.

1 pound small, dried black beans	4 large, fresh (or canned) jalapeno peppers
1 pound small, dried white beans	1/2 cup virgin olive oil
12 medium garlic cloves	salt to taste
10 to 12 summer savory sprigs, or 1 1/2 to 2 teaspoons crumbled, dried savory	Garnish: 6 to 8 nasturtium flowers
6 tablespoons red wine vinegar	

Rinse the beans and soak them separately overnight. Drain, rinse well, and pick over. Put the beans in separate pots and cover by 3 inches with water. Simmer about 1 1/2 hours, or until they are very tender.

Mince the garlic and add half to each pot. Stem the savory, mince it, and add 4 tablespoons (or the dried savory) to the white beans. Seed the jalapenos, mince them, and add to the black beans, along with the red wine vinegar. Add 1/4 cup olive oil to each pot and simmer the soups for about 10 minutes.

Puree each soup separately and return them to their separate pots. Cook over low heat for about 5 minutes. The soups should be rather thin; add a little water if necessary. Adjust the seasoning.

To serve, ladle about 1/2 cup black bean soup in a warm, shallow soup bowl. Carefully ladle 1/2 cup white bean soup in the center of the bowl. Fill 6 to 8 bowls and garnish each with a nasturtium blossom.

Serves 6 to 8.

Pork Chops with Savory Stuffing

Pork chops benefit from a much shorter cooking time than was necessary years ago. Current hog-raising and butchering practices take care of the bacteria, which were the reason for cooking pork until it was dry and tasteless. Pork does have a good amount of fat, but not in the muscle tissue as beef does. It is really much tastier if left a little rare.

6 center loin pork chops, each about 1 1/4 inches thick	1 egg
1/4 pound ground veal	salt and pepper to taste
1 1/2 to 2 tablespoons fresh, minced summer savory, or 1 1/2 to 2 teaspoons crumbled, dried savory	1 tablespoon light olive oil
3 tablespoons freshly grated Parmesan cheese	1 tablespoon unsalted butter
2 tablespoons fine dry bread crumbs	1/2 cup dry white wine

Cut the chops with a sharp knife to make pockets for the stuffing. In a small bowl, mix the veal, savory, cheese, bread crumbs, and egg. Season with salt and pepper. Divide the stuffing among the chops and sew them closed or secure with toothpicks.

Heat the olive oil and butter in a large skillet over medium heat. Salt and pepper the chops and saute them about 4 minutes on each side, until they are nicely browned. Add the wine, cover, and cook very slowly for 15 to 20 minutes. Turn the chops occasionally for even browning. Remove the string or toothpicks and serve very hot.

Serves 6.

Savory Meat Cakes

This recipe can be adapted by rolling the meat into balls and serving them with noodles or as appetizers.

1/2 pound ground lean beef	1 egg
1/4 pound ground veal	1/2 cup fine, dry bread crumbs
1/4 pound ground pork	1 garlic clove, minced
1 small onion, finely diced	2 tablespoons unsalted butter
2 teaspoons minced, fresh winter savory, or 1 scant teaspoon crumbled, dried winter savory	1/2 cup dry white wine
1/2 teaspoon freshly ground allspice	6 peppercorns
3/4 teaspoon salt	2 whole cloves

Blend the meats, onion, savory, allspice, salt, egg, bread crumbs, and garlic together. Pat the mixture into 8 fat cakes, about 2 1/2 inches in diameter.

Melt the butter in a large skillet over medium heat. Saute the cakes 5 to 6 minutes on each side, until the meat is browned.

Add the wine, peppercorns, and cloves. Simmer over medium heat until the wine evaporates, about 7 minutes. Serve hot.

Serves 4.

Savory Pepper Roast

4- to 5-pound, bone-in pot or chuck roast	4 medium potatoes
3 garlic cloves	4 medium carrots
12 to 15 black peppercorns, crushed	3 tablespoons minced parsley
4 4-inch winter savory sprigs	salt and freshly ground pepper to taste
1 cup rich red wine	

Pat the roast dry. Peel and cut the garlic into slivers. Make small slits in the meat on both sides and insert the garlic. Press the crushed peppercorns into both sides of the meat. Put the roast in a casserole with a tight-fitting lid. Put 2 sprigs of winter savory on top of the roast and pour the red wine over it. Marinate for 4 hours at a cool room temperature, turning the meat several times.

Preheat the oven to 375° F.

Salt the meat lightly and braise it in the covered casserole in the oven for 1 hour. Peel the carrots and potatoes. Cut the potatoes lengthwise into sixths and the carrots lengthwise into quarters. Put them on top of the roast, season with salt and pepper, and baste them with the pan juices. Cover and cook for 20 minutes.

Add the remaining savory sprigs and 2 tablespoons parsley. Cook, covered, for 15 to 20 minutes, until the vegetables are just done. Remove the roast to a board and slice it into serving pieces. Arrange the roast and vegetables on a serving platter. Reduce the pan juices over high heat for 1 to 2 minutes and spoon the sauce over the meat. Sprinkle with the remaining parsley.

Serves 6.

Baked Beans with Savory

1 1/2 pounds cannellini beans, or small white beans	2 teaspoons minced, fresh winter savory, or 1 teaspoon crumbled, dried savory
1 bay leaf	1 teaspoon ground mustard seed
1 large onion, cut in a medium dice	1 teaspoon salt
1 14-ounce can plum tomatoes	1/8 teaspoon cayenne pepper
1/3 cup molasses	several grinds black pepper
1/4 cup olive oil	reserved bean stock
4 garlic cloves, minced	

Soak the beans overnight in 2 quarts cold water. Drain, rinse, and pick over the beans. Put them in a pot with the bay leaf and cover by 1 inch with water. Bring to a boil, reduce the heat, cover, and simmer for 30 to 45 minutes, until they are barely tender.

Drain the beans and reserve the stock. Mix the beans with the onion, molasses, olive oil, garlic, savory, mustard seed, salt, cayenne, and black pepper. Stir in 1 cup of bean stock.

Preheat the oven to 250° F.

Put the beans in an oiled, 2-quart bean pot and bake, covered, for 3 hours. Reduce the heat to 200° F. and bake 2 hours longer. After the first two hours, stir the beans once an hour. Add bean stock, 1/2 cup at a time, if the beans become dry. About an hour before they are done, adjust the seasoning and uncover the beans. Serve hot from the bean pot.

Serves 8 to 10.

Green Beans with Savory and Shallots

Whether this dish is served warm or at room temperature, it always disappears quickly. When the green beans come in, you may want to make a double recipe. Make it even if you don't have a red pepper, but use your best olive oil.

1 pound very tender green beans, 1/4 inch thick and 3 to 4 inches long	6 to 8 summer or winter savory sprigs
small red pepper	about 1/4 cup extra virgin olive oil
1/4 cup imported, oil-cured olives	1 1/2 to 2 tablespoons red wine vinegar
2 medium shallots	salt and pepper

Trim and clean the beans. Blanch them in lightly salted water until just tender, about 1 minute. Refresh under cold water and pat dry.

Clean and seed the red pepper. Cut it lengthwise into 1/8-inch strips. Pit and halve the olives. Dice the shallots very finely. Stem the savory and roughly chop the leaves.

Mix the olive oil with 1 1/2 tablespoons vinegar, the shallots, and the savory. Salt and pepper the vinaigrette lightly.

Toss the beans, red pepper, and olives with the vinaigrette. Cover and marinate 3 to 4 hours, or overnight, in the refrigerator. Bring the salad to a cool room temperature before serving. Or heat it gently for a few minutes, until it is warm. Adjust the seasoning with oil, vinegar, salt, and pepper.

Serves 4 to 6.

Summer Savory Potato Corn Fritters

1 1/2 pounds brown potatoes	1 tablespoon snipped chives
1/4 cup milk	salt and pepper
2 cups freshly cut corn kernels	about 1 cup finely ground yellow cornmeal
1/4 cup sour cream	2 tablespoons unsalted butter
2 tablespoons minced summer savory	

Wash and peel the potatoes. Chop them, put them in a pan, and barely cover with lightly salted water. Cover and cook over medium heat until they are tender.

Drain the potatoes, and rice or mash them in a large bowl. Stir in the milk. Add the corn, sour cream, savory, and chives. Season with salt and pepper and combine the mixture well. Pat the potato mixture into patties about 2 1/2 inches by 1/2 inch. Dredge the patties in cornmeal.

Melt the butter in a large skillet over medium heat. Saute half the fritters, cooking them about 4 minutes on each side, until they are golden brown and crisp. Arrange them on a warm platter and hold in a warm oven while cooking the rest of the fritters.

Yields about 15 fritters.

Savory Corn Relish

We use this relish as an accompaniment to grilled meats and spicy dishes from Mexican or Indian cuisines. It makes a special gift.

24 ears fresh sweet corn, husked	*1 tablespoon salt*
2 1/2 cups assorted, chopped sweet peppers (red, green, and yellow)	*2 teaspoons celery seed*
2 cups chopped onion	*4 tablespoons winter savory, finely chopped*
1 1/2 cups water	*1 tablespoon yellow mustard seed*
1/2 cup olive oil	*3 cloves garlic, minced*
1/2 cup honey	*3/4 teaspoon ground turmeric*
1 cup white wine vinegar	*6 3-inch winter savory sprigs*

Bring a large kettle of water to boil and cook 12 ears of corn for 3 minutes. Remove the corn, refresh under cold water, and pat it dry. Cook the other 12 ears the same way. Cut the corn from the cob. There should be at least 10 cups of corn. An extra cup will not affect the recipe.

In a large stainless steel or enameled pot, combine the peppers, onion, water, olive oil, honey, vinegar, salt, celery seed, chopped savory, mustard seed, and garlic. Bring these ingredients to a simmer and cook for 5 minutes.

Add the corn and bring to a boil. Reduce the heat and simmer about 5 minutes, stirring occasionally so that the relish does not stick. Take 2 tablespoons of the liquid and combine it with the turmeric in a small cup, mixing well. Add the turmeric to the pot, stir well, and simmer 2 minutes longer. Ladle the relish into hot pint jars with a sprig of savory in each jar. Seal the jars and process them in boiling water for 15 minutes.

Yields 6 pints.

Savory Peach Butter

6 pounds ripe, unblemished peaches	8 6-inch summer savory sprigs
1 1/3 cups light honey	5 3-inch summer savory sprigs
2 tablespoons lemon juice	

Skin and pit the peaches and slice them into eighths. Cover and cook in a stainless steel or enameled pan, over low heat, for 1 hour. Let stand for 30 minutes.

Puree the peaches and return them to the pan. Add the honey, lemon juice, and 8 savory sprigs. Cook over low heat, stirring frequently, until the mixture is medium thick. The butter will thicken some as it cools.

Remove the cooked sprigs. Ladle the butter into 5 hot, half-pint jelly jars with a small sprig of savory in each jar. Seal the jars.

Yields 5 jars.

Savory Baked Apple Custard

2 cups milk	1/2 teaspoon cinnamon
9 6-inch summer savory sprigs	1/4 teaspoon freshly ground nutmeg
about 1 tablespoon butter	3 eggs
3 medium apples (Winesap, MacIntosh, or Granny Smith)	2 egg yolks
1/4 cup light honey	1/3 cup light honey
2 tablespoons lemon juice	

Scald the milk with 6 savory sprigs and let the mixture stand for 30 minutes. Generously butter a 10-inch glass or ceramic quiche dish. Peel, core, and thinly slice the apples. In a bowl, toss them with 1/4 cup honey, lemon juice, cinnamon, and nutmeg.

Remove the savory from the milk and squeeze the extra liquid from the leaves. In a bowl, combine the eggs, egg yolks, and 1/3 cup honey. Whisk the mixture until blended. In a slow, steady stream, pour the scalded milk into the egg mixture, whisking continually.

Strain the apples and reserve the liquid. Arrange the apples around the bottom of the quiche dish in overlapping concentric circles. Strain the custard through a fine sieve and pour it carefully over the apples.

Preheat the oven to 325° F.

Place the custard dish in a larger dish and add hot water to a depth of half the custard dish. Bake about 35 minutes, testing with a cake tester for doneness. Remove from the pan of water and set on a rack to cool. After the custard has cooled to room temperature, gently loosen the edges with a spatula. Slide a completely flat platter over the custard dish and invert the custard onto it.

Pour the reserved apple liquid, about 3/4 cup, into a small saucepan and add the remaining savory sprigs. Bring the sauce to a simmer and cook over low heat for 15 minutes. Serve the custard at room temperature and pass the sauce separately.

The custard can be made ahead and refrigerated. Allow it to stand at room temperature for 30 minutes before serving. If you refrigerate the custard, reduce the sauce while the custard is standing.

Serves 6 to 8.

TARRAGON

TARRAGON

From times of old,
subtle yet bold,
in sauces fine with meat or fish,
tarragon defines the dish.

THE LATINS named this herb *dracunculus* because its serpentine root structure suggested little dragons. We think the fiery flare that warms the palate sparks more brilliant draconic images. Tarragon's multifaceted flavor recalls rich, glowing tapestries and paintings of dragons, their scales gleaming as greenly as the plant in the garden.

The "little dragon" was the favorite herb of Charlemagne and was cultivated in the gardens of the Tudors. Tarragon is one of the royal herbs, in fact as well as legend. Through the centuries, its regal presence has become more familiar and respected in the kitchen. In its early history, Pliny thought tarragon prevented fatigue. This notion continued through the Middle Ages, when the faithful put it in their shoes before setting out on pilgrimages. Arab doctors used its pleasant flavor and numbing properties to mitigate the effects of swallowing bitter medicines. Evelyn wrote of tarragon as "good for the heart, lungs, and liver."

Tarragon's strongest champions in central Europe have been cooks rather than herbalists or doctors. The French work with tarragon in the most majestic way, although it also finds favor with the Sienese and with some peoples of southern Russia, where it probably originated. The rich, anise-like, peppery flavor of tarragon and its complex aroma of freshly cut hay, mint, and licorice enhance a great variety of foods. Classic in sauces from bearnaise to tartar, and excellent with fish, eggs, and chicken, tarragon also adds much to grilled meats. A light sprinkling goes well with many simply prepared vegetables, notably peas, spinach, cauliflower, and potatoes. Tarragon vinegar is called for in many vinaigrettes and is easily prepared. Bring the desired quantity of good quality white wine vinegar just to the boil; then decant it into bottles containing several sprigs of fresh, healthy tarragon. Cap and store three weeks before using.

Tarragon tastes best on its own or with the classic fines herbes: parsley, chervil, and chives. The strong aromatics—rosemary, sage, and thyme—do not harmonize well with it. The fresh herb is subtler than the dried and should be used accordingly. Heat brings out the flavor of tarragon, so cooked dishes usually need less. In the late spring and early summer, tarragon is often sold in produce markets and at greengrocers.

For cultivation, French tarragon, *Artemisia dracunculus sativa,* is the culinary herb. It must be started from a cutting or by root division and probably should be obtained from an herb supplier. The mature French tarragon will grow from two to two and one-half feet tall. Like rosemary and sage, it will become a handsome bushy plant. Seeds come from Russian tarragon, a close relative; however, Russian tarragon lacks the essential oils necessary for culinary use. The Russian variety can grow up to five feet and will be rangier than French tarragon.

It is best to buy rooted cuttings or small plants in the spring and plant them eighteen inches apart, as tarragon has a shallow, lateral root system. Tarragon likes a well-drained, rich soil, a bit on the sandy side, and a sunny spot free from the shadow of other plants. Fertilization twice a month is necessary, especially the first few months after it has been transplanted. You will have to protect the plants if you set them out while there is still a chance of frost.

To insure the most flavorful tarragon, the roots should be divided in two to three years, after the plants are well established. This spring we devoted a little time to the gratifying task of dividing our three-year-old tarragon. We were rewarded with twelve root divisions, which are now healthy plants in the gardens of happy cooks. To divide the plant, we dug it up when it showed new growth, but before the stems were three inches tall. Carefully, we separated it into pieces that had part of last year's stem and roots on each portion. Such divisions should be treated as plants, and they will thrive with water and fertilization.

Tarragon dies back each winter even in temperate climates; in cold climates, it should be well protected with mulch. Mature tarragon can be grown in the house if it receives at least four hours of sun daily. Place it in a wide pot with good drainage and do not overwater it. A plant brought indoors for the winter may not flourish since tarragon requires a dormant season.

Tarragon can be taken in several cuttings for oils and vinegar, and drying or freezing. The sprigs can be frozen in airtight plastic bags with good results. Snip it as needed for dishes that call for the fresh herb. To dry tarragon best, place the sprigs on a mesh screen in a shady but warm place. Drying emphasizes the hay aroma and licorice taste at the expense of the more volatile oils, so the dried herb will not be as rich in flavor.

A closer acquaintance with tarragon will reveal why kings and cooks have been so enamored of it.

Salmon Cured with Tarragon

All ingredients should be the finest and freshest for this recipe. The easiest way to remove the bones from the salmon is to use a pair of needle-nosed pliers. After it has been cured, the salmon is delicious grilled.

2 whole salmon fillets, each about 2 pounds, with the skin on	*1/4 cup Cognac*
8 to 10 tarragon sprigs	*about 1 1/2 tablespoons kosher salt*

Remove the bones from the fillets. Arrange the tarragon along the flesh side of one of the fillets. Sprinkle this fillet with the Cognac. Scatter the salt evenly over the tarragon. Put the other fillet on top of the tarragon, flesh side down.

Place the salmon on a platter large enough to hold it without crowding and cover it with a damp tea towel. Marinate in the refrigerator for 24 hours, turning the fish at least once and keeping the towel damp.

To serve, remove the tarragon and salt from the fillets. Put the salmon skin side down on a serving board or platter and slice it very thin. Begin at the tail end and hold the knife almost parallel to the flesh.

Serves 12 to 16.

Tarragon Deviled Eggs in Celery

6 large eggs	2 dashes cayenne pepper
1/4 cup sour cream	salt and pepper to taste
2 teaspoons minced tarragon	7 celery ribs
2 teaspoons Dijon mustard	Garnish: capers

Hard-cook the eggs, peel, and cool them. Rub them through a medium sieve into a bowl. Add the sour cream, tarragon, mustard, cayenne, salt, and pepper to taste.

Wash the celery ribs and cut them into 3-inch lengths. Fill the celery with the egg mixture, using a pastry bag or spoon, and garnish with capers.

Yields 26 to 30 appetizers.

Herbed Panettone

12 tablespoons unsalted butter	1 cup sugar
1/3 cup currants	1/3 cup pine nuts
6 to 7 cups unbleached white flour	grated rind of 1 lemon
2 tablespoons dry yeast	1 tablespoon minced tarragon leaves
1/2 cup warm water	1 tablespoon minced fennel leaves
1 1/2 cups milk	1 teaspoon salt

Melt the butter and set aside. Soak the currants in about 1 cup of very warm water. Heap 5 cups of flour in a large bowl and make a well. Pour the yeast into the well. Add 1/2 cup warm water and stir the yeast into it. Let the sponge proof about 10 minutes, until the yeast shows signs of activity. Drain the currants.

Stir the melted butter, drained currants, milk, sugar, pine nuts, lemon rind, tarragon, fennel, and salt into the dough with a wooden spoon. Stir 1/2 cup flour into the dough. Sprinkle 1/2 cup flour on a smooth surface and turn the dough onto the flour. Knead the dough until it is smooth and not sticky, adding flour as necessary. This takes about 10 minutes.

Put the dough into a lightly buttered bowl, cover with a damp tea towel, and rest in a warm place until doubled in bulk. Punch the dough down.

Preheat the oven to 350° F.

For the traditional panettone shape, butter and lightly flour a 3-quart pan or tin whose height is equal to its diameter. Place the dough in the prepared pan and let it rise until two-thirds the height of the pan. Or, shape the dough into a round loaf and let it almost double its bulk on a buttered and floured baking sheet.

Bake for 45 minutes. Reduce the temperature to 300° F. and bake for 30 to 45 minutes longer. The panettone is done when a cake tester tests clean. Watch the panettone as it bakes; if it becomes too brown, cover with foil. Cool the panettone in the pan or on the baking sheet for 20 minutes before turning out or cutting.

Yields 1 large panettone.

Cream of Cauliflower Soup

1 medium-large cauliflower, about 1 1/2 pounds	1 cup half-and-half cream
3 cups vegetable or chicken stock	1 tablespoon minced tarragon
3 small shallots	salt and white pepper to taste
2 tablespoons unsalted butter	1/4 teaspoon freshly ground nutmeg

Wash and break the cauliflower into flowerets. Put them in a soup pot with the stock. Cook until the cauliflower is just tender. Puree the cauliflower with 1 cup of stock in a blender or food processor until smooth. Return the puree to the soup pot.

Finely mince the shallots and sweat them in butter for about 5 minutes. Add the shallots, cream, and tarragon to the soup and stir well. Taste and adjust for salt and pepper, and add the nutmeg. Reheat to serve, but do not allow to simmer.

Serves 6.

Fillet of Sole with Crab

1 cup cooked crabmeat (do not use frozen crab)	1 tablespoon unsalted butter
2 tablespoons creme fraiche	1 tablespoon minced tarragon
pinch of white pepper and cayenne pepper	1/2 cup dry white wine
4 fillets of sole, about 1 pound	salt and white pepper to taste
1 medium shallot	1/2 cup whipping cream

Mix the crabmeat gently with the creme fraiche, and add the pinch of white pepper and cayenne. Roll each fillet around 1/4 cup of crab mixture and tie the fillets with kitchen string or secure with toothpicks.

Mince the shallot and soften it in butter over low heat for 5 minutes. Add the tarragon, wine, and salt and white pepper to taste. Simmer for 5 minutes. Add the rolled fillets and poach gently for about 5 minutes, carefully turning them once.

Remove the fillets with a slotted spoon to a warm plate and keep warm. Increase the heat under the sauce and reduce to 1/3 cup. Add the whipping cream and heat thoroughly. Spoon the sauce into a warm serving dish. Remove the string or toothpicks from the fillets and place the fillets on top of the sauce. Serve immediately.

Serves 4.

Grilled Lamb with Mustard Tarragon Marinade

3-pound boned leg of lamb	2 tablespoons olive oil
2 or 3 garlic cloves	2 tablespoons medium dry sherry
6 fresh tarragon sprigs, or 2 teaspoons dried tarragon	1/2 teaspoon black peppercorns, cracked
4 tablespoons whole grain mustard	salt

Butterfly the lamb. Cut the garlic in thin slivers and insert in small incisions made in the meat with a sharp knife. If fresh tarragon is available, insert a leaf with each garlic sliver.

Stem and mince the fresh tarragon, or soak the dried tarragon in the sherry. Mix the mustard, olive oil, sherry, tarragon, and pepper together, and rub the marinade all over the lamb. Cover and marinate overnight in the refrigerator or a cool place. Four hours before cooking, remove the lamb from the refrigerator and let stand at room temperature.

Prepare a medium-hot charcoal fire. Grill the lamb 5 inches above the coals, turning it 4 or 5 times. For rare lamb, check for doneness after 12 minutes. The lamb will be rare if it is firm yet springy when pressed lightly with a finger (or when the internal temperature is 125° to 128° F.). Let the lamb rest on a platter for 5 minutes before carving.

To serve, slice the lamb into 3/8-inch slices on a diagonal across the grain of the meat. Serve immediately.

Serves 6 to 8.

Sweetbreads with Tarragon and Blu Castello

1 1/2 pounds veal sweetbreads (these should be so young that they do not need blanching)	1 tablespoon minced tarragon
1 medium shallot	1 teaspoon Dijon mustard
1 tablespoon unsalted butter	4 ounces Blu Castello cheese, at room temperature
2 tablespoons dry white wine	

Trim the sweetbreads of any connective tissue. Cut them into 1-inch thick slices. Mince the shallot and soften it in butter over low heat for 5 minutes. Increase the heat to medium-low, add the sweetbreads, and saute about 4 minutes, turning the sweetbreads once. Remove the sweetbreads to a warm platter and keep them warm.

Add the wine, tarragon, and mustard to the pan and reduce the heat. Stir the sauce well and add the Blu Castello cheese. Stir constantly until the cheese has melted to a thick cream consistency. Nap the sweetbreads with the sauce and serve immediately.

Serves 6.

Wild Goose, Cooked in Clay, with Blueberry Tarragon Sauce

Susan's father, Robert Belsinger, goes goose hunting every season. In search of a new recipe for preparing wild goose, we decided to try this method and sauce. We were all very pleased with the result.

4- to 5-pound wild goose, plucked and cleaned	*1/3 cup orange juice*
3-inch tarragon sprig	*2 teaspoons minced tarragon*
2 teaspoons salt	*salt to taste*
1 teaspoon cracked black pepper	*Garnish: fresh tarragon sprigs*
2 cups fresh blueberries	

Rinse the goose and dry it well. Bruise the tarragon leaves and rub the bird inside and out with the sprig. Mix the salt and pepper and rub the bird inside and out with it. Put the tarragon sprig inside the bird.

Follow the directions for soaking a clay roaster.

Put the bird, breast side up, in the roaster and place in a cold oven. Roast for 15 minutes per pound at 500° F. Remove the bird to a warm platter and keep warm.

Carefully decant the juices from the roaster into a skillet, scraping the roaster with a wooden spoon to loosen any bits of meat and skin. Reduce the juices to 1 cup and strain them. Add the blueberries (frozen berries without juice or sugar can be substituted; partially thaw before using), orange juice, tarragon, and salt to taste. Cook over medium-high heat for 5 minutes. Garnish the bird with tarragon sprigs. Pass the sauce separately.

Serves 4 to 6.

Chicken and Vegetable Salad in Tarragon Aspic

1-pound chicken breast	1 small, sweet red pepper
1 cup defatted chicken stock	2 tablespoons gelatin
2 3-inch tarragon sprigs	3 1/2 cups completely clear, defatted chicken stock
2 small turnips	1 1/2 tablespoons tarragon leaves
2 small carrots	1 tablespoon parsley leaves
1/3 pound asparagus	Garnish: tarragon sprigs

Skin and bone the chicken breast. Poach the breast in 1 cup chicken stock along with 1 tarragon sprig for 5 to 8 minutes, until the meat is just done. Remove the chicken from the stock and cool to room temperature. Slice the breast on the diagonal into 3/8-inch strips.

Trim, clean, and peel the turnips and carrots. Trim and clean the asparagus. Blanch the carrots, turnips, and asparagus separately and refresh under cold water. Drain the vegetables and pat them dry. Slice the turnips into 1/4-inch rounds and cut the rounds in half. Slice the carrots into 1/4-inch rounds. Cut the asparagus into 2-inch lengths. Seed and trim the red pepper and cut into 1/4-inch strips.

Soften the gelatin in 1/2 cup of the clear, defatted chicken stock. Bring the remaining 3 cups of clear stock to a boil with the second tarragon sprig. Remove the tarragon and dissolve the gelatin in the stock. Chill the dissolved gelatin for 1/2 hour. Finely mince the tarragon and parsley leaves.

Oil a 2-quart souffle dish or other mold very lightly with vegetable oil. Pour enough of the stock gelatin mixture into the mold to measure 1/4 inch. Chill until set. Decoratively arrange one quarter of the chicken and vegetables on the aspic. Add enough aspic to come half way up the chicken and chill until almost set. Add aspic to just cover the chicken and vegetables and chill until set.

Repeat the process with a second layer of chicken and vegetables, sprinkling the minced herbs over the set layer of chicken and vegetables before covering them completely. Repeat the layering procedure two more times, finishing with a 1/4-inch layer of aspic. Chill at least 2 hours. Unmold onto a chilled platter and garnish with tarragon sprigs.

Serves 8 to 10 as a salad course.

Scallop, Shrimp, and Artichoke Salad

Artichokes

6 medium-large artichokes	juice of 1/2 lemon

Trim the artichokes to the heart. Remove the chokes and pare the hearts so that no green remains. In an enameled or stainless pan, with a tight-fitting lid, steam the hearts over water, with the lemon juice added, for 10 to 15 minutes, until the hearts are tender but still firm. Refresh the hearts under cold water, rub them with lemon juice, cover, and chill.

Court Bouillon

1 cup water	3-inch tarragon sprig
1/2 cup dry white wine	6 parsley sprigs
1 carrot, cut in pieces	6 fennel seeds
1 onion, cut in pieces	8 black peppercorns
1/2 teaspoon salt	

Combine the water, wine, carrot, onion, and salt in a soup pot. Make a bouquet garni from the tarragon, parsley, fennel seeds, and peppercorns. Add to the bouillon and simmer for about 30 minutes.

Shrimp and Scallops

1/2 pound medium shrimp	1/2 pound scallops

Poach the shrimp in their shells in the court bouillon for about 2 minutes, or until they just begin to turn pink. Remove the shrimp with a slotted spoon and spread them to cool. Cut the scallops into 1/2-inch dice and poach in the court bouillon for 1 minute. Remove them with a slotted spoon and spread to cool.

Vinaigrette

3/4 cup reduced court bouillon	1 scant tablespoon minced tarragon
3 tablespoons light olive oil	1 tablespoon minced parsley
salt, pepper, and lemon juice to taste	

Remove the vegetables and bouquet garni from the court bouillon and reduce it to 3/4 cup. Add the olive, oil, salt, pepper, and lemon juice and cook over medium heat for 3 minutes, whisking continually. Pour this dressing into a glass bowl and set aside to cool.

Shell and devein shrimp. Add the shrimp, scallops, and minced herbs to the dressing and toss well. Cover and chill for 2 hours.

Garnish: limestone or butter lettuce   thin slices of red pepper

Before serving, line 6 salad plates with limestone or butter lettuce. Place an artichoke heart on each plate. Divide the salad among the artichokes, spooning the remaining dressing over each. Garnish with red pepper strips.
Serves 6.

Baked Potatoes with Boursault and Tarragon

3 large baking potatoes	*1 tablespoon unsalted butter*
3 1/2 ounces Boursault cheese, at room temperature	*1/2 cup whipping cream*
1 tablespoon minced tarragon	*salt and pepper to taste*

Preheat the oven to 425° F.

Scrub the potatoes and bake them for 50 to 60 minutes, or until the potatoes are tender. Remove from the oven and cut in half lengthwise. Carefully scoop the pulp into a large bowl, leaving 1/4-inch shells.

Mash or rice the pulp and blend in the cheese (there should be some lumps of cheese). Add the tarragon, butter, cream, salt, and pepper and blend well. Mound the potato filling in the skins and place on a baking sheet. Return to the oven for 10 minutes, until the potatoes are golden brown on top.
Serves 6.

Lima Beans with Tarragon

1 pound dried baby lima beans	*3 garlic cloves, minced*
1 tablespoon finely chopped tarragon, or 1 teaspoon crumbled, dried tarragon	*salt and freshly ground white pepper to taste*
2 teaspoons lemon juice	*2 medium-sized ripe tomatoes*
1/2 cup olive oil	

Soak the beans overnight. Pour off the water and add enough fresh water to cover the beans by 2 inches. Cover and cook the beans over medium heat until they are tender.

Add the tarragon, lemon juice, olive oil, garlic, salt, and pepper. Remove from the heat, cover, and allow flavors to mingle at room temperature for at least 1 hour. (Refrigerate if the beans are not to be served after 2 hours at room temperature.) Seed and chop the tomatoes, add them to the beans, and reheat gently until warm.

Serves 6.

Warm Vegetable Salad with Tarragon Vinaigrette

1 small red cabbage	1 small cauliflower
2 large carrots	2 small green peppers

Wash and chop the cabbage. Wash and peel the carrots. Break the cauliflower into flowerets, and cut the peppers into strips. Steam the vegetables slightly so that they are still crunchy. Arrange the vegetables on a platter and keep them warm.

Vinaigrette

2/3 cup virgin olive oil	1 large garlic clove, crushed
1/3 cup light sesame oil	1 teaspoon Dijon mustard
1 tablespoon white wine vinegar	1 teaspoon honey
1 tablespoon plus 1 teaspoon finely chopped tarragon	salt and pepper to taste
4 tablespoons chopped parsley	

Combine all the dressing ingredients in a blender and blend well. Pour over the vegetables and serve warm.

Serves 8.

Tarragon Pickles

The finest *cornichons* we have tried, both for flavor and appearance, were prepared by Patricia Wells in Paris. She shared her recipe with Carolyn, and these pickles are a variation of those memorable cornichons.

Preparing the Cucumbers

about 2 1/2 pounds scrubbed pickling cucumbers (French cucumbers are best)	about 6 cups cold water
1/3 cup kosher salt	

Trim the stem ends of the cucumbers, rinse, and drain them. Put them in a large bowl with the salt and water. Let stand in a cool place for 6 hours or overnight. Drain the cucumbers well.

Making the Pickles

2 1/2 cups tarragon vinegar	8 garlic cloves, peeled
2 1/2 cups water	8 small bay leaves
1 tablespoon sugar	8 small, dried, hot red peppers
16 very small, white pickling onions, or 8 small pickling onions, peeled but with ends intact	32 peppercorns
16 fresh tarragon sprigs, about 2 inches long	

Combine the vinegar, water, and sugar in a saucepan and bring to a boil.

Have ready 8 sterilized half-pint canning jars with lids and rings. Fill the jars with drained cucumbers, layering the onions, herbs, and spices in between. Each jar should have 2 onions, 2 tarragon sprigs, 1 garlic clove, 1 bay leaf, 1 red pepper, and 4 peppercorns.

Pour the boiling vinegar and water into each jar to 1/4 inch from the top. Wipe the rim of each jar and seal. Let the jars cool. Store the pickles at least 3 to 4 weeks before serving. Refrigerate after opening.

Yields 8 half-pints.

THYME

THYME

Honeysweet and handsome thyme,
with what wit you bring to rhyme:
Conceits of cabbage, apple, oyster:
Advance brave cooks, braise, and roister.

OF ALL THE CLASSICAL culinary herbs, thyme is especially endearing to those who love miniatures; its handsome, compact form growing close to the earth perfumes the air around it, seemingly to the heavens. It has a modest appearance, not more than eight to twelve inches from the ground, but a luxurious symmetry to its plump, thickly set leaves and a charm to its rosy lavender or white flowers, which do much to explain why it has entranced herbalists for so long. As the aroma intimates, it is a sweetish yet pungent herb when fresh—a combination to scent and savor.

Thyme is another herb of Mediterranean origin, and the Classical Greeks, who were conservative in the culinary use of many common herbs, embraced thyme wholeheartedly. Perhaps this is so because they discovered the attraction thyme had for bees, and tasted the honey that was the fruit of thyme's perfume and the bees' chemistry. Certainly a taste of the famous Mount Hymettus honey is a sensual recognition of the beauty and power of thyme.

Athenians did not restrict their use of thyme to home and restaurant kitchens; they also made liqueurs with it, burned it in their temples, and bathed in it. The root of thyme's name is definitely Greek, although whether it derives from *thuo*, "to fumigate," "to perfume," or from *thumus*, "courage, without fear of death," is uncertain. Possibly both concepts were fused from the Egyptians, who used thyme in their embalming processes.

Later, thyme became a symbol of energy and acuity, teas and baths of it being especially recommended for the eyes. Culpeper spoke highly of its effects on the lungs, and it is used in cough medicines today. Thyme also had a well-deserved reputation for banishing unpleasant odors, making it, with rosemary and lavender, one of the chief strewing herbs. Renaissance England respected thyme in more elegant social contexts; "to smell as sweet as thyme" was a moral as well as physical compliment. "Punning thyme" was a signal for clever wordplay among the wits and poets of the Elizabethan period.

In uses closer to cooking, the Spanish and Italians grazed sheep and goats on thyme for the flavor it gave their meat. The herb was used in many rich dishes, as it was believed to alleviate the sufferings of gout. Thyme, if used judiciously, will add a soft, plummy fragrance and subtle taste compounded of mint, bay, and marjoram to almost all classes of cooked foods. It is good with cereal grains, especially rice and wheat; all meats, including brains and sweetbreads; eggs; most vegetables, especially potatoes, carrots, squash, onions, and tomatoes; and it enters into an exquisite marriage with shellfish and fish. Although it loses some of its fragrant quality in drying, which emphasizes an earthy aroma and pungent flavor, thyme enriches the simplest soup or stew and gives a delectable accent to fruits and salads. It is indispensable in bouquets garnis used for making stocks, particularly chicken and lamb stocks. A good part of our kitchen wealth is concentrated in freshly harvested bundles of thyme.

Thyme germinates easily from seed; the seeds are tiny and should be covered very lightly in a mixture of half sterile sand or perlite and half potting soil. For culinary use, *Thymus vulgaris* is available in small pots at nursery and herb suppliers. It may be called English, German, or French thyme. Their aromatic properties are very similar, the distinctions being made in the width of their leaves. There are some interesting scented varieties, the lemon thymes and caraway thyme. These should be used fresh, with little or no cooking. They are excellent marinating herbs.

The species of *Thymus serpyllum*, creeping thymes, are beautiful ground covers if there is space for them in the garden. Although they are not particularly useful in the kitchen, we grow some varieties to provide magic carpets for the bees. All thymes grow best in sandy soil, as their fine root structures are unable to find enough nutrients in heavy soil. They are hardy but will not survive very cold winters without mulching.

The time to harvest is when the flower buds just begin to open. Cut about two or three inches of the stems and hang them in small bunches or spread them on screens to dry. In the house, thyme does not require special care if it is transplanted to a wide pot with sandy soil and given plenty of sun.

And now, the time has come to please the palate.

Thyme Mushroom Pate

3 slices whole grain bread	2 tablespoons minced thyme leaves
1/2 cup milk	1/4 cup half-and-half cream
2 pounds fresh mushrooms	1/2 teaspoon salt
2 shallots	1/2 teaspoon freshly ground black pepper
6 tablespoons unsalted butter	2 tablespoons brandy
2 eggs	Garnish: 10 to 12 thyme sprigs
1 tablespoon soy sauce	

Break the bread in large pieces and soak it in the milk for about 5 minutes. Transfer the bread to a colander and drain for 10 minutes. Clean and trim the mushrooms. Mince the shallots and saute them in 4 tablespoons of butter for about 5 minutes.

Divide the mushrooms into 3 batches. Puree 1 batch with half the bread crumbs, the remaining 2 tablespoons butter, 1 egg, the soy sauce, 1 tablespoon minced thyme, and the cream. Transfer the puree to a large bowl.

Puree another batch of mushrooms with the rest of the bread crumbs, the sauteed shallots, 1 egg, the salt and pepper. Add the puree to the bowl.

Puree the last batch of mushrooms with the brandy and remaining minced thyme. Add this to the bowl and blend the puree very well.

Preheat the oven to 350° F.

Butter a 1 1/2-quart terrine or a loaf pan and add the mixture. Cover the pate with foil, then with the terrine lid. Place the terrine on a baking sheet and bake for 1 hour.

Remove the foil and cover with the terrine lid only or loosen the foil over the loaf pan. Bake for 30 minutes, reduce the heat to 300° F., and bake 30 minutes longer. Remove the terrine and let cool to room temperature.

Turn the pate out onto a larger platter and let the liquid drain for an hour or so. Wrap the pate in foil, put in on a platter, and chill it at least 4 hours, or overnight. To serve, remove the foil and slice the pate into 3/8-inch slices. Arrange the slices on a serving platter and garnish with thyme sprigs.

Serves 12 to 16.

Lox Thyme Rolls

1/2 pound natural cream cheese, softened	*salt and freshly ground white pepper to taste*
2 tablespoons minced thyme leaves	*1/2 pound thinly sliced lox, each slice about 6 inches long*
1 1/2 tablespoons lemon juice, or to taste	*Garnish: thyme and parsley sprigs*

Combine the cream cheese, minced thyme, and lemon juice well in a bowl. Season the mixture lightly with salt and pepper.

Spread the lox slices on a work surface. Divide the cream cheese mixture evenly among the slices, spreading it to the edges. Roll the slices, starting with a short side, and transfer the rolls to a platter.

Cover the rolls and chill them for 1 hour, or until they are firm. Cut the rolls into 3/8-inch slices with a sharp knife and arrange them on a platter, cut side down. Garnish the platter with thyme and parsley sprigs.

Yields about 30 hors d'oeuvre.

Oatmeal Bread with Thyme and Walnuts

2 cups boiling water	*1 teaspoon salt*
1 cup rolled oats	*1 tablespoon active dry yeast*
2 tablespoons unsalted butter	*4 1/2 to 5 cups unbleached white flour*
1/4 cup honey	*2 tablespoons minced thyme*
1 tablespoon molasses	*2/3 cup coarsely chopped walnuts*

Pour the boiling water over the oats and butter. Stir in the honey, molasses, and salt. Cool the mixture to warm. Add the yeast and sift in 4 cups of flour. Stir in the thyme and walnuts.

Turn the dough onto a smooth surface and knead until smooth, working in extra flour as necessary. Let the dough rise until doubled in bulk in a lightly buttered and covered bowl.

Punch the dough down and knead it for 2 or 3 turns. Cut it into 4 pieces and shape the pieces into small loaves. Divide the loaves between 2 buttered, 9-by-5-inch loaf pans.

Preheat the oven to 350° F.

When the dough has risen to the top of the pans, bake it for 50 to 60 minutes. Cool the bread in the pans on racks for 10 minutes, then turn it out to cool completely.

Yields 4 small loaves.

Carrot Soup with Thyme

2 pounds carrots	2 cups half-and-half cream
1 medium onion	salt and pepper to taste
4 tablespoons unsalted butter	freshly grated nutmeg to taste
1 1/2 quarts chicken or vegetable stock	Garnish: 1 tablespoon finely chopped thyme leaves mixed with 2 tablespoons chopped parsley leaves
bouquet garni: (6 to 8 Italian parsley sprigs; 3 fresh thyme sprigs or 1 teaspoon dried thyme; 6 to 8 black peppercorns)	

Wash, trim, and peel the carrots, and chop them coarsely. Trim, peel, and chop the onion coarsely. Sweat the vegetables in butter in a soup pot. Add the stock and bring the soup to a simmer. Add the bouquet garni and simmer about 20 minutes.

Remove the bouquet garni and puree the soup in batches. Stir in the cream and season with salt, pepper, and nutmeg. Let the soup warm over very low heat for 5 minutes. Serve in warm soup bowls and sprinkle each with a little chopped thyme and parsley.

Serves 4 to 6.

Herbed Clam Chowder

4 dozen of the smallest littleneck clams	*1 medium onion*
1 28-ounce can plum tomatoes	*2 celery ribs*
4 thyme sprigs, or 1 teaspoon dried thyme	*3 medium, new potatoes*
2 marjoram sprigs, or 1/2 teaspoon dried marjoram	*4 tablespoons unsalted butter*
1 bay leaf	*salt to taste*
cayenne pepper to taste	*Garnish: small thyme sprigs*

Scrub the clams and steam them in 1 cup water until they just open. Shuck them and rinse if necessary. Strain the cooking juices through tripled and rinsed cheesecloth in a sieve. Pour the strained juice over the clams and set aside.

Put the tomatoes and their juice in a soup pot and break them up with a wooden spoon. Add the thyme, marjoram, and bay leaf, and season with cayenne.

Trim and peel the onion and celery ribs. Cut them into medium dice. Peel the potatoes and cut them into medium dice. Cook the vegetables in butter over low heat for about 10 minutes. Add them to the tomatoes, along with most of the juice covering the clams. Simmer until the vegetables are just done, about 10 minutes. Add the reserved clams and remaining juice and heat through. Serve hot in warm soup bowls and garnish with thyme sprigs.

Serves 6.

Tagliolini with Prosciutto and Cream Sauce

1 recipe Egg Pasta (see Index)	*1 tablespoon minced thyme leaves*
1/4 pound prosciutto, thinly sliced	*salt and freshly ground black pepper to taste*
1 cup whipping cream	*1/2 cup freshly grated Parmesan cheese*
1/2 cup half-and-half cream	*2 or 3 eggs*
2 tablespoons unsalted butter	

Cut the pasta into tagliolini, through the fine noodle cutters. Bring abundant salted water to a boil.

Shred the prosciutto and put in a skillet with the creams, butter, and thyme. Heat the sauce over low heat and season with salt and pepper.

Cook the pasta al dente, drain it well, and toss it with the sauce. In a warm serving bowl, toss the cheese and eggs into the pasta. Serve immediately.

Serves 4 to 6.

Spareribs and Potatoes in Thyme Tomato Sauce

When she was growing up, Susan used to ask her mother, Audrey, to make spareribs and potatoes with tomato sauce for her birthday. We have worked with that recipe to make this satisfying, homey dish.

Marinade

1 cup dry white wine	1 teaspoon freshly ground pepper
6-ounce can tomato paste	1/4 teaspoon ground allspice
8 to 10 thyme sprigs	3 pounds country-style spareribs
3 large garlic cloves, mashed	

Mix the wine, tomato paste, thyme, garlic, pepper, and allspice in a large ceramic or glass bowl. Add the spareribs and coat them with the marinade. Cover and chill overnight.

Let the spareribs and marinade come to room temperature. Spread the spareribs on a baking sheet large enough to hold them in one layer. Reserve the marinade.

Potatoes

1 1/2 pounds boiling potatoes	1 teaspoon salt
1 1/2 cups beef or veal stock	reserved marinade

Peel and quarter the potatoes. Put them in a stainless steel or enameled saucepan along with the stock, salt, and marinade. Bring the liquid to a boil, reduce to a simmer, and cook the potatoes until they are just done, 15 to 20 minutes. Transfer the potatoes to a platter, cover them, and keep warm. Reduce the cooking liquid to about 1 cup.

Finishing the Dish

salt and pepper	*about 3 tablespoons chopped parsley*
1/2 cup beef or veal stock	

Preheat the oven to 450° F.

Salt and pepper the ribs lightly and bake them in the upper third of the oven for about 30 minutes, until they are well browned and tender. Turn them once while they are cooking. Transfer the ribs to a large, warm platter.

Pour off the fat in the baking pan. Deglaze the baking pan with the stock and stir the juice into the reduced sauce. Arrange the potatoes around the ribs, pour the sauce over the ribs, and sprinkle the dish with parsley.

Serves 6.

Veal Scallops with Thyme Caper Sauce

2 pounds veal scallops, flattened to about 1/8 inch thick	*2 tablespoons lemon juice*
salt and pepper	*2 tablespoons capers, rinsed and drained*
1/2 cup all-purpose flour	*1 tablespoon minced thyme leaves, or 1 teaspoon dried, crumbled thyme*
1/2 cup clarified butter	*salt and freshly ground black pepper to taste*
1/2 cup veal stock	*Garnish: about 3 tablespoons chopped parsley leaves*

Salt and pepper the veal scallops lightly. Dredge them in flour, shaking off the excess. Heat the butter over moderately high heat in a large skillet. Saute the scallops, a few at a time, for about 1 minute, turning them once. Transfer them to a platter and keep them warm.

Add the veal stock to the pan, along with the lemon juice, capers, and thyme. Season lightly. Deglaze the skillet for 1 or 2 minutes over high heat. Reduce the heat to medium and add the scallops to the pan. Cook them for about 2 minutes.

Transfer the veal to a serving platter and spoon the sauce over it. Sprinkle the dish with parsley.

Serves 4 to 6.

Baked Tomatoes with Jerusalem Artichokes

6 large, firm, ripe tomatoes	1 teaspoon salt
6 ounces Jerusalem artichokes	about 1/4 cup virgin olive oil
1 shallot	1/3 cup fine, dry bread crumbs
1 tablespoon finely chopped thyme leaves	

Wash the tomatoes and cut off the tops. Drain the juice and seeds and scoop out the pulp. Chop the pulp coarsely and put it in a bowl.

Wash the Jerusalem artichokes and peel them if necessary. Chop them in a fine dice. Chop the shallot in a fine dice. Add the vegetables to the tomatoes and stir in the thyme, salt, and olive oil.

Preheat the oven to 400° F.

Stuff the tomatoes loosely with the mixture and brush the outside of each tomato lightly with olive oil. Divide the breadcrumbs among the tomatoes. Put the tomatoes in a baking dish and bake about 15 minutes. Serve hot.

Serves 6.

Butternut Puree with Thyme

1 1/2 pounds butternut squash	2 teaspoons finely chopped thyme leaves
2 to 3 tablespoons unsalted butter	salt and freshly ground white pepper to taste
1 tablespoon honey	

Preheat the oven to 375° F.

Split the butternut squash lengthwise. Place on a baking sheet, cut sides up, and cover them with aluminum foil. Bake for 1 hour, or until it pierces easily with a fork.

Remove the squash from the oven and set aside until it is cool enough to handle. Remove the seeds. Scoop out the meat and puree it through a food mill, or carefully in a food processor.

Increase the oven temperature to 400° F.

Stir the butter, honey, and thyme into the puree and season. Bake the puree in a buttered, ovenproof serving dish for 20 to 25 minutes. Serve the puree hot.

Serves 6.

Greek Salad with Thyme Vinaigrette

Although this is not a traditional Greek salad, the flavors and textures remind us of dining in Greece.

1 1/2 pounds green cabbage	juice of 1 lemon, or to taste
1 medium red onion	2 tablespoons finely chopped thyme leaves
6 ounces Kalamata olives	1 teaspoon salt
12 ounces feta cheese	1 medium bunch spinach
2/3 cup virgin olive oil	freshly ground black pepper

Wash, trim, and shred the cabbage. Cut the red onion in half and slice it thinly. Pit and halve the olives. Crumble the feta cheese. Toss the cabbage, onion, olives, and cheese together in a large bowl.

Whisk the olive oil, lemon juice, thyme, and salt together. Toss the vinaigrette with the salad and let stand at a cool room temperature for 2 hours.

Chill the salad about 30 minutes before serving. Wash and stem the spinach. Just before serving, toss the spinach with the salad and sprinkle with pepper.

Serves 6 to 8.

Thyme Mustard

This is a basic recipe that can be experimented with in many ways. If a sweeter mustard is desired, add more honey. For those who like variety, we suggest trying chives, oregano, savory, or tarragon in place of thyme.

1 1/2 cups fresh, ground mustard seed	1/4 teaspoon freshly ground white pepper
1/2 cup water	1 1/2 teaspoons honey
1/4 cup white wine vinegar	2 teaspoons finely minced fresh thyme, or to taste
1/4 teaspoon salt	

In a small mixing bowl, blend the mustard, water, and vinegar. The mustard powder will absorb the liquid as it stands. Add the salt, pepper, honey, and thyme and blend well. Pack into jars and keep refrigerated until ready to use.

Yields about 2 cups.

Note: The mustard will be hot when it is first prepared, so it must be allowed to mellow at least 3 to 4 weeks before using it or giving it as a gift.

Thyme Grape Jelly

10 to 12 3-inch thyme sprigs	*1 1/2 cups light honey*
2 cups freshly squeezed, unpasteurized grape juice	*1 tablespoon lemon juice*
2 ounces powdered fruit pectin	*3 thyme sprigs*

Put 10 to 12 thyme sprigs and the grape juice in a stainless steel or enameled saucepan. Bring the liquid to a boil, remove from the heat, cover, and steep for an hour. Strain the juice through a sieve.

Heat the strained juice in a stainless steel or enameled saucepan until it is just warm. Stir in the fruit pectin. Bring the juice to a rolling boil and add the honey and lemon juice. Stir the mixture constantly and bring to a boil that cannot be stirred down. Boil for 2 minutes, remove from the heat, and skim the juice.

Have ready 3 8-ounce sterilized jelly jars. Place a thyme sprig in each jar, then ladle the jelly mixture to 1/4 inch from the rim. Wipe the rims clean and seal with the lids and rings. Let the jars cool. The jelly should sit for 24 hours before use.

Yields 3 8-ounce jars.

Fruit Compote

3 Bosc or Comice pears	1/2 cup port wine
2 Winesap or MacIntosh apples	1 tablespoon lemon juice
1 Granny Smith or other tart green apple	1/4 cup light honey
1/4 pound pitted and halved prunes	Garnish: 1/2 pint whipping cream, whipped
6 thyme sprigs	freshly grated nutmeg
1 1/2 cups rich red wine	

Peel and core the pears and apples. Cut them into wedges. Put them in a large stainless steel or enameled pan with the prunes, thyme, red wine, port wine, lemon juice, and honey. Cover the pan and bring the liquid to a boil. Reduce the heat to a simmer and cook, uncovered, about 15 minutes, until the fruit is just done.

Remove the fruit to a large bowl to cool. Strain the poaching liquid and reduce it by about half. Remove from the heat and let the syrup cool. Pour it over the fruit, cover, and chill the compote for 3 to 4 hours. Allow the compote to stand at room temperature for 30 minutes before serving. Serve with whipped cream and freshly grated nutmeg.

Serves 6 to 8.

DRIED HERBS
MINT   SAGE   ROSEMARY

WORKING WITH HERBS

The pleasure of herbal company
is more than just a simple tea.
Herbs extend the cook's domain;
With a balanced hand, a long-lived reign.

Cultivating Herb Plants

When we began to grow herbs, we often followed the books to the letter; this method brings its disappointments as well as its successes. Growing plants must depend on so many factors, such as climate, soil, how the soil is cultivated, light, water, and their proximity to one another, that general guidelines can prove inappropriate. Our notes on cultivation come from our experience of growing herbs, mainly in temperate climates.

The most important advice we can give you is to talk with herb growers in your area. Although the growers may chafe a bit at being asked the same questions, we have found them exceptionally pleasant people who are glad to share their knowledge.

If there is a garden club near you, inquire whether it sponsors lectures on herb growing. Many do, and open these to the public for no fee, or a small one.

All successful gardening depends on preparing the earth well. If you have space in the ground, cultivate the soil deeply, adding sand, organic materials, and fertilizers as necessary. A soil test will provide information as to soil type, pH, and recommended additives.

We think herbs will reward you even if you are new to gardening. They are relatively easy to grow and not fussy in the garden. At first, you will probably be happier, and understand herbs better, if you limit yourself to four or five herbs whose flavor you really like and that you will use often.

Information for the Herb Growing Guide included in this chapter was researched by Thomas De Baggio, owner of Earthworks Herb Garden Nursery. Tom grows some of the finest herbs that we have seen for sale; we are fortunate to count him as a friend and to have had his advice on preparing this chapter. The guide provides the most important information for growing herbs, in the garden or the house.

Those who live in a cold climate need to know the hardiness of the plants. Frost usually occurs below 36° Fahrenheit. Herbs such as basil and summer savory must be harvested before the first frost or all is lost. Chervil, coriander, dill, and parsley withstand some frost. Bay, marjoram, and rosemary must be brought indoors every year if the temperature goes below their cold hardiness.

In warmer climates, you may be able to sow annuals such as chervil or coriander two to three times a year for a continuous crop. Or you might grow a hedge of rosemary plants.

The chart is useful for those who have limited space, as it is necessary to know how large the herbs will grow in order to plan adequate space for them. You must also take into consideration how far apart they should be planted, and whether they prefer sun or shade. Finally, those who must grow herbs in pots will want to know which herbs do best as house plants.

We have discussed the important requirements for growing each herb, as well as its peculiarities, in each chapter introduction. This chapter provides some herb gardening basics. We have divided the herbs into two categories: annuals and perennials (parsley is a biennial, but cultivated as an annual).

Annuals

If you want only a few annuals, it is easier to buy plants. However, if you would like to grow some herbs from seed, annuals are the ones with which to experiment. Basil, chervil, coriander, dill, parsley, and summer savory can all be sown in the same manner.

Seed can be sown directly in the ground after all danger of frost is past. Work up a bed or an area with compost to enrich the soil. The soil should have a fine texture and good drainage.

Indoors, start the seed in small plastic pots or in flats. Prepare these by filling them with half sterile potting mix (we use ProMix) and half perlite or vermiculite. Dampen this medium thoroughly before sowing the seed. It should not be soaking wet. Place two or three seeds in each pot or make rows in a flat. Seeds planted in rows have fewer problems after germination because of better air circulation. Cover the seeds lightly with a thin layer of dampened potting mix. Place the germinating containers in a plastic bag or cover them with plastic wrap to preserve moisture.

Most seeds germinate in a warm, dark place. They should sprout in a week to ten days; parsley may take longer. Once they have sprouted, move them to the light. A twin-tube, fluorescent grow light will speed sturdy development, but a sunny window or cold frame will suffice.

Water the plants with a fine mist. The soil should be kept evenly damp and never allowed to dry out. Take care not to overwater or the plants may rot at the soil level.

When the seedlings are one or two inches tall, fertilize them lightly. Once they reach three or four inches in height, and possess two true leaves, they can be transplanted into pots for further development or into the garden. Before transplanting to the garden, annuals should be hardened-off. Carefully get them used to outdoor conditions for a week, bringing them indoors at night if necessary, before setting them in the garden when danger of frost is past.

Perennials

Unless you have a grow light, cold frame, or greenhouse, we recommend that you purchase perennial herb plants. They will save you time, since it takes a year or more before perennials provide large harvests. To sow perennials, follow the directions for starting annual seeds indoors, keeping in mind that most home gardens will need only one or two of each herb. When sown directly in the garden, perennials, some of which do not come true from seed, are more difficult to grow than are quick-maturing annuals.

Rooting

If you are fortunate enough to have a friend who grows herbs, you might want to try rooting some cuttings of perennials. This is a quick and inexpensive way to obtain plants that are true to type. The best time to do this is in the spring when plants are putting out new growth.

Choose sturdy cuttings, five to six inches long, and remove the leaves from the lower two inches of the stem. Fill small plastic pots with a medium of half sterile potting mix and half perlite. Dampen the mix thoroughly. Dip the leafless part of each stem in a rooting powder such as Rootone, shake off the excess, and place the stem in the moist medium. Mist the cuttings.

Keep these cuttings in a warm place with filtered sun. Mist them several times a day, keeping the foliage damp. They should not be allowed to dry out. If the cuttings dry out and wither in the first two or three weeks, they will not root.

The cuttings should produce a healthy root system in six weeks or less. After this time, the stems should show signs of new growth and, if tugged gently, their new roots should hold them in the soil. If all danger of frost is past, you can now transplant the herbs to new pots or into the garden.

HERB GROWING GUIDE

COMMON NAME (Botanical Name)	Cold Hardy To	Peren- nial	Bien- nial	An- nual	Height in Feet	Full Sun	Part Sun	Shade	Inches Apart	House Plant
BASIL *Ocimum basilicum*	35° F			❦	2	❦			18	❦
BAY *Laurus nobilis*	15° F	❦			40	❦			var.	❦
CHERVIL *Anthriscus cerefolium*	25° F			❦	2		❦		9	❦
CHIVES *Allium schoenoprasum*	−40° F	❦			1½	❦			12	❦
CORIANDER *Coriandrum sativum*	33° F			❦	3	❦	❦		18	
CRESS *Nasturtium officinale*	−20° F	❦			1		❦		6	
DILL *Anethum graveolens*	29° F			❦	3	❦			12	
GARLIC *Allium sativum*	−40° F	❦			2	❦			6	
LEMON BALM *Melissa officinalis*	−20° F	❦			2	❦	❦	❦	18	❦
MARJORAM *Origanum Majorana*	30° F	❦			1	❦			10	
MINT *Mentha species*	−20° F	❦			2	❦	❦		15	❦

HERB GROWING GUIDE

COMMON NAME (Botanical Name)	Cold Hardy To	Perennial	Biennial	Annual	Height in Feet	Full Sun	Part Sun	Shade	Inches Apart	House Plant
OREGANO *Origanum vulgare*	−20° F	●			2	●			12	●
PARSLEY *Petroselinum crispum*	20° F		●		1½	●	●		12	●
ROSEMARY *Rosmarinus officinalis*	10° F	●			6	●	●		36	●
SAGE *Salvia officinalis*	−10° F	●			2½	●			24	
SAVORY, SUMMER *Satureja hortensis*	33° F			●	1½	●			12	
SAVORY, WINTER *Satureja montana*	−10° F	●			1½	●			12	●
SORREL *Rumex acetosa*	−20° F	●			2	●	●		12	
TARRAGON *Artemisia Dracunculus sativa*	−20° F	●			2	●	●		24	
THYME *Thymus vulgaris*	−20° F	●			1	●	●		18	●

Combining Herbs in the Kitchen

Herbs are used with foods to accent particular flavors or to create new ones. The two flavor groups of culinary herbs, robust and mild, tend to follow the perennial and annual classifications. Robust perennials include garlic, rosemary, sage, sorrel, tarragon, and thyme. More delicate annuals are basil, chervil, dill, and parsley. However, some annuals like coriander and summer savory are strong in flavor, while some perennials, notably marjoram and bay, are mild. Mild and robust do not necessarily refer to the taste of the raw leaves. Mild also describes herbs that combine well in cooking, or whose flavors mellow in cooking.

Robust herbs stand up well to cooking and even improve in long-simmered dishes. They are used together or alone for braised or roasted meat or poultry, and in soups or stews. They can be combined judiciously with basil, marjoram, or other mild herbs.

The milder-mannered herbs can often be used in larger quantities and with more variation. Often, three mild herbs are combined if their flavors complement. They frequently appear in salads and dishes in which the leaves are used raw or cooked only briefly.

The best advice we have for combining herbs is to follow your own taste. Experiment with herbs that you like best and that you think might go well together. If too many herbs are used in one dish, their flavors will clash or become muddy. Ideally, they should blend or marry without fighting. Generally, combinations of two or three herbs provide enough flavor interest and balance for most dishes. Bouquets garnis may benefit from using four or five herbs.

Drying an herb usually concentrates some, but not all, of its oils. This means that some flavor elements are more intense, while aromas are weaker. Subtlety and balance are not as great as they are in fresh herbs.

When replacing a fresh herb with a dried herb, the amount of the dried herb is usually one-third that of the fresh. For example, a teaspoon of dried basil can be used for a tablespoon of fresh, minced leaves. Dried robust leaves should be substituted carefully. Often only a half-teaspoon of rosemary, savory, or thyme will be needed in place of a tablespoon of the fresh, minced herb.

It is best to add dried herbs in small amounts. If they have not been sitting on the shelf for a year, their flavor is strong. Usually a teaspoon is enough to flavor a whole dish. Add a small amount, simmer, taste, and adjust accordingly.

We think that garlic, parsley, sorrel, and watercress should not be dried. Delicate herbs, such as chervil, chives, coriander, and dill, tend to lose most of their flavor when dried. Many of our recipes indicate the amount of dried herb when it can be substituted for the fresh. If no substitution is suggested, the flavor of the recipe depends on the fresh herb.

Our suggestions for herb combinations should be used with your culinary preparation in mind. For example, thyme and rosemary go well together in meat dishes, but the rosemary would overpower a delicate cream-based soup such as Carrot Thyme Soup.

Herb Combinations

Basil's inimitable flavor combines well with bay, garlic, marjoram, oregano, savory, and thyme in cooked dishes such as soups, stews, or pastas. In salads, it goes well with chives, cress, dill, garlic, mint, and parsley.

Bay goes well with almost any herb in cooked dishes. It is compatible with basil, chervil, chives, coriander, dill, garlic, marjoram, oregano, parsley, rosemary, sage, savory, tarragon, and thyme. The leaves should be added when the cooking begins.

Chervil's delicate flavor can be used successfully with milder herbs, such as chives, cress, dill, lemon balm, and parsley, or with the complementary herbs, sorrel and tarragon. It is best used fresh, or cooked briefly.

Chives have a versatile flavor that goes well with basil, chervil, coriander, cress, dill, lemon balm, marjoram, oregano, parsley, sorrel, tarragon, and thyme. Chives need little cooking.

Coriander's leaf has such a distinctive, strong flavor that it is often used on its own. In cooked dishes, we find that it creates a subtle flavor with chives, garlic, marjoram, oregano, and parsley.

Cress's peppery flavor is clearest when the herb is eaten raw. It works well with chervil, chives, dill, garlic, parsley, sorrel, and tarragon.

Dill's delicate foliage is most flavorful raw, but it also stands up well to cooking. Dill harmonizes with basil, bay, chervil, chives, cress, garlic, mint, parsley, sorrel, and tarragon.

Garlic's sweet, robust flavor can lend either subtlety or intensity to food. We have used it with all of the herbs and find it good with most. Take care when using it with chives, as it can overpower them. Use it sparingly with the sweeter herbs, such as chervil, lemon balm, and mint.

Lemon balm's sweet, citrus flavor can be overpowered by stronger herbs. It melds successfully with chervil, chives, mint, and parsley, and it can be used very carefully with garlic.

Marjoram is one of the most compatible herbs. Although it is related to oregano, its sweetness combines more successfully with other herbs than does oregano's bite. We like it with basil, bay, chives, coriander, garlic, oregano, mint, parsley, rosemary, sage, savory, and thyme.

Oregano's spicy flavor cooks well and mellows with basil, bay, chives, coriander, garlic, marjoram, mint, parsley, savory, and thyme.

Mints have flavors that vary from peppery to sweet, making them a family of herbs that needs to be used carefully. We like mint alone or with basil, cress, lemon balm, parsley, and tarragon.

Parsley is the most versatile of the culinary herbs. Its fresh, green flavor goes well with all other herbs, either by adding complexity to them or by softening them. Italian parsley has a stronger flavor than the curly variety, so you might like to use less of it. We find it difficult to overuse parsley.

Rosemary's flavor is strong and highly aromatic. We are partial to it for marinating and roasting, though there are some Italian breads and cheeses that would not be the same without it. Rosemary goes well with bay, garlic, marjoram, oregano, parsley, the savories, and thyme.

Sage's pungency is best appreciated when the herb is cooked. It stands with the robust herbs and is used with bay, garlic, marjoram, oregano, parsley, rosemary, the savories, and thyme.

Savories are clean-flavored, sound, strong herbs that blend well. Summer savory is milder than winter savory. Both combine with basil, bay, garlic, marjoram, oregano, parsley, rosemary, sage, tarragon, and thyme.

Sorrel's tart, lemony flavor is especially good in salads. The herb is often used in lightly cooked soups and sauces. It can be used with basil, chives, dill, garlic, parsley, and tarragon.

Tarragon's piquant, anise-like flavor often melds well with the milder herbs. The classic fines herbes blend contains tarragon, parsley, chervil, and chives. We like it as well with bay, cress, dill, garlic, mint, savory, sorrel, and sometimes thyme.

Thyme's sweet and spicy flavor makes it a good herb for combining, although it is stronger than marjoram. It is fine with basil, bay, chives, garlic, marjoram, oregano, parsley, rosemary, sage, savory, and occasionally tarragon.

Enjoying Herbs in Salads

When you pick the tender lettuce you've coddled to perfection, wash and dry it with care, toss it with a bit of good olive oil, and sprinkle it with fine wine vinegar, you have what is fairly called a salad. This salad has the essential elements—freshness, earthiness, sweetness, and tartness—that bring you to appreciate how simple food can be elegant and satisfying.

Freshness is the most important quality, and the hardest to find. Commercial lettuce has barely a shadow of the flavor of garden lettuce. Herbs renew some of this flavor, as restaurateurs who grow chervil, basil, and rocket hydroponically in their basements know quite well. A few sprigs of Italian parsley or dill improve even market lettuce.

If a salad is eaten before the meal, herbs add pleasant flavors that stimulate the palate. If, instead, a salad is served after the meal, as Italians do, herbs help to cleanse and refresh the palate.

When we yearn for the variety and freshness of salad greens that we ate in Europe, we begin to plot our salad garden. One of the best lettuces we know, especially for herb salads, is *mache*. It has a fine sweetness and some delicacy, so it is best used with milder herbs. In English, it is known as corn lettuce or lamb's lettuce.

Some sweet varieties we like for their compatability with herbs are red leaf and oak leaf. We grow these every season, along with other loose-leaved lettuces such as Black-seeded Simpson and Salad Bowl. We prefer these to head lettuces because they provide salad greens until the very hottest part of summer. Tender leaves are harvested continually from each plant, or the entire plant can be cut back to about 2 inches from the soil. In either case new growth is continuous until the plants send up seed stalks. The more leaves you cut, the more salads you will enjoy. Regular cutting also slows the production of seed stalks and inhibits bitterness from developing in the leaves.

Chicory, curly endive, radicchio, young spinach, and rocket are other salad greens we would not be without. Rocket is also known as arugula, ruchetta, roquette, and rucola, and is sometimes classified as an herb. These greens add to the flavor range of a salad, from the pepperiness of rocket, through the pleasant bitterness of curly endive and the chicories, to the earthiness of radicchio and spinach.

Winter is the time to pore over seed catalogs so that you can make the piquant decisions of which salads to eat this year. We order from suppliers that import French and Italian seeds to get the plants we are fond of and to try new varieties as well.

Of the herbs we consider most important for salads—basil, chervil, chives, coriander, cress, dill, Italian parsley, and sorrel—we grow all but watercress. We do allow room for garden cress, and even grow it indoors occasionally. A few leaves of lovage, lemon balm, and mint add an unusual spark to our salads sometimes.

Also, all herb flowers are edible, with the same taste, but more assertive, as the herbs from which they come. We especially like using perennial flowers: thyme, marjoram, oregano, sage, and rosemary. The annual flowers tend to be bitter, but we find chervil and coriander blossoms very tasty and pretty.

Sometimes, particularly for festive occasions, we enjoy making rather extravagant herb salads modeled after those of the Renaissance. We use mild greens to allow the herbs to be savored fully. Handfuls of lettuce and smaller handfuls of Italian parsley, dill or fennel leaves, basil, chervil, and sorrel, with some sprigs of tarragon, marjoram, chives, cress, or lovage, compose a glorious salad. We dress the whole lightly with extra virgin olive oil and lemon juice or wine vinegar, then sprinkle it with nasturtiums, violas, and borage blossoms, or perhaps lavender, sage, or rosemary flowers. Such a fanciful salad might seem excessive, but we have found that it gives us and our guests a sensual appreciation for fresh green things. Experimenting with the amounts of greens and herbs will lead you to the combinations and balance you prefer.

Another true delight is gathering the salad ingredients. Choosing just the right lettuce and spinach, picking a few peppery leaves of rocket and garden cress, snipping the tips of new green dill and parsley, and choosing the blossoms for garnish is like preparing a palette for a painting. The salad forms in your mind and hands as it will appear on your table—a feast for the eyes and a relish for the tongue.

Preserving Herbal Bounty

Like most other growing things, herbs are at their best when they are fresh and in season. In summer, herbs reach the height of their flavor, but we yearn for them in winter, too, when we live in a cold climate. We long for the taste of garden fresh pesto or fresh tarragon for sauces and vinaigrettes. To prepare for these cravings, we store summer's bounty in our freezers and pantries. We enjoy the time spent preserving our herbs, knowing that we will be thankful to savor their flavor all year.

Harvesting

Harvest the herbs before the plants are about to bloom. Choose a sunny day and pick the herbs in the morning, when their oils are strongest. Cut them back to about three inches from the ground, or just above the bottom set of leaves. Do not leave the cut herbs out in the sun; take them into a shady area for sorting and tying into bunches.

Remove the brown bottom leaves and any spotted or bug-eaten ones. If the herbs are dirty, brush away the dirt. If you must wash them, rinse them quickly and pat dry.

Drying

You can dry herbs by hanging them or laying them on screens. To dry herbs by hanging, tie the stalks into small bundles with string or twine and hang them in a dry, well-ventilated place. An attic or shed is usually a good location. If you are drying herbs on screens, remove the large leaves from their stems and lay them on the screens. Small leaves, like thyme or savory, should be left on their stems and spread on the screens.

If you are drying herbs for seed, such as coriander or dill, follow the directions for hanging to dry. Since they tend to drop some seeds as they dry, it is best to hang the bunches over a screen that will catch the seed. Or, you can hang each bundle in a paper bag with a few air holes cut in it.

Herbs can take from a few days to a week or more to dry, depending on the climate and humidity. Check the herbs daily—if left too long, especially in humid weather, they lose their green color and turn brown. A dried herb should crackle and crumble when rubbed between your fingers. If it bends and is not crisp, it has not dried sufficiently. To remove excess moisture, spread the herbs on baking sheets and place them in a very low oven, not over 200° F., for 3 to 5 minutes.

When the herbs are dried, strip them for their stems and pack them in clean jars with tight-fitting lids. Do not crumble the leaves but pack them whole to retain the finest flavor. Label the jars and store them away from heat and light. If the herbs are not completely dried when you pack them in jars, they will mold and spoil.

Home-dried herbs can be stored in jars or tins for up to one year, when next season's crop will take their place.

Freezing

Cut the herbs before they bloom in the morning of a sunny day. If the herbs are not clean, give them a quick rinse and pat them dry, or remove excess moisture in a salad spinner.

To freeze whole leaves, remove the leaves from the stems and pack them in a small freezer bags or airtight freezer containers. We think this is the simplest method and it provides the best flavor. We prefer to use pint bags and pack a handful into each bag. You might want to pack some herbs in larger plastic containers and remove a few leaves as you need them.

To freeze chopped herbs in small amounts, we remove them from their stems, chop them with a knife or *mezzaluna,* and pack them into freezer bags or plastic containers. When we are working with larger amounts, we use the food processor to chop the herbs and pack them in freezer bags in one-half cup quantities. We harvest chives frequently, snip them with scissors, and pack them in plastic containers that we keep on the freezer door.

Be sure to label your herbs before putting them in the freezer because they tend to look alike when chopped and frozen. We keep our herbs sorted by placing the small, labeled bags of each kind of herb into larger freezer bags with a large label. Frozen herbs keep a reasonable flavor and texture for about four months. If you have a separate freezer unit, the herbs can be kept for up to a year, but they will not be as tasty.

Concentrating Herbal Flavor

Perhaps nothing, other than shiny little vials of exotic spices, give such a sense of imminent kitchen alchemy as an array of fresh herbs floating in good quality white wine vinegar. Picking sprigs of different herbs when the plants are at their aromatic peak and putting them into vinegar for a month or so are all you have to do to have this agreeable satisfaction.

Making herbal infusions is a pleasure for the herb gardener, as well as a simple way to concentrate herb flavor and store it for the year. Bottles of opal basil vinegar, shining rosy lavender, and pale, golden green, tarragon vinegar gleaming in the sunlit garden are two of our summer traditions. They enhance salads and sauces throughout the winter.

Each year, we experiment with different herbs for making vinegars and oils; often a combination of two herbs offers a pleasant surprise to our palates. Our herbal oils are precious to us—we use them for special dishes and give them to appreciative friends. The rewards are worth the small effort it takes to make herbal oils and vinegars.

Herbal Oils

We find the best herbs for preparing culinary oils are basil, bay, garlic, lavender, marjoram, oregano, rosemary, and thyme.

Cut the herbs in the morning of a sunny day. Bring the herbs inside and clean them. If you wash them, be absolutely sure that all the moisture is dried from the leaves before placing them in oil. Bruise the herb sprigs and fill clean quart jars with them. The jars should be fairly full of the herb so that you will get a strong infusion. Pour a good quality olive oil over the herbs and seal the jar. Place the jars in a cool, dark place for two to three weeks.

At this point, remove the infused herb sprigs from the jars by straining the oil through cheesecloth. Pour the oil into smaller bottles or jars, adding one small, fresh sprig or leaf if you like, label, and store in a cool place. Use the oil within one year.

Herbal Vinegars

Some of the herbs that we like for vinegars are: basil, especially the purple varieties; chive with chive blossoms; dill; garlic; lavender; lovage; marigold; mint; tarragon; and savory.

Cut your herbs on a sunny morning, clean the sprigs if necessary, and pat them dry. Fill large, clean jars full of the herbs you have chosen and cover them with a good quality white wine vinegar. We have found that red wine vinegar is too strong for most herbs except garlic.

Set the jars out in the herb garden and let the sun do its work with the herbs and vinegar for three to four weeks.

After this time, bring the jars inside and remove the herbs by straining the vinegar. Pour the vinegar into smaller bottles, adding a fresh sprig of the herb if desired, and label. Keep the vinegars away from direct sunlight and use them within one year.

Basil Leaves Packed in Oil

In Italy, we learned of this method for preserving basil. If you are a basil lover, follow these instructions.

Cut the herbs, before the buds form, on a sunny morning. Brush them free of dirt. Rinse and pat them dry only if absolutely necessary. Remove the leaves from the stems.

In a half-pint canning jar, add enough olive oil to cover the bottom. Place a few leaves, about five or six, in the jar and press them down lightly with a wooden spoon. Add a little more oil, a pinch of salt, and another layer of leaves. Repeat this process until the jar is filled. Place the lid on the jar and keep it in the refrigerator for up to one year.

Once refrigerated, the leaves will turn a bit darker and the oil will coagulate. It is surprising how much basil will be needed when packing the leaves in this manner. Use the leaves as needed; they can be used whole or chopped. The oil can be used as well.

APPENDIX: HERB SOURCES

We have included this comprehensive listing to make it easier for the reader to find herbs. We make no endorsement of quality for any of the companies listed. Because of publication lag-time, some companies may be out of business or may have moved. When we have encountered such cases, we have found a very helpful attitude in directing us to other growers in the area.

Some herb growers sell by mail order and at their shops or farms; others sell only by mail order or only on the premises. Usually this is noted in the grower's catalog. The catalogs differ in size, and, as the legend shows, there is a range in what they offer. There is a charge for almost every catalog listed.

Part of the pleasure of working with herbs is choosing the particular plants you like. If there is a greenhouse or herb farm in your area, you should pay it a visit. Not only will you be able to select special plants, but you can also benefit from the advice of the grower. In fact, meandering through an herb farm is so enjoyable for us that we have only one caution: you may not have enough room for all the plants that you bring home.

Herb Sources	Catalog	Plants	Seeds	Dried Herbs	Mail Order
CANADA					
Richters Goodwood, Ontario Canada LOC 1A0	🌿		🌿		🌿
Sanctuary Seeds 2388 West 4th Vancouver B.C. Canada V6K 1P1	🌿		🌿	🌿	🌿
UNITED STATES					
CALIFORNIA					
Hoover Herb Shoppe 115 West Green Street Pasadena, CA 91105	🌿	🌿	🌿	🌿	🌿
J. L. Hudson, Seedsman P. O. Box 1058 Redwood City, CA 94064	🌿		🌿		🌿
Redwood City Seed Company P. O. Box 361 Redwood City, CA 94064	🌿		🌿		🌿
Clyde Robin Seed Company, Inc. P. O. Box 2855 Castro Valley, CA 94546	🌿		🌿		🌿
Taylor's Herb Gardens, Inc. 1535 Lone Oak Road Vista, CA 92083	🌿	🌿	🌿		🌿
COLORADO					
Applewood Seed Company P. O. Box 10761 Edgemont Station Golden, CO 80401	🌿		🌿		🌿
CONNECTICUT					
Caprilands Herb Farm Silver Street Coventry, CT 06238	🌿	🌿	🌿	🌿	🌿
Catnip Acres Farm Christian Street Oxford, CT 06483	🌿	🌿	🌿		🌿
Comstock, Ferre & Company 263 Main Street Wethersfield, CT 06109	🌿		🌿		🌿
Gilbertie's Herb Gardens Sylvan Avenue Westport, CT 06880	🌿	🌿			

Herb Sources	Catalog	Plants	Seeds	Dried Herbs	Mail Order
Charles C. Hart Seed Company 304 Main Street Wethersfield, CT 06109	✓		✓		✓
Hemlock Hill Herb Farm Hemlock Hill Road Litchfield, CT 06759	✓	✓			✓
Sunrise Enterprises P. O. Box 10058 Elmwood, CT 06110	✓		✓		✓
White Flower Farm Litchfield, CT 06759	✓	✓			✓
DISTRICT OF COLUMBIA					
Herb Cottage Washington Cathedral Mount Saint Alban Washington, DC 20016	✓		✓	✓	✓
GEORGIA					
Hastings 434 Marietta Street P. O. Box 4274 Atlanta, GA 30302	✓	✓	✓		✓
ILLINOIS					
Maple Hill Herb Farm Route One Anna, IL 62906	✓	✓	✓	✓	✓
IOWA					
De Giorgi Company, Inc. P. O. Box 413 Council Bluffs, IO 51502	✓		✓		✓
KANSAS					
J. A. Demonchaux Company 827 North Kansas Avenue Topeka, KA 66608	✓		✓		✓
KENTUCKY					
Rutland of Kentucky P. O. Box 16 Washington, KY 41096	✓	✓	✓	✓	✓
MAINE					
Johnny's Selected Seeds Albion, ME 04910	✓		✓		✓
Merry Gardens Camden, ME 04843	✓	✓			✓

Herb Sources	Catalog	Plants	Seeds	Dried Herbs	Mail Order
Monk's Hill Herbs P. O. Box 8200 RFD #2 Winthrop, ME 04364	❧	❧	❧		❧
MARYLAND					
Bittersweet Hill Nurseries Route 424 & Governors Bridge Road Davidsonville, MD 21035	❧	❧			
Carroll Gardens P. O. Box 310 444 East Main Street Westminster, MD 21157	❧	❧			❧
Smile Herb Shop 4908 Berwyn Road College Park, MD 20740	❧		❧	❧	❧
Solar Gardens 14400 New Hampshire Avenue Silver Spring, MD 20904		❧	❧	❧	
Stillridge Herb Farm 10370 Route 99 Woodstock, MD 21163	❧	❧	❧	❧	❧
MASSACHUSETTS					
Borchelt Herb Gardens 474 Carriage Shop Road East Falmouth, MA 02536	❧	❧	❧		❧
Country Herbs P. O. Box 357 Stockbridge, MA 01262	❧	❧	❧	❧	❧
Cricket Hill Herb Farm, Ltd. Glen Street, P. O. Box 229 Rowley, MA 01969	❧	❧		❧	❧
Fern Hill Herb Garden 177 Taylor Street Pembroke, MA 02359	❧	❧			
Hartman's Herb Farm Old Dana Road Barre, MA 01005	❧	❧		❧	❧
Herb's Etc. 108 College Avenue Arlington, MA 02174	❧		❧	❧	❧
Herb Patch Gardens 57 Anson Road Concord, MA 01742		❧	❧		
Mount Vernon Farm Herbs Hummock Pond Road Nantucket, MA 02554	❧	❧			❧

Herb Sources	Catalog	Plants	Seeds	Dried Herbs	Mail Order
Thunderhill Farm Petticoat Hill Road Williamsburg, MA 01096		✿			
MICHIGAN					
Far North Gardens 15621 Auburndale Avenue Livonia, MI 48154	✿		✿		✿
Fox Hill Farm P. O. Box 7 Parma, MI 49269	✿	✿			✿
International Growers Exchange P. O. Box 397 Farmington, MI 48024	✿	✿			✿
MISSOURI					
ABC Nursery and Greenhouse Route 1 P. O. Box 313C Lecoma, MO 65540	✿	✿		✿	✿
NEW HAMPSHIRE					
The Herb Garden Haynes Road Deerfield, NH 03037	✿	✿	✿		✿
NEW JERSEY					
Thompson & Morgan P. O. Box 100 Farmingdale, NJ 07727	✿		✿		✿
Well Sweep Herb Farm 317 Mount Bethel Road Port Murray, NJ 07865	✿	✿	✿		✿
NEW YORK					
Back of the Beyond 7233 Lower East Hill Road Colden, NY 14033	✿	✿			
Epicure Seeds Ltd. P. O. Box 23568 Rochester, NY 14692	✿		✿		✿
Joseph Harris Company, Inc. Moreton Farm Rochester, NY 14624	✿		✿		✿
Herbst Seedsmen, Inc. 1000 North Main Street Brewster, NY 10509	✿		✿		✿
Stokes Seeds, Inc. 737 Main Street P. O. Box 548 Buffalo, NY 14240	✿		✿		✿

Herb Sources	*Catalog*	*Plants*	*Seeds*	*Dried Herbs*	*Mail Order*
Van Bourgondien Brothers 245 Farmingdale Road & Route 109 Babylon, NY 11702	✿	✿			✿
NORTH CAROLINA					
Sandy Mush Herb Nursery Route 2 & Surrett Cove Road Leicester, NC 28748	✿	✿	✿		✿
Wyatt-Quarles Seed Company P. O. Box 2131 Raleigh, NC 27602	✿		✿		✿
OHIO					
Mellingers 2310 West South Range North Lima, OH 44452	✿	✿	✿		✿
Quailcrest Farm 2810 Armstrong Road Wooster, OH 44691	✿	✿			
Sunnybrook Farms Nursery 9448 Mayfield Road P. O. Box 6 Chesterland, OH 44026	✿	✿	✿	✿	✿
OREGON					
Casa Yerba Star Route 2 P. O. Box 21 Days Creek, OR 97429	✿	✿	✿		✿
Dutch Mill Herb Farm Route 2 P. O. Box 190 Forest Grove, OR 97116	✿	✿			
Nichols Garden Nursery 1190 North Pacific Highway Albany, OR 97321	✿	✿	✿	✿	✿
PENNSYLVANIA					
Burpee Seed Company 2123 Burpee Building Warminster, PA 18974	✿	✿	✿		✿
Dionysos' Barn P. O. Box 31 Bodines, PA 17722	✿	✿			✿
Rosemary House 120 South Market Street Mechanicsburg, PA 17055	✿	✿	✿		✿
RHODE ISLAND					
Meadowbrook Herb Garden Wyoming, RI 02898	✿	✿	✿	✿	✿

Herb Sources	Catalog	Plants	Seeds	Dried Herbs	Mail Order
SOUTH CAROLINA					
George W. Park Seed Company P. O. Box 31 Greenwood, SC 29647	🌢		🌢		🌢
SOUTH DAKOTA					
Gurney Seed and Nursery Company Yankton, SD 57079	🌢	🌢	🌢		🌢
TEXAS					
Hilltop Herb Farm P. O. Box 1734 Cleveland, TX 77327	🌢	🌢	🌢	🌢	🌢
Yankee Peddler Route 1 P. O. Box 251 A Burton, TX 77835	🌢		🌢	🌢	🌢
VERMONT					
Herb Patch P. O. Box 1111 Pawlet Road Middletown Springs, VT 05757	🌢			🌢	🌢
Highlander Farm Bragg Hill Road Norwich, VT 05055	🌢	🌢			🌢
Le Jardin du Gourmet West Danville, VT 05873	🌢	🌢	🌢		🌢
Putney Nursery, Inc. Putney, VT 05346	🌢	🌢			🌢
VIRGINIA					
Earthworks Herb Garden Nursery 923 North Ivy Street Arlington, VA 22201	🌢	🌢	🌢		🌢
Stillcopper Herb Farm P. O. Box 186 Route 1 Brookneal, VA 24528	🌢	🌢	🌢		🌢
WASHINGTON					
Abundant Life Seed Foundation P. O. Box 772 Port Townsend, WA 98368	🌢		🌢		🌢
WEST VIRGINIA					
Hickory Hollow P. O. Box 52 Route 1 Peterstown, WV 24963	🌢		🌢		🌢

Herb Sources	Catalog	Plants	Seeds	Dried Herbs	Mail Order
WISCONSIN					
Flintridge Herb Farm P. O. Box 187 Route 1 Sister Bay, WI 54234	❦	❦	❦	❦	❦
MacFarland House 5923 Exchange Street McFarland, WI 53558	❦	❦	❦		❦
Sunnypoint Gardens Route 1 Egg Harbor, WI 54209	❦	❦	❦	❦	❦

BIBLIOGRAPHY

Boxer, Arabella, and Back, Phillipa. *The Herb Book,* London: Octopus Books, 1980.

Claiborne, Craig. *Cooking with Herbs and Spices.* New York: Harper and Row, 1963.

Collin, Mary A. *Everyday Cooking with Herbs.* New York: Doubleday and Company.

Foster, Gertrude, and Louden, Rosemary. *Park's Success with Herbs.* Greenwood, South Carolina: George W. Park Seed Company, 1980.

Fox, Helen Morgenthau.*Gardening with Herbs for Flavor and Fragrance.* New York: Dover Publications, 1972.

Garland, Sarah. *The Complete Book of Herbs and Spices.* New York: Viking Press, 1979.

Grieve, Maud. *Culinary Herbs and Condiments.* New York: Dover Publications, 1971.

Grieve, Maud. *A Modern Herbal.* New York: Dover Publications, 1971.

Hatfield, Audrey Wynne. *A Complete Culinary Herbal.* North Hamptonshire, England: Thorsons Publishers Limited, 1978.

Hersey, Jean. *Cooking with Herbs.* New York: Charles Scribner's Sons, 1972.

Hoffmann, Irene Botsford. *The Book of Herb Cookery.* Boston: Houghton Mifflin Company, 1975.

Howarth, Sheila. *Herbs with Everything.* New York: Holt, Rinehart and Winston, 1976.

Hylton, William H., ed. *The Rodale Herb Book.* Emmaus, Pennsylvania: Rodale Press, 1979.

McNair, James K. *The World of Herbs and Spices*. San Francisco: Ortho Books, 1979.

Mazza, Irma Goodrich. *Herbs for the Kitchen*. Boston: Little, Brown and Company, 1975.

Meyer, Joseph E. *The Herbalist*. Glenwood, Illinois: Meyerbooks, 1976.

Rohde, Eleanour Sinclair. *A Garden of Herbs*. New York: Dover Publications, 1969.

Simmons, Adelma Grenier. *Herb Gardening in Five Seasons*. New York: Hawthorn Books, 1964.

Simmons, Adelma Grenier. *Herb Gardens of Delight*. New York: Hawthorn Books, 1974.

Sounin, Leonie de. *Magic in Herbs*. New York: Pyramid Books, 1977.

Stobart, Tom. *Herbs, Spices, and Flavorings*. New York: Overlook Press, 1982.

Woodward, M., ed. *Leaves from Gerard's Herball*. New York: Dover Publications, 1969.

INDEX